Student Workbook to accompany

Psychology

Its Principles and Meanings

Bourne / Ekstrand

FIFTH EDITION

Arthur Gutman
Florida Institute of Technology

Frank Webbe
Florida Institute of Technology

Holt, Rinehart and Winston
New York   Chicago   San Francisco   Philadelphia   Montreal   Toronto
London   Sydney   Tokyo   Mexico City   Rio de Janeiro   Madrid

ISBN 0-03-069818-9

Address correspondence to:
383 Madison Avenue
New York, NY 10017

Printed in the United States of America
5 6 7 8 016 9 8 7 6 5 4 3 2 1

CBS COLLEGE PUBLISHING
Holt, Rinehart and Winston
The Dryden Press
Saunders College Publishing

Introduction: How to Use This Workbook

This workbook has three main parts. First, each chapter includes a section containing Learning Objectives, a synopsis, and key terms and phrases. This section is designed to help you organize the material as you study it. Second, there are between twelve and twenty-one exercises per chapter, which are to serve as your intermediate test. They will tell you how well you have succeeded in organizing the material. Finally, each chapter contains three multiple-choice self-tests. These are your final tests before the class tests. Let's examine each part in detail.

COMPONENT 1

Component 1 can be viewed as the organizational component of this workbook. Each chapter begins with a set of Learning Objectives, which are closely tied to the major headings in the chapter outlines in the textbook itself. As you are reading the text, you should be asking yourself the objectives questions. If the answers do not become clear as you are reading, then something is wrong. For example, you may have overlooked a term you cannot define, or you may have read too fast. Go back! You should not continue to read if the objectives are not being learned.

The remainder of this component consists of a chapter synopsis and key terms and phrases. The synopsis is an overview of the chapter which emphasizes the key points of each of the Learning Objectives.

The key terms are listed according to the Learning Objective number. We have done this so that you do not confuse the terms from one part of the chapter with those from another part. This is important. You may give incorrect answers on exams because you forget some piece of information, but more often these mistakes are caused by confusion. You remember a concept, but you just can't place it. We call this *interference*. As you will see in Chapter 5, "forgetting" is mainly due to poor organization of material which, in turn, promotes confusion regarding "what goes where." So, keep the key terms together with the objectives. It is also important that you try to define these terms and phrases. (Use a separate sheet of paper.)

In summary, Component 1 is mainly for organization. You should use it mostly before and during your reading of the text.

1. Step 1 is to read the objectives and the outline in the text.
2. Read the synopsis.
3. Thumb through the chapter so that you get a mental picture of the line between the objectives and the outline and the material itself.
4. Look at the key words and phrases.
5. Read the text. If it's going slowly, read the material relating to only a single Learning Objective and then return to Step 1. If your reading is going well, then, by all means, continue.
6. When you're finished reading, read the chapter summary in the text.

7. Go beck to the objectives and outline. At this point you should have a good mental outline of the chapter.
8. Write your own synopsis and compare it with ours.
9. Write your own key words and phrases and compare them with ours.
10. Finally, look at the key terms and phrases--you should know them fairly well. But don't trust your mental map--write out your thoughts on each one on a separate sheet of paper.

COMPONENT 2

At this point you may feel confident that you know the material. The chances are that you do. However, as you will learn in Chapter 4, there's a big difference between learning and performance (or knowledge versus deeds). *Knowing* is a prerequisite for showing that you know (that is, good performance), but knowing does not guarantee performance. We have included the next two components--the testing components--so that you can practice the transfer from knowledge to performance and know how well you're transferring.

Component 2 is your intermediate test. Each chapter contains between twelve and twenty-one exercises. These exercises may include identification, fill-ins, matching, essays, and true-false tests. They test both your knowledge of material and your ability to apply knowledge to real-world problems. We have provided a variety because we do not want you to become fixed on a given mode of testing. We also thought it would be more interesting that way.

Remember that these exercises are probably more difficult than are the questions you will see on exams. Why? Because they break down the material very carefully and therefore force you to make fine distinctions. If you do these exercises well, you will find the multiple-choice questions a snap. Don't be quick to test yourself with the multiple-choice questions in Component 3. Indeed, leave some time between Component 2 and Component 3--at least a day. We advise this for two reasons. First, your performance on the exercises may require you to reexamine the text (as well as the organizational material in Component 1). If that is the case, go back to the text. Second, there is going to be a time lapse between your home study periods and your class tests. Consequently, you will almost never be tested just after you have studied. So you will need to carry the information for long periods of time. Therefore, you need to practice doing so. Again, don't be quick to take the self-tests.

COMPONENT 3

These are your "acid tests." After Chapter 1, each chapter contains at least two thirty-question multiple-choice tests--more questions in all than you will receive on a given chapter in any single test. Moreover, these questions are representative of the organizational structure in Component 1. Your performance here will be a good predictor of your performance in class --*but* only if you've taken the time to work through our earlier suggestions. Occasionally students who do poorly in class tests tell us that they did perfectly on the self-tests. On closer look, it appears that almost invariably these students failed to allow time between the organizational and the testing components. Again, time between study and testing is a feature of the real world. Make it a feature of your study habits too!

Take the first self-test and see how you do. If you've studied efficiently up to this point, you should get a perfect score. If you do not, analyze your mistakes. Why did you get the question(s) wrong? Usually, it's because you failed to make an important distinction. If this is the case, go back and drill yourself on that distinction. Then do the second self-test. Remember that multiple-choice tests force you to make distinctions.

What should you do the night before an exam? Review your notes and read over the three components. Be on the lookout for things you *do not* know. Make up your own questions. The point is that your period of intensified study is over. What you are doing now is proving to yourself that you know what you think you know.

Finally, if you feel you know the material but will still perform poorly, you might be suffering from "test anxiety" (much the same as stage fright). Don't be embarrassed--it's a common affliction. Tell your instructor. Your college or university may have a system for dealing with this (for example, a counseling center). In most cases, the prognosis for test anxiety is excellent. Treating it usually involves some relatively simple behavioral relaxation techniques (see Chapter 12). The real problem, usually, lies not in the treatment of "test anxiety" but in the identification of it. So, please, if you have (or think you have) this problem, identify yourself. Learning can be fun, but not if you cannot show what you know.

If you follow our suggestions we predict that you will earn a grade in the course that reflects your knowledge. More important (at least from *our* point of view), you will learn about psychology. Psychology is a fascinating area of study, but not just for its own sake. Psychology *is* a scientific discipline--the textbook will demonstrate that to you repeatedly--but it is also a discipline that teaches you things that will be useful to yourself and others. But be on guard: one psychology course will not make you a psychologist. There are dangers in thinking that you know more than you know. (Alexander Pope in his "Essay on Criticism" said, "A little learning is a dangerous thing.") Therefore, we have included in this introductory material a section that illustrates what it takes to become a psychologist. It plots the careers of three fictitious psychologists. The demands are great, but some of you taking the course now will become psychologists. Those of you who choose other careers may be surprised to learn how often the knowledge gained here will help you in those areas--and with daily matters that are not necessarily career related. We hope that you will enjoy the course and that this workbook will enhance your thinking about psychology.

Some General Study Tips and Techniques

Now that you have a step-by-step description of how to use this guide, let's examine some general pointers that apply to any course.

1. There is a difference between storage and retrieval (see Chapter 5 of your textbook). For example, one thousand books can be placed in a library either randomly or in alphabetical order. Either way, the volumes are stored. But *organized* storage makes it easier to retrieve the information later on. Similarly, when you study, a good organization facilitates your subsequent recall of the material. That's why we recommend that you pay extra attention to the Learning Objectives, outline, synopsis, and keys. They represent our way of helping you put your "library" in order. In general, good memory begins with organized learning!

2. A similar principle holds for lecture notes. What you take down in class is usually a small part of what you heard. So you must reorganize this material (outline it) *after* class, and as soon after as possible, in order to be able to find--and fill in--the gaps in information. By the way, why not tape the lecture, jot down only important points in class, listen carefully during class, and then write up your notes?

3. When reading (or listening), look up (or ask about) words or concepts you don't understand. Also, pay extra attention to tables and graphs, and study them until they are clear.

4. Do not cram. It's almost impossible to create much of an organization by cramming. You are better off studying for an hour a few days a week than several hours one day a week. If you are having difficulty understanding the reading assignments, it's particularly important to study less at shorter intervals. What's so special about a whole chapter? Why not take part of a chapter and treat that part as a mini-chapter? YOu can use the outline to create between three and five minichapters per regular chapter.

5. Keep the conditions of study close to the conditions of testing. Don't study on the beach or while eating dinner. This is not the context in which you will be tested. If you tense up a little during tests, try to build a little tension into your study time. Most important, don't stay up late while stimulated with caffeine, No-Doz, or whatever. Actually, your best study time is in the morning, after a good sleep.

6. Don't be quick to test yourself with multiple-choice questions. Your class tests will quiz you on materials you studied as much as two to three weeks earlier, not a half hour earlier.

7. As a true "acid test," see if you can play teacher. Explain what you've learned to someone not taking the course. If you cannot find a co-operative friend, use the mirror.

8. Use the resources available to you. If you don't understand something, see your instructor. Your problems may seem unique to you. However, the chances are that your instructor has seen them before.

Careers in Psychology

You are taking a course in psychology. Doubtless, you have been finding this course interesting--even exciting. Did you know that in U.S. colleges and universities, psychology is the largest single undergraduate major? The chances are that many of you who are not psychology majors now will end up specializing in that field. What does a career in psychology mean? Your textbook, Bourne/Ekstrand, *Psychology*, fifth edition, gives you a superb introduction. But how does this knowledge relate to you, your career choices, your employability, and your long-term happiness and satisfaction? We shall address these issues.

Unless you are independently wealthy, you will eventually be working. Your area of specialization should certainly help you in seeking employment and in your employment itself. In psychology there are three levels of degrees that you can earn, and you can pursue different paths based on the level you reach. The degrees are the bachelor's, the master's, and two doctorates-- the doctor of philosophy (Ph.D.) and the doctor of psychology (Psy.D). The bachelor's is the most flexible degree. It allows you entry into many different occupations and careers, some that are related to psychology and some that are not. The master's degree is a more specialized degree that will direct you more toward the profession of psychology. Because the degree is more specialized, there are fewer employment opportunities. However, those opportunities are likely to be at higher professional levels and are likely to pay a higher salary than are those obtainable with the bachelor's degree. The doctor of philosophy degree is primarily a research degree. The holder has completed a dissertation, which represents a large amount of research, and is qualified to conduct research, to supervise others in research, and to teach other candidates in the field. Professors of psychology in universities, particularly, have Ph.Ds. The doctor of psychology degree is what is called a practitioner's degree. The holder usually specializes in assessing why people are troubled and the kinds of treatments that are likely to help them. Although the Ph.D. holder may also be qualified to do clinical work, the doctor of psychology is especially trained for this area.

Let's take a look at three individuals, each holding a different degree in psychology and each involved in a particular facet of the field.

Let us first share a few minutes with Elizabeth Wilson. Elizabeth graduated from a state university with a bachelor of arts degree in psychology. As part of her course work, she took experimental psychology, industrial and organizational psychology, statistics, and research design. She also had courses in abnormal psychology, theories of personality, and clinical psychology. Elizabeth, by nature an analytical person, enjoyed the research aspects of psychology. When she graduated from the state university, she wasn't quite sure what she wanted to do, but she knew that she had certain skills in areas such as research design and program evaluation and that she had a facility for statistical analyses. Upon returning home, Elizabeth had very little trouble in obtaining a position with a group of marketing con- sultants. She was hired to generate market analyses before the development and introduction of new products. She surveys people's attitudes toward potential products, analyzes the data, and then recommends characteristics that the products should have for the widest acceptability.

Barry Goldberg received a bachelor of arts degree in psychology from a small private college. He followed the usual program, which included psychology, humanities, and science courses. Like Elizabeth, Barry was not entirely sure what he wanted to do after graduation, but he knew he wanted to work with people. What made him decide on a choice of career was a newspaper article about a seven-year-old child who had been beaten to death by his parents--a death that was the culmination of years of parental abuse. Appalled by such a tragedy, Barry decided that he would enter a career in which he could do something about such social problems. One possibility was being an intervention worker in the county juvenile court. In applying for this position, Barry found that a bachelor's degree in psychology was highly desirable. Now in this position, he derives great satisfaction from both a career and personal view. He knows that some of his recommendations have probably saved the lives of several children and contributed to greater happiness in the lives of others.

Melanie Lawton also earned a bachelor's degree in psychology. Long before she graduated, she knew that she wanted an advanced degree in psychology so that she could become a practicing clinical psychologist. After graduation, Melanie applied for and was accepted into a program in psychology leading to the degree of doctor of psychology. In her four years of graduate training, which included both course work and supervised experience dealing with people, Melanie gradually acquired the skills that she would have to use when practicing psychology independently. After a year's internship at a community mental health center, Melanie obtained the doctor of psychology degree. Because she enjoyed the experience during her year's internship, she applied for and was hired as a psychologist at a mental health center in a town along the Pacific coast of California, an area in which she had always wanted to live. As a psychologist in the day treatment program at the mental health center, Melanie includes in her case load several clients who are functioning well enough to live at home and to engage in many normal activities. However, these clients are still troubled by a variety of problems and must see Melanie on an ongoing basis for therapy. Melanie herself is gratified that she is contributing to the long-term happiness of her clients. She finds satisfaction in the fact that with her help, "her people" are able to live at home in their community instead of in a state mental institution.

Each person depicted above is fictitious. But any one of them could be you reading this workbook. The employment outlook for persons with bachelors, masters, and doctorates in psychology is excellent. Additionally, the variety of employment available, particularly at the bachelor's degree level, lets people find positions that suit them and in which they may find substantial satisfaction. If you are interested in exploring areas of employment in psychology, write to the Administrative Services Department of the American Psychological Association for their booklet *Careers in Psychology* (1979). Also, be sure to read through the "What Does It Mean?" section of Chapter 1 in your textbook. It includes a list of the various subdivisions of psychology and where to obtain information about these interest areas.

1 The Nature of Psychology

OBJECTIVES

1. What are the three components in the definition of psychology?
2. What are the four goals of psychology?
3. What are the six examples of modern controversies in psychology?
4. What are the five specific nonexperimental methods, and what is the correlational approach?
5. What are the defining features of the experimental method, and what are its strengths and weaknesses?
6. When is quasi experimentation used, and what are its major weakness and strength relative to the true experiment?
7. What are the five historical schools of psychology, what issues did they study, and what methods did they use?
8. What are the two contemporary trends in psychology, and what are their contributions to psychology?

SYNOPSIS

This chapter introduces you to psychology. You will learn how psychology is defined, its goals, some of the major controversies, the methods that make it a science, its historical roots, and some contemporary trends.

The definition of psychology has three components. First, psychology is a body of knowledge about behavior rather than a set of half-truths, old wive's tales, slogans, intuitions, wild guesses, bold assertions, and unsubstantiated common sense. Second, this knowledge is obtained through scientific research methods. Third, this knowledge is applied to psychological problems so as to improve the welfare of all people.

There are four goals. First, behavior must be described and measured with instruments that are reliable and valid. Second, these measurements are used to predict what people will do in the future. Third, methods such as behavior modification are used to control and modify predictable behaviors that are undesirable. And fourth, theories are used to organize known facts so as to make reasonable guesses as to the explanations of these facts.

There are six major controversies that cut across several areas of psychology: free will versus determinism, mind versus body, heredity versus environment, conscious versus unconscious control, general laws versus individual differences, and determination of behavior by past versus persent circumstances.

The methods of psychology can be broken down into nonexperimental, experimental, and quasi experimental. The nonexperimental methods include the case study, which entails individual biographical measurements used primarily for application purposes; naturalistic observation, which involves systematic but unobtrusive measurements in natural settings; and tests, interviews, and surveys, which may be used for either applied or research purposes. The correlational approach, which can use any of these methods, is intended as a way of finding positive and negative relationships among variables.

The strength of the experimental method is its potential for determining cause and effect among variables. The independent variable is manipulated, and the effect of this manipulation on the dependent variable is observed. This method requires control groups as well as the random assignment of subjects to these groups.

In circumstances in which manipulation is impossible, or possible but unethical, there are quasi experimental methods such as the time-series design. In general, this method is weaker than the true experiment on causality is, but stronger on generalizability.

Historically, the science and application of psychology grew from the ideas and methodologies of the early "schools" of psychology. Included among these schools are structuralism, functionalism, behaviorism, Gestalt psychology, and psychoanalysis.

Two of the more contemporary trends are human information processing and humanism. The former has contributed greatly to the areas of human learning, memory, and cognition, and the latter represents a clear protest against the prevailing mechanistic trend in contemporary psychology.

KEY WORDS AND PHRASES

OBJECTIVE 1

psychology
knowledge
research
application

OBJECTIVE 2

description/measurement
reliability
validity
prediction
control/modification
explanation

OBJECTIVE 3

free will versus determinism
mind versus body
nature versus nurture
conscious versus unconscious
general laws versus individual differences
past versus present causes of behavior

OBJECTIVE 4

individual case study
naturalistic observation
unobtrusive measurement
tests
interviews
surveys
variable
correlation coefficient

OBJECTIVE 5

experiment
independent variable
dependent variable
cause-effect relationship
operational definition
control groups
random selection
random assignment
internal validity
external validity
generalization
placebo
demand characteristics
blind
double blind
confounding

OBJECTIVE 6

quasi experiment
time-series design

OBJECTIVE 7

consciousness
structuralism
    introspection
    sensations/images/feelings
functionalism
    stream of consciousness
behaviorism
organizational processes
Gestalt psychology
psychoanalysis
    unconsciousness motivation

OBJECTIVE 8

cognition
information processing
stages of memory
limited capacity processor
humanistic psychology

EXERCISES

EXERCISE 1: Objectives 1 and 2

TITLE: DEFINITION AND GOALS
TASK: Fill in the blanks

1. _____ is best defined as a science of behavior.
2. Psychology contains a body of _____.
3. Psychology uses _____ methods to obtain this knowledge.
4. Psychology _____ this knowledge for the welfare of society.
5. The first goal of psychology is to _____ and measure behavior.
6. Measurements in psychological research must be consistent in repeated testing; that is, they must be _____.
7. Measurements in psychological research must also measure what they are supposed to measure; that is, they must be _____.
8. The second goal of psychology is to _____ future behavior.
9. The third goal of psychology is to _____ and modify behavior with methods such as behavior modification.
10. The fourth and final goal of psychology is to _____ behavior by formulating theories that group facts and pose reasonable guesses.

EXERCISE 2: Objective 3

TITLE: CONTROVERSIES IN PSYCHOLOGY
TASK: Match letters to numbers

____1. Physical versus nonphysical causes
____2. Science of behavior versus individual uniqueness
____3. Hidden causes versus full awareness
____4. Self-determination versus outside forces
____5. Early childhood versus current circumstances
____6. Heredity versus environment

A. free will versus determinism
B. mind versus body
C. nature versus nurture
D. conscious versus unconscious
E. general laws versus individual differences
F. past versus present causes of behavior

EXERCISE 3: Objectives 4, 5, and 6

TITLE: METHODS OF PSYCHOLOGICAL INVESTIGATION
TASK: Match letters to numbers

____1. General opinions, attitudes, or feelings regarding a given issue.
____2. Systematic and unobtrusive measures in the real world.
____3. They may be structured or unstructured.
____4. Manipulation and control of variables and random selection and assignment of subjects.
____5. An individual and biographical account that often combines information from tests and interviews.

_____ 6. Obtaining relationships between two (or more) variables.
_____ 7. With methods such as time-series designs, it permits greater generalizability than the experiment does.
_____ 8. Can be used to measure many things such as general ability, intelligence, and traits.

A. case study
B. naturalistic observation
C. psychological tests
D. interviews
E. surveys
F. experiment
G. quasi experiment
H. correlational approach

EXERCISE 4: Objective 3

TITLE: POSITIVE VERSUS NEGATIVE CORRELATIONS
TASK: Match letters to numbers

_____ 1. Two variables whose values move in opposite directions.
_____ 2. Two variables whose values move in the same direction.
_____ 3. There is a tendency for weight to increase as height increases.
_____ 4. There is a tendency for weight to decrease as height decreases.
_____ 5. There is a tendency for weight to decrease as the number of hours of exercise increases.

A. positive correlation
B. negative correlation

EXERCISE 5: Objective 4

TITLE: A RESEARCH SCENARIO
TASK: Fill in the blanks

Suppose I were interested in the effects of a drug on anxiety and as a result of this interest did the following research. I used a psychological test as my operational definition of anxiety, and for my major manipulation I randomly assigned twenty subjects with high anxiety scores to one of two groups. Group 1 received the psychoactive antianxiety drug (called anxiorelief), whereas Group 2 received a sugar pill. Of course, both groups were led to believe that they were receiving anxiorelief, and it is important to note that the researcher was unaware of which group received which treatment. After taking the pills, both groups were tested for anxiety again, using the same method as before.

1. This study should be classified as a(n) _____.
2. Anxiety is the _____ variable.
3. The drug anxiorelief is the _____ variable.
4. The group receiving the sugar pill is a control group, and this type of control is called _____.
5. Another control condition here is the fact neither the researcher nor the subjects knew which group received which treatment. This type of control is called _____.

5

6. If the subjects knew what this research was for, they might act in a way that they thought the researcher wanted them to act. This type of behavior defines _____.

7. Assuming that the only difference between groups is drug versus sugar pills, we could conclude that there were no confounds. In other words, the results would be _____ valid.

8. Moreover, if the results were generalizable to students from many different colleges and universities, then the results would also be _____ valid.

EXERCISE 6: Objective 4

TITLE: WHAT'S WRONG WITH THIS EXPERIMENT?
TASK: Essay

Dr. Wise is the head administrator at a drug treatment center named Happy House. Recently, he's been under pressure to show that the treatment offered at Happy House is effective in "curing" drug addiction. In order to demonstrate this, Wise selected 100 drug addicts: 50 had volunteered for treatment at Happy House, whereas the other 50 were addicts found in the streets. After six months, Wise found that 80 percent of the addicts receiving treatment were cured (that is, they were no longer dependent on drugs). In comparison, only 15 percent of the "street" addicts were cured (that is, they showed spontaneous remission). Wise's conclusion was that the difference between the 80 percent and 15 percent cure rates was entirely a function of the Happy House treatment. What do you think?

EXERCISE 7: Objectives 7 and 8

TITLE: HISTORY AND CONTEMPORARY TRENDS
TASK: Match letters to numbers

_____1. The goal is to find lawful stimulus-response relationships.
_____2. Each individual is unique and has a free will.
_____3. Use of introspection to determine basic elements or building blocks of the mind.
_____4. Stages of memory, top-down processing, limited capacity processor, and the like.
_____5. The importance of early childhood experiences.
_____6. The whole is different from the sum of the parts.
_____7. Action rather than contents of the mind.
_____8. Sensations, images, and feelings.
_____9. Protest against the prevailing mechanistic trend in contemporary psychology.
_____10. Learning and problem solving as functions of the mind's organizational processes.
_____11. Learning in terms of classical conditioning.
_____12. How the mind permits us to adapt to the environment.
_____13. Currently the strongest influence on learning, memory, language, and cognition.
_____14. Conflicting unconscious motives.

A. structuralism
B. functionalism
C. behaviorism
D. Gestalt psychology

E. psychoanalysis
F. human information processing
G. humanism

EXERCISE 8: Objectives 7 and 8

TITLE: KEY NAMES
TASK: Fill in the blanks

1. The structuralist who used introspection to study the elements of consciousness was _____.
2. The functionalist who believed that mind was a "stream of consciousness" was _____.
3. The names of three functionalists other than James are _____, _____, and _____.
4. The scientist who espoused evolutionary principles that greatly influenced functionalism was _____.
5. The behaviorist who espoused the need for lawful relations between stimuli and responses was _____.
6. The scientist whose research on classical conditioning greatly influenced behaviorism was _____.
7. The Gestalt psychologists who were interested in how the mind's organization influences learning and problem solving were _____, _____, and _____.
8. Two contemporary humanists who reacted against the prevailing deterministic and mechanistic trends in psychology are _____ and _____.

MULTIPLE-CHOICE TESTS

SELF-TEST 1

1. A body of knowledge, a set of research methods, and application of the knowledge are the three major aspects of:
    a. the philosophy of psychology
    b. the science of psychology
    c. the application of psychology
    d. the teaching of psychology
    (page 2)

2. If little Johnny consistently obtained the same IQ score every time that he took the same intelligence test, we would say that this test is:
    a. powerful
    b. reliable
    c. valid
    d. confounded
    (page 2)

3. If a researcher developed a test to measure anxiety and people with known differences in anxiety level got the same exact score, we would call this test:

a. powerless
b. unreliable
c. invalid
d. predictive
(page 2)

4. Which is the final goal of psychology?
a. measurement or description
b. prediction
c. control or modification
d. explanation
(page 3)

5. Which of the following is not a contemporary controversy in psychology?
a. nature versus nurture
b. past versus present causes
c. perception versus extrasensory perception
d. mind versus body
(pages 3 and 4)

6. The *Diary of Anne Frank* might be of particular interest to a psychologist interested in:
a. basic research
b. a case study
c. naturalistic observation
d. a psychological test
(page 5)

7. If your goal as a researcher is to chronicle behavior without altering it, then you would probably use the method called:
a. case study
b. structured interview
c. survey
d. naturalistic observation
(page 5)

8. Opinion polls and marketing research are two forms of the general research method called:
a. survey
b. psychological test
c. naturalistic observation
d. experiment
(page 6)

9. Correlation coefficients allow us to fulfill one of the goals of psychology. More specifically, they allow us to _____ behavior.
a. explain
b. control
c. describe
d. predict
(page 6)

10. Which of the following methods of research manipulates and controls variables?
a. naturalistic observation
b. survey

c. experiment
d. case study
(page 7)

11. If a researcher examined the effect of a change in temperature on the growth of a plant, the change in temperature would be called:
a. a dependent variable
b. an independent variable
c. an uncorrelated variable
d. a control variable
(page 9)

12. The measure of plant growth in the experiment described in the question above would be called:
a. a dependent variable
b. an independent variable
c. an uncorrelated variable
d. a control variable
(page 9)

13. Potentially, the greatest strength of a true experiment is the ability to determine:
a. a placebo effect
b. internal validity
c. external validity
d. unintrusiveness
(page 10)

14. Potentially, the greatest weakness of a true experiment is often the failure to obtain:
a. a placebo effect
b. internal validity
c. external validity
d. unintrusiveness
(page 10)

15. External validity is potentially maximized in:
a. an experiment
b. manipulative studies
c. laboratory studies
d. quasi experiments
(page 13)

16. The search for the elements of the mind was a characteristic of the psychologists who are referred to as:
a. structuralists
b. functionalists
c. behaviorists
d. psychoanalysts
(page 14)

17. Emphasis on the role of individual perception as controlling the mind's organizational processes was characteristic of the psychologists who are called:

a. structuralists
b. functionalists
c. Gestaltists
d. humanists
(page 16)

18. Because of its reliance on a deterministic framework for the control of behavior, behaviorism was most like:
    a. structuralism
    b. humanism
    c. psychoanalytic theory
    d. functionalism
    (page 17)

19. The shortest "memory" of an event is said to occur in:
    a. sensory memory
    b. short-term memory
    c. long-term memory
    c. limited capacity processor
    (page 18)

20. The leading contemporary proponents in psychology of the concept of free will are called:
    a. behaviorists
    b. humanists
    c. elitists
    d. cognitivists
    (page 19)

SELF-TEST 2

1. The basic knowledge of the discipline of psychology comes from:
   a. scientific facts
   b. self knowledge
   c. philosophy
   d. religion
   (page 2)

2. Reliability would be exemplified in which of the following:
   a. a test that measures what it is supposed to measure
   b. getting the same TV channel every time you push the same button on the tuner
   c. a psychological scale that predicts who will be the best salesperson out of a group of friends
   d. the behavior of a dog that is controlled by events similar to those that control the behavior of a cat
   (page 2)

3. The scientific aim of control is exemplified in the area of psychology called:
   a. humanism
   b. psychoanalysis
   c. behavior modification
   d. information processing
   (page 3)

4. Questions about the causes of mental illness would probably be discussed in:
    a. the mind versus body controversy
    b. the nature versus nurture controversy
    c. the conscious versus unconscious processes controversy
    d. all of the above
    (pages 3 and 4)

5. A case study would most likely involve:
    a. structured interview
    b. unstructured interview
    c. quasi experimentation
    d. double blinds
    (page 5)

6. Suppose that you sat in a tree overlooking some children playing on swings in a playground. You measured how frequently they jumped off the swings and when. You were not seen by the children. This would be:
    a. a case study
    b. a naturalistic observation
    c. a quasi experimention
    d. a true experiment
    (page 5)

7. A researcher discoveres that the neater the home environment is, the more intelligent the child will be. Which correlation coefficient below best describes this relationship?
    a. +.50
    b. -.50
    c. 0
    d. -1.00
    (page 6)

8. If intelligence is defined as "what IQ tests measure," this definition is:
    a. explanatory
    b. predictive
    c. descriptive
    d. operational
    (page 9)

9. Random assignment of subjects and control of variables are the hallmark of:
    a. quasi experimentation
    b. case studies
    c. true experiments
    d. correlational methods
    (page 9)

10. If the results of an experiment apply to populations other than the one sampled, the experiment is said to have great:
    a. external validity
    b. internal validity
    c. reliability
    d. insight
    (page 10)

11. If a researcher wanted to discover the effect of watching pornography on moral development in children, for ethical reasons she would probably NOT use which method?
    a. case study
    b. survey
    c. quasi experiment
    d. true experiment
    (page 11)

12. If you clapped and cheered every time the children jumped off the swing and measured the change in jump frequency, the research would be:
    a. a case study
    b. a naturalistic observation
    c. a quasi expeimentation
    d. a true experiment
    (page 11)

13. If you measured the change in highway accidents following introduction of a new DWI law, the procedrue to use would be:
    a. double blind
    b. time series
    c. single blind
    d. correlation
    (page 12)

14. Which school of psychological thought was LEAST concerned with the mind?
    a. structuralism
    b. functionalism
    c. behaviorism
    d. Gestalt psychology
    (page 15)

15. The school of psychological thought that was greatly influenced by Darwin's theories was:
    a. functionalism
    b. structuralism
    c. behaviorism
    d. psychoanalysis
    (page 15)

16. Who among the following could be characterized as a behaviorist?
    a. Freud
    b. James
    c. Wundt
    d. Watson
    (page 15)

17. The method of introspection to investigate sensations, images, and feelings was used extensively by the school of psychological thought called:
    a. functionalism
    b. behaviorism
    c. structuralism
    d. humanism
    (page 15)

18. Freud's research primarily was of what kind?
    a. experiment
    b. naturalistic observation
    c. case study
    d. survey
    (page 17)

19. The view that human beings are rational and in full conscious command
    of their behavior was threatened by which trend in psychology?
    a. structuralism
    b. psychoanalysis
    c. information processing
    d. humanism
    (page 17)

20. Our inability to recall large amounts of information at one time can be
    traced to which role of the human information-processing system?
    a. input
    b. output
    c. processor
    d. memory bank
    (page 18)

WHAT DOES IT MEAN?

OBJECTIVES

1. What are the seven major specialty areas in psychology?
2. What kind of training is necessary to earn the various degrees in
   psychology?
3. How is psychology applied in law, medicine, and advertising?
4. Why is there an ethical code in psychology?
5. What are the common misconceptions about psychology?

SELF-TEST

1. Psychologists who study how people interact with one another, often
   focusing on attitudes, beliefs, and values, are called _____
   psychologists.
   a. developmental
   b. social
   c. clinical
   d. industrial/organizational
   (page 21)

2. Psychologists who study changes in behavior over an individual's life
   span are called _____ psychologists.
   a. clinical
   b. social
   c. developmental
   d. experimental
   (page 21)

3. Psychologists who study how the nervous system, hormones, and genes influence behavior are called _____ psychologists.
   a. clinical
   b. developmental
   c. experimental
   d. biological
   (page 21)

4. Psychologists who study learning, sensation and perception, human performance, motivation and emotion, and language, thinking, and communication are usually called _____ psychologists.
   a. industrial/organizational
   b. biological
   c. experimental
   d. educational
   (page 21)

5. Psychologists who specialize in the assessment and treatment of emotional and/or adjustment problems are called _____ psychologists.
   a. clinical and counseling
   b. social
   c. developmental
   d. biological
   (page 21)

6. Psychologists who study work-related behaviors, job satisfaction, employee morale, and similar topics are called _____ psychologists.
   a. clinical and counseling
   b. social
   c. educational
   d. industrial/organizational
   (page 22)

7. Psychologists who specialize in applying psychology to the design, development, and evaluation of training materials and programs are called _____ psychologists.
   a. social
   b. developmental
   c. industrial/organizational
   d. educational
   (page 22)

8. Psychologists who focus on the treatment of individual alcoholics would probably be called _____ psychologists.
   a. biological
   b. clinical
   c. developmental
   d. social
   (page 22)

9. Psychologists who focus on the reinforcement value of alcohol for alcoholics would probably be called _____ psychologists.
   a. biological
   b. educational
   c. developmental
   d. experimental
   (page 22)

10. The genetic basis of alcoholism might be the interest of _____ psychologists.
    a. biological
    b. clinical
    c. social
    d. educational
    (page 22)

11. In most states, a person could advertise as a psychologist if he or she:
    a. had a doctoral degree in psychology
    b. had a doctoral degree in psychology and at least one year of supervised internship
    c. had a doctoral degree and at least one year of supervised internship and passed a licensing examination
    d. had a doctoral degree and at least one year of supervised internship, passed a licensing examination, and was certified to practice by the American Psychological Association
    (page 23)

12. Which degree usually requires the most practical experience, as compared with research experience?
    a. B.A.
    b. M.A.
    c. Ph.D.
    d. Psy.D.
    (page 23)

13. The degree that affords the fewest opportunities to practice psychology is the:
    a. bachelors
    b. masters
    d. doctor of psychology
    d. doctor of philosophy
    (page 23)

14. Which of the following is NOT an activity of the American Psychological Association?
    a. fostering ethical principles in psychology
    b. accrediting graduate programs in psychology
    c. certifying psychologists for licensure
    d. promotion of the public welfare
    (page 23)

15. Psychological research suggests that juries are least likely to convict a person if the _____ reminds them at the _____ of the trial that the accused is presumed innocent until proven guilty.
    a. defense attorney; beginning
    b. defense attorney; end
    c. judge; beginning
    d. judge; end
    (page 24)

16. Psychological research suggests that _____ can be traced directly to a person's life-style.
    a. cancer
    b. accidents
    c. Addison's disease
    d. mononucleosis
    (page 24)

17. Innuendo and inference are used extensively in the application of psychological principles to:
    a. law
    b. medicine
    c. advertising
    d. teaching
    (page 25)

18. Which of the following behaviors would NOT be an ethical violation by a psychologist?
    a. concealing the purpose of an experiment from a subject
    b. having a sexual relationship with a client
    c. insisting that employees and students adhere to the ethical code
    d. holding clinical information confidential
    (page 27)

19. Trying to discover why you behave as you do is an important feature of:
    a. attribution theory
    b. clinical theory
    c. reciprocal theory
    d. developmental theory
    (page 28)

20. Which of the following is correct?
    a. children of low intelligence usually are just slow starters and become brighter as they mature
    b. most geniuses are mentally disturbed
    c. red-headed people are no more temperamental than anyone else
    d. animals cannot think
    (page 28)

ANSWER KEY

EXERCISES

Exercise 1

1.	psychology	5.	describe	9.	control
2.	knowledge	6.	reliable	10.	explain
3.	research	7.	valid		
4.	applies	8.	predict		

Exercise 2

1. B   2. E   3. D   4. A   5. F   6. C

Exercise 3

1. E   5. A
2. B   6. H
3. D   7. G
4. F   8. C

Exercise 4

1. B   2. A   3. A   4. A   5. B

Exercise 5

1. experiment   5. double-blind
2. dependent   6. demand characteristics
3. independent   7. internally
4. placebo   8. externally

Exercise 6

Let's assume that we have no problem with the operational definition of "cure" (that is the amount of time off drugs). The real problem here is one of selection bias. The subjects were not randomly assigned to the two groups. There could be, and probably is, a good reason that some addicts seek help and others do not. This difference (rather than treatment versus nontreatment) could be responsible for the difference in the cure rate. Thus, the experiment is confounded (that is, lacks internal validity). The only way to unconfound this study would be to assign subjects who want treatment into treatment and no-treatment groups. However, this would raise ethical issues about withholding treatment from those who want or need it.

Exercise 7

1. C   5. E   9. G   13. F
2. G   6. D   10. D   14. E
3. A   7. B   11. C
4. F   8. A   12. B

Exercise 8

1. Wundt
2. James
3. Cattell, Dewey, and Thorndike
4. Darwin
5. Watson
6. Pavlov
7. Kohler, Koffka, and Wertheimer
8. Maslow and Rogers

MULTIPLE CHOICE

Self-Test 1

1.	b	5.	c	9.	d	13.	b	17.	c
2.	b	6.	b	10.	c	14.	c	18.	c
3.	c	7.	d	11.	b	15.	d	19.	a
4.	d	8.	a	12.	a	16.	a	20.	b

Self-Test 2

1.	a	5.	a	9.	c	13.	b	17.	c
2.	b	6.	b	10.	a	14.	c	18.	c
3.	c	7.	a	11.	d	15.	a	19.	b
4.	d	8.	d	12.	c	16.	d	20.	c

WHAT DOES IT MEAN?

Self-Test

1.	b	5.	a	9.	d	13.	a	17.	c
2.	c	6.	d	10.	a	14.	c	18.	c
3.	d	7.	d	11.	c	15.	c	19.	a
4.	c	8.	b	12.	b	16.	b	20.	c

2 Biological Foundations of Behavior

OBJECTIVES

1. How is the control and flow of information in the nervous system analogous to the control and flow of information in a computer?
2. What are the major anatomical and neurochemical components of the neuron?
3. How are neuronal circuits organized to code information?
4. How do neurons develop, and what are the implications of physical damage and environmental enrichment?
5. What are the major divisions and subdivisions of the nervous system?
6. What are the specific structures and functions of the brain?
7. What are the implications of lateralization, brain sexuality, and biological clocks?
8. What are the major components of the endocrine system, and how do endocrine hormones and chemical modulators interrelate with the nervous system to control behavior?
9. What methods are used in behavioral genetic research to discover the relative contributions of heredity and environment to behavior?

SYNOPSIS

This chapter introduces you to the biological foundations of behavior. You will learn about the structures and functions of both the nervous system and the endocrine system, as well as the methods and issues important to behavioral genetics.

In many ways the nervous system is analogous to a computer. Information enters the system by way of the sensory systems (input). It is then processed, and appropriate responses may be initiated by way of neuromuscular junctions (output). Also like a computer, there are "hard-wired" circuits that are preprogrammed to carry out automatically functions such as breathing and "soft-wired" circuits that can be programmed according to the organism's experiences.

The elementary unit of the nervous system is the neuron, and its major anatomical parts are the soma (or cell body), dendrite, and axon. Action potentials cause the release of fast-acting chemical transmitters from axon terminals into the synaptic space, and these transmitters then excite or inhibit the postsynaptic cell. There are also slower-acting chemical modulators that are released by the pituitary and that interact with transmitters at various synapses.

A single neuron can provide information by increasing or decreasing its base firing rate. The brain can interpret this change in state, and it can also interpret the number of neurons that have changed state as well as the area in the nervous system in which these changes have occurred. When neurons act in groups, it is often possible for one group to have the opposite effect on a neighboring group (lateral inhibition). In the sensory cortex, there are hard-wired circuits preprogrammed to react to specific kinds of visual stimuli (for example, lines, angles). Moreover, the cells of these circuits (simple, complex, and hypercomplex) have different functions with respect to the specific stimuli.

It is thought that we are born with all or most of our neurons in place and that with growth, the brain develops by completing the connections between the neurons. However, more recent evidence suggests that with growth, some neurons are also eliminated (pruning) to streamline the neural circuits. In either event, neurons do not reproduce and dead neurons are not replaced, but damaged axons can regenerate. Regeneration is more likely to occur in the younger organism and in the peripheral rather than in the central nervous system. Also, there is some evidence that environmental enrichment can facilitate, whereas sensory isolation can retard, the development of the nervous system.

The two major divisions of the nervous system are the central (CNS) and the peripheral (PNS) nervous systems. In the CNS, composed of the brain and the spinal cord, the most basic life functions are at fairly low levels, and more complex functions such as thinking are organized at higher levels. The PNS is divided into a somatic division that serves the voluntary muscles and an autonomic division that serves the involuntary muscles and glands. The autonomic division is further divided into a sympathetic division that controls energy expenditures associated with emergency reactions and emotions and a parasympathetic division that maintains equilibrium and conserves energy.

In the "split-brain" operation, the corpus callosum is severed, leaving two independent hemispheres. The experiences of split-brain patients reveal the extent to which each side controls different cognitive and emotional processes (a phenomenon called *lateralization*). There are also sexual differences in the brain's function and even structure in both the nervous and endocrine systems. Finally, there is a biological "clock" that controls the various mechanisms, the most common of which (circadian rhythm) cycles every twenty-four hours.

The endocrine system is a collection of glands that secrete hormones into general circulation. The hypothalamus controls the pituitary gland which, in turn, controls other endocrine glands by way of the trophic hormones such as ACTH. Some of the major activities under endocrine control are growth, metabolism, sexual development, fluid regulation, and temperature regulation. Additionally, activation of the autonomic nervous system may stimulate the release of stress hormones from the adrenal gland, and modulators can act both locally and systemically to alter potentials at receptor sites on neurons or other cells. Finally, recent interest has centered on a group of peptides known as cortical steroids (secreted from the adrenal cortex).

Behavioral genetics is the study of the degree and nature of inherited aspects of behavior. By controlling both the environment and subject selection, scientists attempt to separate genetic from environmental determinants and interactions. Selective breeding and inbred strain comparisons are two typical methods used with animals, and comparisons among identical twins, fraternal twins, and other siblings represent a nonintrusive way of studying humans.

KEY WORDS AND PHRASES

OBJECTIVE 1

input function
processing function
output function
transduction
afferent nerves
efferent nerves
hard-wired systems
programmable systems

OBJECTIVE 2

neuron
soma
dendrites
axon
myelin sheath
synapse
chemical transmitter substances
action potentials
modulators
receptor sites

OBJECTIVE 3

base rate of firing
neural codes
lateral inhibition
detector circuits
receptive field
simple cells
complex cells
hypercomplex cells

OBJECTIVE 4

equipotentiality
regeneration
sprouting
pruning
enrichment
isolation

OBJECTIVE 5

central nervous system (CNA)
peripheral nervous system (PNS)
somatic division
autonomic division
sympathetic nervous system
parasympathetic nervous system
spinal cord
PET scan

OBJECTIVE 6

brain stem
pons
medulla oblongata
cerebellum
reticular formation
thalamus
hypothalamus
cortex
corpus callosum
motor cortex
sensory cortex
association cortex
frontal lobe
occipital lobe
temporal lobe
parietal lobe
basal ganglia
caudate nucleus
putamen
globus pallidus
limbic system
pleasure centers

OBJECTIVE 7

split-brain operation
lateralization
brain sexuality
biological clock
zeitgeber
circadian rhythm
period of a rhythm
biorhythms
chronobiology

OBJECTIVE 8

endocrine system
endocrine glands
hormones
pituitary gland
thyroid-stimulating hormone
growth hormone
ACTH
gonadotropic hormones
ADH
peptides
thyroid gland
thyroxin
adrenal glands
adrenal medulla
adrenal cortex

cortisol
ovaries
testes

OBJECTIVE 9

behavioral genetics
chromosomes
DNA
RNA
phenylketonuria (PKU)
recessive gene
dominant gene
selective breeding
inbred strains
twin/sibling comparisons

EXERCISES

EXERCISE 1: Objective 1

TITLE: INFORMATION FLOW
TASK: Fill in the blanks

1.   The various sensory systems bring information from the outside world
     into the nervous system. This is termed the _____ function.
2.   The actual conversion of physical energy into nervous energy is called
     _____ .
3.   The _____ nerves carry information to the spinal cord and brain.
4.   Once information is centralized, it is compared with other information
     so that decisions can be made. This is known as the _____ function.
5.   After a decision has been made, the system must carry messages to the
     sites of action--what is known as the _____ function.
6.   It is the _____ nerves that carry information from the brain and
     spinal cord to the muscles and glands.
7.   Many biologically vital functions such as breathing are genetically
     _____ so that tney may be carried out automatically.
8.   In comparison, other functions can be programmed by _____, much
     like a computer software.

EXERCISE 2: Objective 2

TITLE: THE NEURON
TASK: A typical neuron is pictured below. Draw lines from the lables
        to the corresponding parts in the diagram.

Axon terminals

Myelin sheath

Axon

Dendrites

Soma (cell body)

Nucleus

EXERCISE 3:   Objective 2

TITLE: ANATOMY AND NEUROCHEMISTRY OF THE NEURON
TASK: Match letters to numbers

_____1. After an action, potential information is conducted to this portion of the axon.
_____2. These act like receiving stations that pick up information from other neurons.
_____3. Free-floating hormonelike substances that interact with the faster-acting transmitter substances.
_____4. Contains the nucleus that, in turn, controls cellular activities such as oxygen utilization and energy production.
_____5. The lipid (fatty) substance separated by nodes that speeds up conduction in the axon.
_____6. Conducts information away from the cell body during an action potential.
_____7. The fast-acting substances that are released from the axon terminals into the synaptic space after an action potential.
_____8. The postsynaptic effect of transmitters.
_____9. The junction of an axon terminal of one cell with the dendrite (for example) of a second cell.
_____10. The basic information conducted in an axon.

A.	soma (cell body)	F.	terminals
B.	dendrites	G.	synapse
C.	axon	H.	transmitters
D.	action potential	I.	excitation/inhibition
E.	meylin sheath	J.	modulators

EXERCISE 4: Objective 3

TITLE: CODING OF INFORMATION
TASK: Fill in the blanks

1.   A single neuron can code information by increasing or decreasing its _____ rate of firing.
2.   In addition, information is coded by _____ of neurons that are firing and their _____.
3.   When neurons A, B, and C react in a chain and they all report to neuron X, we call this a _____ circuit.

4. Within dectector circuits, when inhibition comes from neurons alongside one another, this is known as _____ inhibition.
5. In a given detection circuit, a _____ cell might respond to a vertical line, but only in a given portion of the visual field.
6. A _____ cell might respond to the vertical line, regardless of its location in the visual field.
7. A _____ cell might require a pattern of vertical lines such as a right angle.

EXERCISE 5: Objective 4

TITLE: NEURON DEVELOPMENT, DAMAGE, AND REPAIR
TASK: Short essays

1. What is the principle of equipotentiality?
2. Why are neurons not replaced?
3. What is sprouting, and what are its implications?
4. How complete is our nervous system at birth, and how is it thought to develop with age?

EXERCISE 6: Objective 5

TITLE: DIVISIONS AND SUBDIVISIONS OF THE NERVOUS SYSTEM
TASK: Fill in the blanks

1. The _____ consists of the brain and the spinal cord.
2. The _____ consists of nerves that run to and from the brain and spinal cord.
3. Specifically, there are 12 pairs of _____ nerves and 31 pairs of _____ nerves.
4. The _____ division of the PNS consists of nerves that primarily serve the voluntary muscles.
5. The _____ division of the PNS serves the involuntary muscles and glands.
6. The _____ division of the autonomic nervous system becomes more dominant as the intensity of emotion increases.
7. The _____ division of the autonomic nervous system dominates during relaxation and calmness.
8. The _____ is like a cable that sends information to and from the brain and to effectors.
9. _____ nerves carry sensory information to the brain.
10. _____ nerves carry information to muscles.

EXERCISE 7: Objective 6

TITLE: THE BRAIN
TASK: Draw lines from the labels on the left to the brain structures they refer to.

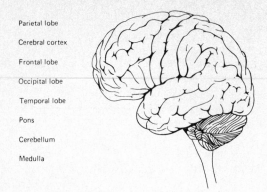

Parietal lobe

Cerebral cortex

Frontal lobe

Occipital lobe

Temporal lobe

Pons

Cerebellum

Medulla

EXERCISE 8: Objective 6

TITLE: THE BRAIN STEM
TASK: Match letters to numbers

_____1. Involved in the control of muscles and muscle coordination.
_____2. Involved in the control of sleep and wakefulness.
_____3. Contains many nuclei that control behavioral functions such as
         sleeping, eating, emotional control, and sexual behavior.
_____4. The major sensory relay station carrying incoming information to
         the cortex.
_____5. Involved in controlling vegetative functions.

A. pons and reticular formation
B. medulla oblongata and pons
C. cerebellum
D. thalamus
E. hypothalamus

EXERCISE 9: Objective 6

TITLE: THE CORTEX
TASK: Fill in the blanks

1. The _____ is like "bread dough overlying a buried fist" and is
    separated down the middle into two hemispheres.
2. The band of fibers that separates the two hemispheres is called the
    _____.
3. In terms of function, the _____ cortex controls the movements of
    particular body parts.
4. The _____ cortex receives incoming information from the body's sense
    organs.
5. The _____ cortex is all the rest of the cortex that is programmable.
6. The cortex is divided into four _____.
7. The _____ lobe is largely association and motor cortex.
8. The _____ lobe is largely sensory cortex for the visual system.
9. The _____ lobe is largely sensory cortex for audition and
    association cortex.

10. The _____ lobe is largely somatosensory cortex and association cortex.
11. The _____ contain three major nuclei called the caudate nucleus, putamen, and globus pallidus.
12. The basal ganglia are involved in the control of movement, and their degeneration leads to _____ and _____.
13. The _____ consists of several areas and connections, and these areas control many functions such as eating, drinking, and aggression.

EXERCISE 10: Objective 7

TITLE: LATERALIZATION, BRAIN SEXUALITY, AND THE BIOLOGICAL CLOCKS
TASK: Short essays

1. What is the split-brain operation, and what have the results of this procedure told us about the brain organization of intellectual and emotional behavior?
2. What are the major male and female brain differences, and what implications do they have for biology and behavior?
3. What are the rhythmic activities that are built into our systems?

EXERCISE 11: Objective 8

TITLE: THE ENDOCRINE SYSTEM AS A WHOLE
TASK: Fill in the blanks

1. The endocrine system consists of a number of glands that secrete chemical messengers known as _____.
2. The "master" gland, or the _____, consists of the andenohypophysis, which secretes four hormones, and the neurophypophysis, which secretes two hormones.
3. In the adenohypophysis, thyroid-stimulating hormone controls the release of _____ from the thyroid gland, and this hormone controls the rate of metabolism of body cells.
4. _____ hormone serves metabolic functions involved in the growth rate of bones and soft tissues.
5. _____ acts on the adrenal cortex to secrete the release of hormones such as cortisol, which increases the rate of energy production in the cells.
6. The adenohypophysis secretes a group of sex hormones known collectively as the _____.
7. _____, secreted from the neurohypophysis acts on kidney cells to decrease amount of water passed to the bladder.
8. _____, secreted from the neurohypophysis, acts on mammary tissue to promote milk ejection and also causes smooth muscles in the uterus to contract.
9. The pituitary and hypothalamus are also implicated in the manufacture and release of peptides known as _____.
10. One neuromodulator, which acts like morphine, is _____.
11. Body metabolism is regulated by the _____.
12. The _____ glands are located above the kidney and release hormones that mobilize our defenses in times of stress.

13. In particular, the adrenal _____ releases epinephrine and norepinephrine, which increase blood pressure, divert blood from internal to external organs, and so forth.
14. The adrenal cortex, which is stimulated by ACTH, releases _____ which regulate body metabolism and help us contend with stressors, ward off infection, and combat injury.

EXERCISE 12: Objective 8

TITLE: FOCUS ON THE SEX HORMONES
TASK: Fill in the blanks

1. Collectively, follicle-stimulating hormone (FSH), luteinizing hormone (LH), and prolactin are called the _____.
2. In females, FSH and LH stimulate the ovaries to secrete _____.
3. In males, LH (and perhaps FSH) stimulate the testes to secrete the androgens and, in particular, _____.
4. In the male, castration reduces sexual behavior, even though the ability to _____ may not be impaired.
5. In the castrated male, replacement therapy with _____ restores normal sexual desires.
6. In the female, removal of the _____ does not alter the sex drive.
7. The onset of _____ in females does not alter the desire for sex.
8. In both males and remales, it is thought that the sex drive is controlled by _____.
9. In addition to sexual behavior, the male hormone testosterone has been implicated in _____ behavior.
10. Aggression may depend in part on exposure to androgens during a _____ before birth in both males and females.

EXERCISE 13: Objective 9

TITLE: GENETIC STRUCTURES
TASK: Match letters to numbers

____1. A genetic disease transmitted by a single dominant gene.
____2. A genetic disease (also called trisimony and Down's syndrome) in which there is an extra chromosome on the twenty-first pair.
____3. A genetic disease transmitted by recessive genes, which can be controlled early in life with a proper diet.
____4. The large molecules that compose the genes.
____5. Controls the production of enzymes.
____6. Implies transmission of a condition to one-quarter of all offspring.
____7. Implies transmission of a condition to one-half of all offspring.
____8. Structures found in the cells of all nuclei that carry the genes.

A.   DNA
B.   chromosomes
C.   RNA
D.   PKU
E.   Huntington's chorea
F.   Down's syndrome
G.   recessive gene
H.   dominant gene

EXERCISE 14: Objective 9

TITLE: GENETIC RESEARCH
TASK: Fill in the blanks

1. On the average, siblings and fraternal twins share _____ of their
    genes.
2. In comparison, identical twins share _____ of their genes.
3. A major behavioral genetic research method used with humans is to
    _____ the degree of behavioral similarity with the degree of known
    genetic similarity.
4. Many methods of behavioral genetics that require manipulation would
    be _____ if done with humans.
5. Most human studies on behavioral genetics have focused on the topic
    of _____.
6. Recently, techniques of behavioral genetics have been applied to
    _____ traits.
7. In general, the most commonly used technique in behavioral genetics is
    to compare _____ reared together versus apart.
8. With animals, subjects may be chosen for reproduction according to the
    degree of possession of a given trait (such as intelligence). This
    technique is called _____.
9. Another technique used to study behavioral genetics in animals is to
    mate related animals across many generations. This results in _____.
10. Although results implicate genetic contributions to behavior, there is
    also evidence that environmental _____ and impoverishment also
    contributes.

EXERCISE 15

TITLE: IMPORTANT NAMES
TASK: Match letters to numbers

_____1. Discovery of the pleasure centers.
_____2. Selective breeding for bright and dull rats.
_____3. Theory of how hormones differentially affect the brains of males and
         females.
_____4. Principle of equipotentiality.
_____5. Discoveries relating to cells in the sensory cortex.
_____6. Review of all published studies relating to genetics versus environ-
         ment and intelligence.
_____7. Use of human genetics methodology to study shyness.
_____8. Split-brain research.
_____9. Studies on environmental enrichment and impoverishment in rats.

A. Hubel and Wiesel
B. Lashley
C. Krech and Rosenzweig
D. Olds and Milner
E. Sperry
F. Levy
G. Gouchard and McGue
H. Plomin
I. Tryon

MULTIPLE-CHOICE TESTS

SELF-TEST 1

1. Which of the following is NOT a basic function of the nervous system as an information-processing system of the body?
   a. output function
   b. input function
   c. mediating function
   d. processing function
   (page 30)

2. The process by which physical energy is converted to nervous energy is called:
   a. transduction
   b. input
   c. output
   d. modulation
   (page 31)

3. Which of the following represents a programmable function in the brain?
   a. control of heart rate
   b. pathways leading from nose to brain
   c. feeling fear when a car almost hits you
   d. learning to touch type
   (page 32)

4. The part of the neuron that receives messages from outside the cell is the:
   a. dendrite
   b. axon
   c. synapse
   d. myelin sheath
   (page 33)

5. The substances that allow neurons to communicate with one another are called:
   a. receivers
   b. transmitters
   c. synapses
   d. enzymes
   (page 34)

6. A substance that occurs naturally in the body and that reduces the sensation of pain is:
   a. pain enzyme C
   b. THC
   c. beta-endorphin
   d. substance P
   (page 35)

7. Which of the following is NOT a way that neurons code information that is transmitted within the nervous system?
   a. changes in the size of action potentials
   b. changes in the rate of firing of individual neurons
   c. the total number of neurons that are firing
   d. which particular neurons are firing
   (page 36)

8. Lateral inhibition refers to:
    a. alternating muscle movements
    b. decrease in the firing rate of neurons exposed to toxic substances
    c. edge and corner detectors in the cortex
    d. oppositional effects of adjacent neurons on each other
    (page 37)

9. Simple, complex, and hypercomplex cells are located in the:
    a. retina
    b. visual cortex
    c. hypothalamus
    d. thalamus
    (page 38)

10. A 50-year old man is involved in an automobile accident that causes
    brain damage. What is the most likely aftermath?
    a. much of the damage will probably be irreversible
    b. the functions of the damaged areas will be taken over by adjacent
       areas
    c. the man will suffer continuous hallucinations
    d. physical and occupational therapy will cause a complete recovery
    (page 40)

11. The brain is divided into two major parts, the _____ and the
    _____.
    a. cerebellum; cortex
    b. spinal cord; cerebrum
    c. medulla; cortex
    d. brain stem; cerebrum
    (page 42)

12. The nervous system division that would be activated during an emergency
    is the:
    a. central nervous system
    b. sympathetic nervous system
    c. parasympathetic nervous system
    d. peripheral somatic nervous system
    (page 42)

13. An important area in the brain stem for the relay of sensory messages to
    the cerebrum is the:
    a. hypothalamus
    b. thalamus
    c. basal ganglia
    d. limbic system
    (page 44)

14. An important area in the brain stem for the control of movement is the:
    a. hypothalamus
    b. cerebellum
    c. thalamus
    d. limbic system
    (page 44)

15. Which lobe of the cerebrum receives direct input from the auditory pathways?
    a. frontal
    b. parietal
    c. temporal
    d. occipital
    (page 45)

16. In the split-brain operation, what major brain structure is severed?
    a. limbic system
    b. pituitary gland
    c. reticular formation
    d. corpus callosum
    (page 46)

17. The left side of the brain has been shown to control _____, whereas the right hemisphere seems to be more involved in _____.
    a. positive feelings; negative feelings
    b. parallel processing; serial processing
    c. spatial relationships; language
    d. artistic ability; logical reasoning
    (page 47)

18. Based on Levy's research on gender differences in brain organization, we might expect women to be more visually responsive to events occurring:
    a. on their left
    b. on their right
    c. directly in front
    d. slightly above eye level
    (page 49)

19. Which of the following is NOT an example of a biological rhythm?
    a. body temperature
    b. menstrual cycle
    c. sexual desire
    d. sleep pattern
    (page 49)

20. Which of the following glands is part of the endocrine system?
    a. thyroid
    b. salivary
    c. gall bladder
    d. liver
    (page 51)

21. The posterior pituitary gland secrets two hormones, one is oxytocin and the other is _____.
    A. ACTH
    b. thyroxin
    c. antidiuretic hormone
    d. cortisol
    (page 52)

22. Which of the following hormones is NOT secreted by the adrenal gland?
    a. epinephrine
    b. ACTH
    c. cortisol
    d. norepinephrine
    (page 53)

23. The hormones beta-endorphin, cholecystokinin, angiotensin, and substance P all are examples of:
    a. endocrine hormones
    b. transmitters
    c. peptides
    d. analgesics
    (page 54)

24. Which of the following hormones is NOT secreted by the pituitary gland?
    a. FSH
    b. ADH
    c. cortisol
    d. oxytocin
    (page 54)

25. Normal human males have which of the following arrangements of chromosomes?
    a. XX
    b. XY
    c. YY
    d. XYX
    (page 55)

26. The genes are composed of:
    a. large molecules of DNA
    b. transmitters and RNA
    c. peptides
    d. modulators
    (page 56)

27. A genetic disorder that is transmitted by a recessive gene and causes mental retardation is:
    a. Huntington's chorea
    b. phenylketonuria
    c. Down's syndrome
    d. diabetes
    (page 57)

28. Which of the following methods would be used in studying the role of genes in determining human behavior?
    a. selective breeding
    b. inbred strains
    c. psychosurgery
    d. identical twin studies
    (page 57)

29. Which of the following is a disorder that was NOT shown to have a clear genetic basis?
    a. cancer
    b. Down's syndrome
    c. Huntington's chorea
    d. PKU
    (page 57)

30 The development of the pit-bull terrier and other fighting dogs is a good example of:
    a. natural selection
    b. selective breeding
    c. psychosurgery
    d. the role of peptides in controlling behavior
    (page 60)

SELF-TEST 2

1. A neuron with a dendrite but no axon would function in the _____ mode, but not in the _____ mode:
    a. processing; input
    b. action potential; synapse
    c. input; output
    d. hard-wired; programmable
    (page 33)

2. Transmitters are released from axon terminals at locations called:
    a. action potentials
    b. synapses
    c. somas
    d. ganglia
    (page 33)

3. Many axons are covered with a fatty coating called:
    a. myelin
    b. node of Ranvier
    c. modulin
    d. beta-endorphin
    (page 33)

4. It is thought that the neuromodulators are probably manufactured in the:
    a. hypothalamus
    b. spinal cord
    c. peripheral nerves
    d. medulla
    (page 34)

5. Unlike most other cells in the body, neurons:
    a. do not have a nucleus
    b. never stop growing
    c. require no nutrients
    d. do not reproduce
    (page 39)

6. Because of differences in the regeneration of tissue in the central and peripheral nervous systems, we would expect the most recovery of function following which of the events listed below?
   a. numbness of the ring and little fingers of the hand after a blow to the "funny bone"
   b. loss of memory following a brain injury
   c. paralysis caused by a stroke in the frontal lobe of the brain
   d. recovery would be about the same in each case
   (page 40)

7. Krech's and Rosenzweig's studies of effects of environment on brain development showed that:
   a. the brain never stops growing
   b. environment has no effect on brain development
   c. an enriched environment can result in more extensive brain growth
   d. the brain grows best in the absence of external stimulation
   (page 41)

8. Spinal nerves form part of the _____ nervous system.
   a. peripheral
   b. central
   c. cranial
   d. sacral
   (page 41)

9. If you were attacked by a mugger in a dark alley at night, which of the following would you expect to be controlling the stressful emotions that you would experience?
   a. central nervous system
   b. parasympathetic nervous system
   c. sympathetic nervous system
   d. somatic nervous system
   (page 42)

10. Sensory information would travel through _____ fibers, whereas motor information would travel through _____ fibers.
    a. large; small
    b. muscle; nerve
    c. afferent; efferent
    d. cortical; somatic
    (page 42)

11. If you were interested in finding some cranial nerve roots in the brain, where would be a good place to look?
    a. cerebellum
    b. cortex
    c. basal ganglia
    d. medulla oblongata
    (page 42)

12. Which of the following is a brain stem structure?
    a. pons
    b. basal ganglia
    c. limbic system
    d. frontal lobe
    (page 44)

13. Which of the following is NOT a functional classification of cerebral cortex?
    a. sensory
    b. association
    c. motor
    d. olfactory
    (page 45)

14. Parkinson's disease involves symptoms that include uncontrollable movement. Which brain structure would be a good candidate for involvement with Parkinson's?
    a. limbic system
    b. basal ganglia
    c. medulla
    d. superior colliculus
    (page 45)

15. Which of the following is NOT a major lobe in the neocortex?
    a. limbic
    b. frontal
    c. parietal
    d. occipital
    (page 45)

16. If you were listening to music instead of taking this test, which hemisphere of your brain would be the more active, and which hand might be moving in time with the music?
    a. right; left
    b. left; right
    c. right; right
    d. left; left
    (page 47)

17. As you read this test, which hemisphere of your brain would you expect to be the most active?
    a. left
    b. right
    c. top
    d. bottom
    (page 47)

18. The male sex hormones, such as testosterone:
    a. are present only after puberty
    b. have been found to affect spatial abilities
    c. are not present in females
    d. seem only to activate sexual behavior
    (page 49)

19. A circadian rhythm:
    a. requires an external stimulus to drive it
    b. is found only in lower mammals and invertebrates
    c. is exemplified by the menstrual cycle
    d. repeats itself about every 24 hours
    (page 49)

20. Which of the following should help a traveler avoid jet lag?
    a. resetting one's watch even before reaching the new destination
    b. eating a heavy meal the day before the flight
    c. stay awake as long as possible after arriving
    d. on the plane, adopt the behaviors appropriate to the time of day of the destination
    (page 50)

21. Just as a faucet turns a flow of water on and off, so also does the hypothalamus turn on and off a flow of _____ through use of the _____.
    a. blood; liver
    b. hormones; pituitary
    c. modulators; heart
    d. lymph; thyroid
    (page 51)

22. Which of the following pairs is NOT an endocrine gland and its associated hormone?
    a. pituitary; ADH
    b. thyroid; thyroxin
    c. liver; bile
    d. adrenal medulla; adrenalin
    (page 52)

23. Blockage of communication in neural circuits that carry pain information seems to be accomplished by a _____ called _____.
    a. hormone; nopaine
    b. transmitter; acetylcholine
    c. cell; glia
    d. modulator; beta-endorphin
    (page 52)

24. Which of the following is NOT a hormone secreted by the pituitary gland?
    a. ACTH
    b. LH
    c. thyroxin
    d. oxytocin
    (page 54)

26. Which of the following procedures would result in a decrease in estrogen production in women?
    a. removal of the ovaries
    b. abstinence from sexual behavior
    c. injections of small amounts of testosterone
    d. engaging in excessive sexual behavior
    (page 55)

27. Humans have _____ pairs of chromosomes.
    a. 23
    b. 46
    c. 92
    d. 184
    (page 57)

28. Phenylketonuria (PKU):
    a. is a genetically based disorder caused by a recessive gene
    b. is a genetically based disorder caused by a dominant gene
    c. affects males only
    d. affects females only
    (page 57)

29. According to Plomin's research, which behavioral tendency seems to be inherited?
    a. wariness of strangers
    b. aggressiveness
    c. friendliness
    d. humor
    (page 59)

30. In assessing the effects of an enriched environment on cortical development in rats, the subjects should be _____ in order to control for genetic variables.
    a. fully mature
    b. from inbred strains
    c. from different strains
    d. male exclusively
    (page 61)

WHAT DOES IT MEAN?

OBJECTIVES

1. What is psychosurgery, and why is it used only as a last resort?
2. How has brain stimulation been used to help control brain-based disorders?
3. What kinds of brain activities are measured with EEG, evoked potentials, and PET scans, and how have these techniques contributed to our understanding of behavioral and mental disorders?
4. How has pharmacological research contributed to our understanding of alcohol and drug abuse and mental disorders?
5. What are the implications of behavioral genetics research for combating mental retardation, schizophrenia, alcoholism, and dyslexia?
6. What are the possible contributions of biopsychological knowledge for treating obesity, sleep disorders, and stress?

SELF-TEST

1. Brain surgery in which the frontal cortex is removed is called:
   a. lobotomy
   b. lobectomy
   c. split-brain operation
   d. lesion operation
   (page 64)

2. Brain surgery in which the connections between the frontal cortex and the rest of the brain are cut is called a:
   a. lobotomy
   b. lobectomy

c. split-brain operaton
d. lesion operation
(page 64)

3. Lobotomies and lobectomies frequently produce:
   a. normally functioning people
   b. human vegetables
   c. extreme anxiety
   d. no noticeable effect
   (page 64)

4. Some psychiatrists and surgeons believe that psychosurgery should never be used to treat mental illness unless:
   a. the patient is very violent
   b. all other therapies have proved unsuccessful
   c. the patient is quite old
   d. malfunctioning brain structures can be identified
   (page 64)

5. Electrical stimulation of the brain has been used successfully in all of the following applications EXCEPT:
   a. suppressing violent behavior
   b. producing relief from pain
   c. treating epilepsy
   d. treating stress
   (page 65)

6. Computer-generated electrical stimulation of the lower centers in the brains of monkeys has been used to:
   a. stop aggressive behavior
   b. control eating
   c. control muscle movements
   d. release beta-endorphin
   (page 65)

7. Computer-generated electrical stimulation of the _____ has been used to help blind people "see."
   a. optic nerve
   b. eyes
   c. occipital cortex
   d. lower brain centers
   (page 65)

8. Electrical stimulation of the _____ has been used to treat epilepsy and chronically psychotic patients.
   a. hypothalamus
   b. cerebellum
   c. motor cortex
   d. hippocampus
   (page 65)

9. The EEG can be used to:
   a. stimulate the brain electrically
   b. detect and localize brain damage
   c. correct brain malfunctions
   d. treat epilepsy
   (page 65)

10. The method that may prove to aid in the early identification of dyslexic children is:
    a. EEG
    b. evoked potential
    c. electrical stimulation
    d. PET scan
    (page 66)

11. Evoked potentials are electrical signals recorded from the brain in response to:
    a. injuries to the brain
    b. evoked memories
    c. sensory stimulation
    d. hyperkinesis
    (page 66)

12. In order to record an evoked potential from a person, one must:
    a. place electrodes on the surface of the scalp
    b. drill several small holes in the skull
    c. x-ray the brain after injecting a dye
    d. inject radioactive-labled glucose and monitor its passage through the brain
    (page 66)

13. Evoked potentials can be used to diagnose hyperkinesis because hyperkinetic children have _____ evoked potentials in response to _____ stimulation than do normal children.
    a. less frequent and lower amplitude; auditory
    b. more frequent and higher amplitude; kinetic
    c. less frequent and higher amplitude; auditory
    d. more frequent and lower amplitude; visual
    (page 67)

14. The P-300 wave form that is recorded by way of the evoked potential is thought to indicate what phenomenon in the brain?
    a. epileptic attack
    b. preseizure syndrome
    c. humor
    d. a decision process
    (page 67)

15. Brain activity relates directly to:
    a. blood volume in carotid artery
    b. P-300 wave form
    c. glucose metabolism
    d. magnitude of evoked potential
    (page 67)

16. One way that heredity may be involved in narcotics abuse is that addicts may have inherited nervous systems that have:
    a. fewer than the normal number of receptors sensitive to the drug and therefore use more than normal for the same effect
    b. more than the normal number of receptors sensitive to the drug and therefore use fewer than normal
    c. more than the normal number of receptors sensitive to the drug and therefore are more susceptible to addiction

d. fewer than the normal number of receptors sensitive to the drug and therefore use fewer with the same effect
(page 68)

17. The "disuse" theory of drug dependence says that when drugs are withdrawn, certain parts of the nervous system:
a. may no longer work because of disuse
b. may be insensitive owing to disuse
c. may be supersensitive owing to disuse
d. may be depressed because of disuse
(page 68)

18. Because the _____ appears to be involved in the starting and stopping of eating behavior, drugs that affect it may be developed to control obesity.
a. hippocampus
b. hypothalamus
c. thalamus
d. cerebellum
(page 70)

19. Research has shown that when narcoleptics fall asleep, such as in the middle of a class, they:
a. do not dream
b. experience increased muscle tension
c. are having an epileptic seizure
d. go directly into a REM state
(page 71)

20. Although brain grafts are a technique whose application lies in the future, one of the disorders for which researchers are expected to use a modification of the procedure is:
a. epilepsy
b. Parkinson's disease
c. schizophrenia
d. alcoholism
(page 72)

ANSWER KEY

EXERCISES

Exercise 1

1. input
2. transduction
3. afferent
4. processing
5. output
6. efferent
7. hard-wired
8. experience

Exercise 2

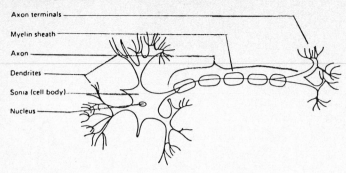

Axon terminals

Myelin sheath

Axon

Dendrites

Soma (cell body)

Nucleus

Exercise 3

1.	F	6.	C
2.	B	7.	H
3.	J	8.	I
4.	A	9.	G
5.	E	10.	D

Exercise 4

1. base
2. number; location
4. detector
4. lateral
5. simple
6. complex
7. hypercomplex

Exercise 5

1. Equipotentiality means that neurons have an equal potential for doing the same thing. Thus, particularly in soft-wired areas, if a neuron is damaged, the undamaged neurons stand ready to take over the functions of damaged ones.

2. There are two reasons that neurons are not replaced. First, cells are so tightly packed they cannot start the process of regeneration. Second, support cells in the CNS may release chemicals that block regeneration. The latter opens the possibility for injecting drugs (like amphetamine) to inhibit this blocking.

3. After destruction of neurons in the hippocampal region of rat brains, researchers discovered that neighboring neurons sprout axons in an attempt to connect with the damaged neurons. Interestingly, more sprouting occurred in females than males, a factor that implicates hormonal differences.

4. We are born with all our neurons in place, and it would appear that their connections are formed with experience. However, it is also possible that we are born with many unnecessary connections and that another role of experience is to "prune" them out. Either way, the implication is that early environmental enrichment facilitates, whereas early environmental isolation retards, neural development.

Exercise 6

1. central nervous system
2. peripheral nervous system
3. cranial; spinal
4. somatic
5. autonomic
6. sympathetic
7. parasympathetic
8. spinal cord
9. afferent
10. efferent

Exercise 7

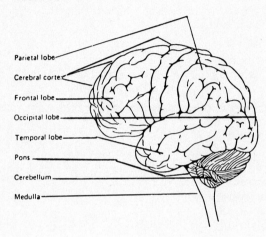

Parietal lobe

Cerebral cortex

Frontal lobe

Occipital lobe

Temporal lobe

Pons

Cerebellum

Medulla

Exercise 8

1. C   2. A   3. E   4. D   5. B

Exercise 9

1. cortex
2. corpus callosum
3. motor
4. sensory
5. association
6. lobes
7. frontal
8. occipital
9. temporal
10. parietal
11. basal ganglia
12. Parkinson's disease; Huntington's chorea
13. limbic system

Exercise 10

1. In the split-brain operation, the corpus callosum is severed, usually
    to prevent epilepsy from spreading from one hemisphere to the other.
    For cognitive functions, the left hemisphere is verbal, whereas the
    right is spatial. For emotional functions, the right hemisphere tends
    to engage in negative feelings, whereas the left tends to engage in
    positive feelings. Thus, there are essentially two brains functioning
    at the same time, and they tend to function differently.

2. The major differences are the amount of area in the corpus callosum (females have more) and the differential role of circulating hormones. Recently, it has been found that men tend to excel in spatial reasoning, and women in language. However, it is unclear whether these differences are due to differences in the corpus callosum, differences in hormonal balance, or differences in cultural expectations.

3. The most common rhythm is the circadian rhythm, which cycles every 24 hours and seems to be driven by external forces such as the light/dark cycle (zeitgebers). Many of the metabolic and physiological functions seem to follow this cycle (body temperature, levels of blood constituents, and so on). Other cycles of importance are the 28-day menstrual cycle in women and the 90-minute dream cycle. The rhythms exist in the nervous and endocrine systems, with the nervous system seemingly in control. There is no evidence, however, that inflexible cycles (biorhythms) are established at birth.

Exercise 11

1.	hormones	6.	gonadatrophins	11.	thyroid gland
2.	pituitary	7.	ADH	12.	adrenal
3.	thyroxin	8.	oxytocin	13.	medulla
4.	growth hormone	9.	neuromodulators	14.	steroids
5.	ACTH	10.	beta-endorphin		

Exercise 12

1.	gonadatropins	6.	ovaries
2.	estrogen and progesterone	7.	menopause
3.	testosterone	8.	androgens
4.	copulate	9.	aggressive
5.	androgens	10.	critical period

Exercise 13

1.	E	5.	C
2.	F	6.	G
3.	D	7.	H
4.	A	8.	B

Exercise 14

1	50 percent	6.	personality
2.	100 percent	7.	identical twins
3.	co-relate	8.	selective breeding
4.	unethical	9.	inbred strains
5.	intelligence	10.	enrichment

Exercise 15

1.	D	4.	B	7.	H
2.	I	5.	A	8.	E
3.	F	6.	G	9.	C

MULTIPLE-CHOICE TEST

Self-Test 1

1.	c	6.	c	11.	d	16.	d	21.	c	26.	a
2.	a	7.	a	12.	b	17.	a	22.	b	27.	b
3.	d	8.	d	13.	b	18.	b	23.	c	28.	d
4.	a	9.	b	14.	b	19.	d	24.	c	29.	a
5.	b	10.	a	15.	c	20.	a	25.	b	30.	b

Self-Test 2

1.	c	6.	a	11.	d	16.	a	21.	b	26.	a
2.	b	7.	c	12.	a	17.	a	22.	c	27.	a
3.	a	8.	a	13.	d	18.	b	23.	d	28.	a
4.	a	9.	c	14.	b	19.	d	24.	c	29.	a
5.	d	10.	c	15.	a	20.	d	25.	b	30.	b

WAHT DOES IT MEAN?

Self-Test

1.	b	6.	c	11.	c	16.	c
2.	a	7.	c	12.	a	17.	c
3.	b	8.	b	13.	a	18.	b
4.	b	9.	b	14.	d	19.	d
5.	d	10.	a	15.	c	20.	b

3 Sensation and Perception

OBJECTIVES

1. What is the difference between sensation and perception, and what concepts are common to both?
2. What are the structures of the eye, and how do they transduce light?
3. What are the rods and cones, and what are their respective locations and functions?
4. What are thresholds, and what laws and theories have been developed to study them?
5. Why are cones so important to both visual acuity and color vision?
6. How do receptive fields (in ganglion cells) influence both brightness constancy and brightness contrast?
7. What are the various theories and principles of object (or pattern) recognition?
8. What are binocular and monocular cues, and what role do they play in depth perception?
9. Why do we perceive constancies, and why are we subject to illusions?
10. What is the transduction process in audition, and what are the three main sound experiences?
11. What are the two sensory systems involved in sensing the position and movement of our bodies?
12. What are the four skin senses, and how are their sensations mediated?
13. What are the two chemical senses, and how do they interact?
14. What is the role of attention in determining what is perceived?

SYNOPSIS

Together, sensation (initial sensory reception) and perception (cognitive processes stimulated by receptor activity) allow us to represent internally the outside world. The basic concepts in sensation and perception include outside physical stimulation, internal physiological (nerve cell) activity, performance activities, and subjective experiences. These processes begin with transduction, which is the conversion of physical stimulation from the outside world into neural activity. These processes have been outlined best for vision. Thus our detailed discussion of vision will be followed by briefer discussions of audition, body position and movement, the skin senses, and the chemical senses.

In the visual system, light enters the eye through the cornea. The amount of light entering is determined by the size of the pupil, which is controlled by the iris. The lens bends the light to different degrees based on the size and distance of the object viewed (accommodation) so that the image focuses on the retina. The retina contains photoreceptors (rods and cones) which, when stimulated, undergo chemical changes that lead to the activation of the axons of the ganglion cells. These axons make up the optic nerve.

Rods are more sensitive to light and therefore are the receptors that we depend on most at night. Cones function best when light sources are more intense, and thus they are used more often in daylight. Both rods and cones are connected to ganglion cells through a network that includes horizontal, bipolar, and amacrine cells. The connections are more direct for the cones, however, because of their location in the foveal region in the retina. There are areas in the retina that influence receptive fields in both the ganglion cells and the cells of the visual cortex.

Experientially, the criterion for discriminating between the presence and absence of light is called *absolute threshold*, whereas the criterion for discriminating among different stimuli is called *differential threshold*. There are three psychophysical laws relating changes in physical stimulation to changes in perceptions (Weber's, Fechner's, and Steven's). But these laws consider only the sensory process involved in detecting the stimulus. In comparison, signal detection theory also considers the criteria for responding to sensory stimulation.

Visual acuity is better in the cones than the rods because the cones converge more directly on ganglion cells. The cones are also responsible for the perception of color. The three types of cones form channels, and the combination of signals from these channels is believed to produce the color experiences.

The experience of brightness depends on the relative intensities of the incoming light. Brightness constancy is determined by the constancy in intensity of the light hitting the center, as opposed to the surrounding regions of receptive fields in the ganglion cells. This effect is also responsible for brightness contrast.

The cells in the visual cortex serve detection and decision functions and, in this way, may recognize patterns from incoming bits and pieces of information (in bottom-up fashion). It is also possible that the cells may associate with one another to form cell assemblies and that these cell assemblies may group to form phase sequences. From the top-down perspective, it is possible for some "demons" to determine which detection processes predominate at a given time. Although these cells are part of the genetic blueprint, there is evidence that their type and number are influenced by our experiences.

The "demon" approach is clearly dominated by the bottom-up processing of specific features. Nevertheless, it is important to understand how these features combine to form whole perceptions. The Gestalt principles of Pragnanz, proximity, similarity, and closure serve such a function.

The combination of features is also important to locating objects in space, particularly in depth perception. Here, we must recognize the importance of both monocular and binocular cues.

Despite the variation of inputs to our visual system, we manage to perceive a constant environment (brightness, shape, and size constancy). The illusions occur when this constancy breaks down.

Next to seeing, we know most about hearing. Sound waves pass through the outer ear and cause vibrations in the eardrum. These vibrations are then transmitted to the inner ear (or cochlea) via the bones of the middle ear. In the cochlea, hair cells on the basilar membrane are bent and distorted, which leads to action potentials in the auditory nerve. There are three main sound experiences: loudness, pitch, and timbre. These qualities are coded according to the intensity, frequency, and complexity of the sound waves and also to which hair cells are active. The ear also helps us locate the source of sound through the perception of time-delay differences in the arrival of sound at each ear and through the differences in loudness at each ear.

Kinesthesis refers to a diffuse system of receptors in the muscles, tendons, and joints that allows us to sense body position. The vestibular system is located in the cochlea, and it allows us to sense head and body movement. Both work independently of vision.

The sense of touch is really four senses: pressure, pain, warmth, and cold. These senses are mediated by different kinds of deep and surface receptors. Of these, pain has received the most attention, probably because of the discovery of enkephalins and endorphins. Although we are beginning to understand the basic processes of analgesia, there is still far too little scientific evidence available.

Taste and smell are chemically mediated by means of the absorption of molecules by receptors on the tongue and in the nose. Taste buds on the tongue respond to dissolved substances with the sensory experiences we call sweet, sour, bitter, and salty. Smell seems to depend on the shape of the molecules absorbed, and there appear to be seven primary and seven secondary oders. Smell also influences taste and is used for communication (via pheromones) among lower animals, and some such similar communication may occur among humans.

In the final analysis, sensations are constantly received from each modality. What we perceive is influenced by what we attend to, and our selective attention is influenced by both peripheral and central processes.

KEY TERMS AND PHRASES

OBJECTIVE 1

sensation
perception
bottom-up versus top-down processing
physical concepts
physiological concepts
performance concepts
experiential concepts
transduction
receptors
photoreceptors
mechanoreceptors
chemoreceptors

OBJECTIVE 2

light
photons (quanta)
intensity
wavelength
reflectance
cornea

lens
iris
pupil
accommodation
retina

OBJECTIVE 3

rods
cones
photopic versus scotopic vision
R-, G-, and B-type cones
sensitivity
fovea
ganglion cells
receptive fields
visual cortex
retinotopic mapping

OBJECTIVE 4

dark adaptation
absolute threshold
differential threshold (jnd)
Weber's law
Stevens's psychophysical law
signal detection theory
detection versus decision
false alarm
miss
hit
correct rejection
signal-plus-noise distribution
noise-only distribution

OBEJCTIVE 5

acuity
convergence on ganglion cells
visual gratings
hue
saturation
brightness
opponent-process channels
complementary colors
color blindness

OBJECTIVE 6

brightness constancy
brightness contrast
color contrast
center versus surround
Mach bands
Herman grid

OBJECTIVE 7

object (pattern) recognition
Pandemonium
demons
hierarchical structure
image, feature, cognitive, and decision "demons"
call assembly model
phase sequences
set (expectation)
context
schemas
nature versus nurture
direct versus constructed perception
Gestalt
Pragnanz
proximity
similarity
closure

OBJECTIVE 8

depth perception
monocular versus binocular cues
partial overlap
size
shading
texture gradients
linear perspective
motion parallax
accommodation
convergence
retinal disparity

OBJECTIVE 9

constancy
illusion
shape versus size versus brightness
impossible forms
moon illusion
Herring-Helmholtz illusion
Ponzo illusion
Muller-Lyer illusion
Zollner illusion

OBJECTIVE 10

sound waves
compression and rarefaction
tone
period
frequency
hertz (Hz)
amplitude

dynes/cm squared
decibel (Db)
sine wave
fundamental frequency
harmonics
outer ear
middle ear
inner ear
eardrum
ossicles: incus, malleus, and stapes
cochlea
basilar membrane
hair cells
cochlea nerve
hertz (Hz)
loudness versus pitch versus timbre
frequency versus intensity versus place
spatial localization

OBJECTIVE 11

kinesthesis
muscles, tendons, and joints
stretching versus contracting
vestibular sense
semicircular canals versus vestibular sacs
gravity
fluid motion

OBJECTIVE 12

touch (pressure, pain, warmth, and cole)
specialized nerve endings
two-point threshold
discrete spots on the skin
free nerve endings
enkephalins and beta-endorphins
substance P
acupuncture
gate control theory
active versus passive touch
Braille

OBJECTIVE 13

taste (gustation)
taste buds (salty, sweet, bitter, and sour)
smell (olefaction)
primary versus secondary odors
molecular shape (stereochemical theory)
olfactory bulb

OBJECTIVE 14

selective attention
peripheral versus central selection
expectancy (altered "demon")
cocktail party phenomenon
automatization

EXERCISES

EXERCISE 1: Objective 1

TITLE: OVERVIEW OF SENSATION AND PERCEPTION
TASK: Fill in the blanks

1. _____ refers to stimulation impinging on a sense organ.
2. _____ refers to the systemic effects of receptor activity.
3. _____ concepts describe characteristics of the outside world such as wavelength and intensity of light.
4. _____ concepts describe the behavior of nerve cells.
5. _____ concepts are used to describe activity of the organism.
6. _____ concepts represent what is private and subjective.
7. A receptor is a specialized cell that _____ or converts physical stimulation into electrical stimulation.
8. _____ receptors are sensitive to light energy.
9. _____ receptors are sensitive to mechanical forces and are found in the skin, the joints, and the inner ear.
10. _____ receptors are sensitive to chemical substances, and they mediate taste and smell.

EXERCISE 2: Objective 2

TITLE: THE PHYSICAL NATURE OF LIGHT
TASK: Identify each of the follwoing

1. What light is composed of.
2. The physical property of photons.
3. The visual spectrum (in nanometers).
4. The number of quanta per second.
5. The number of quanta per second at each wavelength.
6. The type of object that light passes through.
7. The type of object that absorbs light.
8. The ratio of number of quanta reflected from a surface to the number of quanta falling on the surface.

EXERCISE 3: Objective 2

TITLE: THE EYE
TASK: Match letters to numbers

1. The curved transparent surface on the front of the eye.

_____2. The colored part of the eye that controls how much light enters the opening.
_____3. The opening itself.
_____4. The network of photoreceptors at the rear of the eye.
_____5. It bends light so as to focus it properly.

A. retina
B. cornea
C. lens
D. pupil
E. iris

EXERCISE 4: Objective 3

TITLE: FOCUS ON THE RETINA
TASK: Fill in the blanks

1. When photons reflected from objects impinge on the retina, they are transduced into electrical signals by _____.
2. The concept of _____ refers to the amount of light energy needed to excite a receptor.
3. In general, _____ are the most sensitive receptors to light and are maximally sensitive at 510 nm.
4. Rods function best at night, or in _____ vision.
5. Cones function best in day, or in _____ vision.
6. There are three types of cones. The _____ is maximally sensitive to 570 nm, the _____ type to 535 nm, and the _____ type to 445 nm.
7. The densest concentration of cones occurs in the _____.
8. The 120 million rods are located more in the _____ of the retina, as compared with the cones.
9. There is massive convergence as many receptors funnel their information into a single _____ cell.
10. Each ganglion cell is indirectly connected to a circular _____ field on the retina.
11. Receptive fields are divided into _____ and _____ regions having opposing (excitatory versus inhibitory) effects on incoming light.
12. Each ganglion cell is also connected to higher-level cells all the way up to the _____ cortex.
13. Retiontopic _____ reveals that each region of the visual field is represented by a corresponding region in the visual cortex.

EXERCISE 5: Objective 4

TITLE: EXPERIENTIAL SENSITIVITY TO LIGHT
TASK: Match letters to numbers

_____1. This type of adaptation is virtually complete within the first ten minutes in the dark.
_____2. The amount of physical stimulus required to achieve a certain level of correctness in a detection task.
_____3. The magnitude of a sensation is a power function of stimulus intensity, and the exponent is different for each sensory modality.

_____ 4. In addition to the sensory process involved, one must also consider the decision criterion.

_____ 5. This type of adaptation is slower (about 30 minutes in the dark) but reaches a more sensitive final level.

_____ 6. Increased sensitivity to light as you remain in the dark.

_____ 7. The measure of a person's ability to discriminate one stimulus from another (also known as jnd).

_____ 8. The jnd is a constant proportion of the percentage of the stimulus's intensity.

_____ 9. The measure of a person's ability to discriminate between the presence and absence of a stimulus.

A. dark adaptation	F. difference threshold
B. adaptation of cones	G. Weber's law
C. adaptation of rods	H. Steven's law
D. threshold	I. signal detection theory
E. absolute threshold	

EXERCISE 6: Objective 4

TITLE: FOCUS ON SIGNAL DETECTION THEORY
TASK: Essay

In reality, a person may be guilty or innocent of a crime. If he or she is guilty, there will be a signal over and above noise. If he or she is innocent, there is only noise. The jury must make the yes (guilty) or no (innocent) decision. Given a very conservative criterion (such as we should never convict an innocent person), discuss the alternatives according to signal detection theory.

EXERCISE 7: Objective 5

TITLE: VISUAL ACUITY
TASK: Essay

Earlier we learned that less light energy is needed to excite rods than cones. If this is true, then why are cones more important for visual acuity than rods are?

EXERCISE 8: Objective 5

TITLE: COLOR VISION
TASK: Identification

In the following exercise, trun to COLOR PLATE 3 in the text and determine which color is going to be perceived.

1. The B-cone is much more active than R+G, and the R- and G-cones are equally active.

2. B-cone activity equals R+G, and R- and G-cone activity are equal to each other.

3. R+G is much greater than B-cone activity, and R- and G-cone activity are equal to each other.

4. R+G is much greater than B-cone activity, and the R-cone is slightly more active than the G-cone is.
5. R+G is moderately more active than B-cone activity, and the G-cone is much more active than the R-cone is.
6. R+G is moderately less active than B-cone activity, and the G-cone is much more active than the R-cone is.
7. R+G is moderately more active than B-cone activity, and the R-cone is much more active than the G-cone is.
8. B-cone activity is much more active than R+G, and R-cone activity is slightly greater than G-cone activity is.
9. R+G activity is much greater than B-cone activity, and the R-cone is much more active than the G-cone is.

EXERCISE 9: Objective 6

TITLE: BRIGHTNESS CONSTANCY AND CONTRAST
TASK: Essays

1. Why does the brightness of an object remain constant despite changes in luminance?
2. In Figure 3-14 in the text, you will see the Hermann grid. What do you see in the grid and why?

EXERCISE 10: Objective 7

TITLE: FOCUS ON PATTERN RECOGNITION
TASK: Fill in the blanks

1. Currently, pattern (or object) recognition is believed to be a function of circuits that act like _____.
2. These circuits form the basis of a psychological model of _____ perception called *Pandemonium*.
3. The model itself is based on neural detectors (or "demons") that are organized into a _____.
4. On the bottom rung, the _____ demons make a simple record, or photograph of the stimulus.
5. Next, the _____ demons look for specific features in the image such as vertical lines, curved lines, and right angles.
6. Next, the _____ demons put the features together and respond (or "shout") when they recognize what they are looking for.
7. Finally, the _____ demon (the executive decides who is "shouting" the loudest and decides on the pattern.
8. In a closely related theory by Hebb, it was previously argued that _____ assemblies were formed when different feature detectors were frequently excited in close temporal contiguity.
9. Hebb also proposed that _____ sequences were created when assembiles became associated into larger groupings of neurons.
10. From a top-down perspective, the important concept in pattern recognition is _____, or expectation.
11. When decisions are difficult, the decision demons must combine what is known (in memory) with the current _____.

12. Psychology has adopted the concept of _____ in order to capture the impact of context on our thoughts and perceptions.
13. Each schema is like a _____ into which we incorporate information from our past experiences.

EXERCISE 11: Objective 7

TITLE: FEATURE DETECTORS--ADDITIONAL CONSIDERATIONS
TASK: Essay

1. Given the evidence, what are the respective roles of heredity and environment in feature detection?

2. Using depth perception as an example, what is meant by direct versus constructed perception?

EXERCISE 12: Objective 7

TITLE: GESTALT ORGANIZATIONAL PRINCIPLES
TASK: Identify each of the following

1. The tendency is to see 8 pairs of x's rather than 16 separate x's.

2. The tendency here is to see separate columns of x's and o's rather than mixed rows of x's and o's.

3. The dashes would be completed and a circle would be perceived.

4. All three could be perceived as three-dimensional, but the first one is more simply seen as two-dimensional.

EXERCISE 13:   Objective 8

TITLE: MONOCULAR VERSUS BINOCULAR CUES IN DEPTH PERCEPTION
TASK: Fill in the blanks

1. Your ability to represent the distance and depth of objects is called
    _____ perception.
2. _____ cues for depth include partial overlap, size, shading, texture
    gradients, linear perspective, and motion parallax.
3. An example of _____ is the apparent convergence of parallel lines.
4. In the case of _____, closer things look coarser.
5. _____ is the relative motion of objects created when the head moves
    from side to side.
6. When objects are close to the eyes, the shape of the lens changes to
    focus the image on the retina. In other words, there will be _____.
7. Also, with close objects, the orientation of the eyeballs is changed to
    keep each eye pointed at the object, a process known as _____.
8. Artists use monocular cues to achieve a three-dimensional effect on flat
    canvas. For example, consider the _____ figures.
9. Cues requiring both eyes are called _____ cues.
10. The most important of these cues involves differences between images on
    the two retinas, or _____.

EXERCISE 14:   Objective 9

TITLE: CONSTANCY AND ILLUSION
TASK: Essays

1. What is size constancy, and what are the two processes involved?

2. Which of these two processes is responsible for illusions, and how?

EXERCISE 15:   Objective 10

TITLE: THE AUDITORY STIMULUS
TASK: Match letters to numbers

_____1. The unit (per centimeter squared) for air pressure.
_____2. The logarithmic conversion of pressure.
_____3. Cycles per second (hertz).
_____4. Alternative vibrations of sound waves.
_____5. Overtones.
_____6. The time to complete one cycle of compression and rarefaction.
_____7. The simplest possible tone.
_____8. The lowest frequency of a complex sound.
_____9. A composite of many simple tones.
_____10. The simplest possible sound (produced by a tuning fork).

A.	compression and rarefaction	F.	decibels
B.	pure tone	G.	sine waves
C.	period	H.	complex sounds
D.	frequency	I.	fundamental frequency
E.	dynes	J.	harmonics

EXERCISE 16: Objective 10

TITLE: THE EAR--TRANSDUCTION, SENSITIVITY, AND SPATIAL LOCALIZATION
TASK: Fill in the blanks

1.   Sounds enter the outer ear and cause the _____ to vibrate.
2.   Vibrations are then transferred to the inner ear by three _____
      called the malleus (hammer), incus (anvil), and stapes (stirrup).
3.   The inner ear is called the _____.
4.   The inner ear contains the _____ membrane.
5.   And this membrane contains _____ cells.
6.   Bending of these cells causes action potentials on the acoustic or
      cochlear _____.
7.   The place on the basilar membrane where the maximum bending of hair cells
      occurs is determined by the _____ of sound.
8.   The psychological experience corresponding to the intensity of sound is
      _____.
9.   The experience corresponding to frequency is _____.
10.   And the experience that allows you to distinguish sounds of equal
      loudness and pitch is _____.
11.   In addition to auditory experience, the time difference between arriving
      sounds at the two ears allows you to determine the _____ localization
      of a sound.

EXERCISE 17: Objective 11

TITLE: BODY POSITION AND MOTION
TASK: Essays

1.   What are the receptors in kinesthesis, and how do they function?

2.   What are the receptors in the vestibular sense, and how do they function?

EXERCISE 18: Objective 12

TITLE: THE SENSE OF TOUCH
TASK: Fill in the blanks

1.   The sense of touch is really four separate skin senses that rely on a
      variety of specialized nerve _____.
2.   One of these senses, _____, is measured by two-point thresholds.
3.   The senses of _____ and _____ are mediated by discrete spots on
      the skin as well as by current temperature.
4.   Pain is mediated by _____ nerve endings.
5.   Regarding pain, the body produces natural pain killers known as _____
      and _____.
6.   These analgesics operate by _____ impulses in sensory nerves that
      register pain.
7.   The transmitter that conducts these impulses is _____.
8.   Nobody knows how _____ works to relieve pain.
9.   One theoretical account of natural pain control is called the _____
      control theory.

10. According to this theory, touch impulses reach the spinal cord before pain impulses do and, as a result, have priority, or _____ the gate.
11. There are two types of touch. In _____ touch, we are more aware of the nature of the touch experience.
12. In _____ touch, we are more oriented toward identifying the objects producing the experience.
13. The latter experience forms the basis for _____, which allows blind people to read.
14. Currently, computer devices are being used to transform _____ stimulation into patterns of vibration on the skin.

EXERCISE 19: Objective 13

TITLE: TASTE AND SMELL
TASK: Fill in the blanks

1. Taste and smell depend on the absorption of _____ and, for this reason, are known as the chemical senses.
2. Receptors for taste (gustation) are _____ located on the tongue.
3. The sides of the tongue are sensitive to _____ tastes.
4. _____ tastes predominate throughout the tongue, but slightly more on the front sides.
5. _____ predominates on the tip of the tongue.
6. And _____ predominates at the back of the tongue.
7. Smell (olfaction) depends on the _____ of molecules.
8. There are seven _____ and seven _____ smells.
9. Smell helps us evaluate _____.
10. It has also been implicated in _____.
11. In the latter case, it is known that lower animals have special glands that produce (for example) territorial _____.
12. These chemicals have also been implicated in _____ behavior in mice.
13. But it is not clear that they serve similar functions in _____.

EXERCISE 20: Objective 14

TITLE: ATTENTION
TASK: Essay

1. Why is selective attention necessary?

2. What are the two ways in which selective attention occurs?

3. What happens when we attend to multiple sources of information?

EXERCISE 21

TITLE: KEY NAMES
TASK: Match letters to numbers

____1. Won the Nobel Prize for his work on the basilar membrane.
____2. The jnd is a constant proportion of the percentage of the stimulus's intensity.
____3. A believer in direct, as opposed to constructed, perception.
____4. Feature detection circuits.

_____5. The magnitude of sensation is a power function of stimulus intensity.
_____6. A theory based on cell assemblies and phase sequences.
_____7. Hierarchical decision makers for pattern recognition.
_____8. Taste sensations are merely points on different taste dimensions.

A. Weber
B. Stevens
C. Hubel and Wiesel
D. Selfridge
E. Hebb
F. Gibson
G. von Bekesy
H. Schiffman and Ericson

MULTIPLE-CHOICE TESTS

SELF-TEST 1

1. Sensation refers to:
   a. the effect on the nervous system of receptor activity
   b. the immediate effects on receptors of incoming information
   c. the processing of information from the external environment
   d. top-down processing
   (page 74)

2. Which of the following does NOT influence the process of perception?
   a. current motivational states
   b. stimulus meaning
   c. expectations about incoming information
   d. the sensory pathway through which information enters the system
   (page 74)

3. Which four concepts combine to produce the complex process called
   perception?
   a. physical, physiological, performance, experiential
   b. incoming, routing, processing, outgoing
   c. sense, experience, process, concept
   d. intensity, duration, frequency, harmonics
   (page 74)

4. The receptors in the retina of the eye are:
   a. mechanoreceptors
   b. chemoreceptors
   c. photoreceptors
   d. hair cells
   (page 77)

5. Which of the following structures is NOT part of the optical system of
   the eye?
   a. cornea
   b. lens
   c. iris
   d. fovea
   (page 77)

6.   We primarily use _____, mainly located in the _____ of the
     retina for _____ vision.
     a. cones; fovea; daytime
     b. rods; fovea; daytime
     c. cones; periphery; nighttime
     d. rods; fovea; nighttime
     (page 78)

7.   If a bright light stimulated the entire receptive field of a ganglion
     cell, we might expect to observe:
     a. not much change in the activity rate of the ganglion cell
     b. an increase in the activity rate of the ganglion cell
     c. a decrease in the activity rate of the ganglion cell
     d. an increase followed by a decrease in the activity rate of the
        ganglion cell
     (page 79)

8.   The orderly mapping of the visual world onto the surface of the visual
     cortex is called:
     a. visual mapping
     b. retinotopic mapping
     c. stereoscopic mapping
     d. binocular vision
     (page 79)

9.   In long wavelength (red) light, which of the receptors are the most
     sensitive?
     a. R-type cones
     b. Y-type cones
     c. B-type cones
     d. G-type cones
     (page 80)

10. When a person either sees or does not see a light toward which he or
     she is looking, we refer to the concept of _____ to describe the
     phenomenon.
     a. visual acuity
     b. resolution
     c. absolute threshold
     d. brightness contrast
     (page 81)

11. The study of the relationship between external stimulation and the
     resulting sensation is called:
     a. psychology
     b. psychophysics
     c. perception
     d. environmental sensation
     (page 81)

12. In a signal detection task, the higher the decision criterion is, the
     _____ the likelihood of _____ will be.
     a. lower; false alarms
     b. higher; false alarms
     c. lower; correct rejections
     d. higher; hits
     (page 83)

13. In a signal detection task, mistaking the background noise for a signal would be called:
    a. a hit
    b. a miss
    c. a correct rejection
    d. a false alarm
    (page 83)

14. Visual acuity refers to:
    a. the ability to see a stimulus when it is present
    b. the ability to see fine detail in a stimulus
    c. the ability to see a stimulus at a distance
    d. the ability to perceive color in a stimulus
    (pate 84)

15. Which of the following is NOT referred to as an experience of color?
    a. luminance
    b. brightness
    c. hue
    d. saturation
    (page 84)

16. Which factor does NOT enter into our experience of color?
    a. absorption of light photons in cones
    b. different combintations of signals from the R/G and Y/B channels
    c. the location in the retina of the cones that are responding to light
    d. the wavelength of the light energy that strikes the eye
    (page 85)

17. Color blindness results when:
    a. there are more rods than cones in the retina
    b. there is a defect in the function of one or more kinds of cone in the retina
    c. the relative locations of rods and cones are reversed in the retina
    d. the iris lets in too little light
    (page 86)

18. The relative intensities of light reflected from objects defines:
    a. the experience of brightness
    b. brightness constancy
    c. color contrast
    d. brightness parallax
    (page 86)

19. Modern research such as that by Hubel and Wiesel suggests that the basic perceptual process is one that involves:
    a. feature detection
    b. direct interpretations of external stimuli
    c. abstract impression
    d. retinal disparity
    (page 88)

20. At which level of perception does context seem to be most taken into account?
    a. feature
    b. cognitive
    c. image
    d. decision
    (page 88)

21. Which of the following would NOT constitute a level of feature detection in Selfridge's model of perception?
    a. image
    b. cognitive
    c. interpretive
    d. decision
    (page 90)

22. The research done with kittens in which exposure to visual stimuli was controlled in the early months of life suggests that:
    a. infants should be exposed to a varied visual environment
    b. the visual environment of infants should be kept as constant as possible
    c. infants should not be exposed to bright lights
    d. infants can see only red and green lights
    (page 92)

23. Proximity, similarity, and closure are associated with the more general term:
    a. Pragnanz
    b. edge receptor
    c. orientation detector
    d. hallucination
    (page 94)

24. Motion parallax would be exemplified by:
    a. our inability to see a bullet after it is fired from a gun
    b. a sensation that you are moving when you are really not
    c. the perception that objects at different distances from you move at different speeds
    d. the perception that celestial bodies such as the sun are moving in circular directions
    (page 95)

25. If you were to look at Michelangelo's statue of David from several distances, it would still appear to be the same height. We call this phenomenon:
    a. shape consistency
    b. motion parallax
    c. size contrast
    d. size constancy
    (page 98)

26. The stimulus that we perceive as sound consists of:
    a. air compressions and rarefactions
    b. electromagnetic radiations
    c. air rarefactions
    d. vibrations
    (page 100)

27. The psychological dimension of hearing that allows us to hear a difference in two musical instruments that are playing the same note is:
   a. tone
   b. pitch
   c. loudness
   d. timbre
   (page 103)

28. The system that is called kinesthesis:
   a. provides information about the orientation of the body in space
   b. is very diffuse like the sense of touch
   c. reauires no movement in order to be activated
   d. has hair cells as its basic receptors
   (page 104)

29. The two major functions of the sense of smell are:
   a. communication and the evaluation of food
   b. evaluation of food and sexual satisfaction
   c. territorial defense and territorial marking
   d. communication and species differentiation
   (page 109)

30. When you are attending a cocktail party and try to listen to two separate conversations at the same time:
   a. you are unlikely to hear either
   b. you will hear both but understand neither
   c. you will probably understand one and only attend to fragments of the other
   d. you will probably hear, attend to, and understand both conversations
   (page 110)

SELF-TEST 2

1. Perception refers to:
   a. the immediate effects of incoming stimulation
   b. the reception of informational input from the external environment
   c. the sense and nervous system effects of receptor activity
   d. bottom-up processing
   (page 74)

2. If top-down processes are playing the major role in determining a perception, we call that perception:
   a. conceptually driven
   b. data driven
   c. feature driven
   d. image driven
   (page 74)

3. Which adjective below best describes the process of perception?
   a. passive
   b. reactive
   c. dynamic
   d. static
   (page 74)

4. The range of wavelengths that our visual system can convert into neural signals is:
   a. from 100 to 200 nm
   b. from 100 to 400 nm
   c. from 400 to 700 nm
   d. from 700 to 1,000 nm
   (page 76)

5. The ratio of the number of quanta of light reflected from a surface to the number of quanta falling on the surface is called:
   a. reflectance
   b. refractance
   c. parallax
   d. luminance
   (page 77)

6. When you look at a far object, the lens of your eye is quite thin. When your focus shifts to this page, your lens gets fatter. This process of adjustment is called:
   a. distance contrast
   b. accommodation
   c. parallax
   d. depth perception
   (page 78)

7. The order, from most to least, of rods, cones, and ganglion cells in the retina is:
   a. rods, cones, ganglion
   b. cones, rods, ganglion
   c. cones, ganglion, rods
   d. ganglion, cones, rods
   (page 78)

8. Which of the following is correct?
   a. the electrical signal generated by a rod or a cone depends on the wavelength of light, not the number of quanta absorbed
   b. the electrical signal generated by rods and cones depends mainly on the distance of the object being percieved
   c. the electrical signal of the rods and cones depends only on the rate of quanta being absorbed
   d. the electrical signal generated by the rods and cones depends on the size of the viewed object
   (page 78)

9. If you walk from a well-lit to a dark room, about how long will it take for the rods maximal dark adaption?
   a. five minutes
   b. ten minutes
   c. thirty minutes
   d. one hour
   (page 80)

10. The reason that red light can be used as nightlights without destroying dark-adapted vision is:
    a. red light is sensed only by R-type cones
    b. red light activates cones and not rods
    c. rods are least sensitive to red light
    d. rods are most sensitive to red light
    (page 80)

11. We seem to have problems detecting the presence of very weak lights because:
    a. light must be above a threshold intensity in order to pass through the lens
    b. the response to weak light is not much different from the random response of the receptors in the dark
    c. most weak lights are at wavelengths that cones do not detect
    d. only the left eye will be stimulated, which results in retinal disparity
    (page 81)

12. To which of the color experiences do we assign different qualities?
    a. saturation
    b. intensity
    c. brightness
    d. hue
    (page 84)

13. If you mixed varying amounts of white paint pigment into a red pigment, which color experience would also vary?
    a. saturation
    b. hue
    c. intensity
    d. brightness
    (page 84)

14. If the mixture of two colors resulted in white, we would call the colors:
    a. luminant
    b. refractive
    c. contrasting
    d. complementary
    (page 85)

15. According to Selfridge's model of perception, which kind of detector-level cells converge on the cognitive-level cells?
    a. image
    b. feature
    c. decision
    d. executive
    (page 88)

16. According to Hebb's theory of perception, a cell assembly comes into being through what mechanism?
    a. association
    b. direct sensation
    c. concept formation
    d. feature analysis
    (page 90)

17. The context in which a perceptual decision is made contributes most to
    the decision when:
    a. the situation is emotional
    b. the situation is dangerous
    c. the situation contains much ambiguity
    d. the situation has occurred before
    (page 91)

18. The term *schema* is used to describe how context affects our thoughts
    and perceptions. Which of the following describes a schema in action?
    a. recollection of how we acted at last night's party
    b. recognition of the correct answer to this question
    c. mistaking a stick for a snake while out hiking
    d. ability to learn a foreign language
    (page 91)

19. The two major theories of perception emphasize either _____ or
    _____.
    a. direct perception; internal representations
    b. demons; objects
    c. context; constructs
    d. nature; nurture
    (page 83)

20 An ambiguous stimulus does not permit a unique perceptual organization.
    Therefore our perception of the stimulus:
    a. remains incomplete
    b. shifts between different representations
    c. cannot occur
    d. reduces the stimulus's overall size
    (page 84)

21. Size, shading, texture gradients, and linear perspective all contribute
    to our perception of:
    a. shape
    b. brightness
    c. color
    d. depth
    (page 84)

22. Top-down processing is especially pertinent in explaining:
    a. motion parallax
    b. the perception of subjective contours
    c. retinal disparity
    d. monocular cues for vision
    (page 100)

23. We might expect the noise from a band to begin damaging our hearing
    when the intensity reached about:
    a. 30 dB
    b. 60 dB
    c. 90 dB
    d. 120 dB
    (page 101)

24. The actual receptors that transduce sound are _____ and are located in the _____.
    a. rods; ears
    b. membranes; cochlea
    c. hair cells; cochlea
    d. buds; dermis
    (page 102)

25. As the frequency of a 5,000 Hz tone _____, the intensity necessary for us to hear it _____.
    a. decreases; increases
    b. decreases; decreases
    c. increases; increases
    d. decreases; stays the same
    (page 102)

26. As notes ascend a musical scale, the psychological dimension of sound that varies is called:
    a. timbre
    b. pitch
    c. loudness
    d. frequency
    (page 103)

27. A blind person reading a Braille book would be engaged in:
    a. sensory disparity
    b. passive touch
    c. active touch
    d. sensory comparison
    (page 105)

28. It is estimated that taste buds have a life span of about:
    a. 30 minutes
    b. 8 hours
    c. 4 days
    d. 1 year
    (page 106)

29. Which of the following statements is NOT correct?
    a. both taste and smell are chemical senses
    b. a large part of the sense of taste depends on the sense of smell
    c. a large part of the sense of smell depends on the sense of taste
    d. smell seems to depend at least in part on the shape of the molecules
    (page 109)

30. The alarm reaction that bees show when their have is disturbed seems to be communicated by:
    a. pheromones
    b. buzzing
    c. hormones
    d. a special kind of flying "dance"
    (page 109)

WHAT DOES IT MEAN?

OBJECTIVES

1. What are the common impairments of vision, and how can they be corrected?
2. How are visual illusions created, had how does the study of illusions contribute to our understanding of perceptual processes?
3. What treatments are available for normal and traumatic hearing loss?
4. How does deafness sometimes contribute to psychopathology?
5. How can improvement of listening skills contribute to more effective and productive work behavior?
6. What is the mechanism for a perceptual conflict, and what effects can such conflicts have on behavior in everyday life?

SELF-TEST

1. In nearsightedness, or _____, the image of distant objects is focused _____ the retina.
   a. myopia; in front of
   b. myopia; behind
   c. hyperopia; in front of
   d. hyperopia; behind
   (page 113)

2. Nearsightedness can be corrected by placing a _____ in front of the eye. This type of lens is _____ at its edges than in its center.
   a. negative; thicker
   b. positive; thinner
   c. negative; thinner
   d. positive; thicker
   (page 113)

3. In farsightedness, or _____, the image of near objects is focused _____ the retina.
   a. myopia; in front of
   b. myopia; behind
   c. hyperopia; in front of
   d. hyperopia; behind
   (page 113)

4. Farsightedness can be corrected by placing a _____ lens in front of the eye. This type of lens is _____ at its edges than in its center.
   a. negative; thicker
   b. positive; thinner
   c. negative; thinner
   d. positive; thicker
   (page 113)

5. Blindness caused by disruption of the visual system does NOT necessarily destroy visual ability completely in which disorder below?
   a. cataracts
   b. damage to the retina
   c. damage to the optic nerve
   d. damage to the visual cortex
   (page 115)

6. Someday blind people may wear eyeglasses fitted with small TV cameras that send signals directly to the:
   a. eyes
   b. optic nerve
   c. visual cortex
   d. retina
   (page 115)

7. When our perceptual processes create an internal representation based on misleading information, we would say that _____ has occurred.
   a. an illusion
   b. a hallucination
   c. a mystical experience
   d. direct perception
   (page 115)

8. Some of the difficulties that pilots encounter in perceiving aspects of the environment might be caused by:
   a. overreliance on their instruments
   b. the fact that humans did not develop perceptual systems that had to support flight
   c. the effects on the vestibular system of having to look up at the instrumentation rather than down
   d. the different densities of air at normal flight levels
   (page 116)

9. A normal result of the aging process is the gradual loss of the ability to perceive _____ sounds.
   a. high-frequency
   b. low-frequency
   c. low-amplitude
   d. high-amplitude
   (page 116)

10. Progressive hearing loss usually begins by about the age of:
    a. 20
    b. 30
    c. 40
    d. 50
    (page 116)

11. Much of the progressive hearing loss that is reported can be traced to environment, as _____ have larger hearing losses than _____ do.
    a. males; females
    b. factory workers; office workers
    c. young people; old people
    d. pilots; musicians
    (page 116)

12. Someday deaf people may wear microphones that send signals directly to the:
    a. auditory cortex
    b. cochlea
    c. auditory nerve
    d. ossicles
    (page 116)

13. An "artificial ear" might be of use when:
    a. the existing ear has been severed
    b. the eardrum has been punctured
    c. the hair cells on the basilar membrane have died
    d. the auditory nerve has been severed
    (page 117)

14. Paranoia has been related to which perceptual deficit?
    a. blindness
    b. deafness
    c. loss of balance
    d. inability to feel pain
    (page 118)

15. Humans are able to attend to how many channels of information at a time?
    a. one
    b. two
    c. five
    d. seven
    (page 119)

16. The Sperry Corporation has established programs aimed at improving:
    a. communication skills
    b. visual detection skills
    c. listening skills
    d. sensitivity skills
    (page 119)

17. According to the Sperry Corporation program for developing good listening skills:
    a. bad habits built up in childhood must be overcome
    b. most people have no listening skills upon reaching adulthood
    c. males are better listeners than females are
    d. young people listen better than older people do
    (page 119)

18. Ventriloquists are able to create the illusion of "throwing their voice" because the observer's _____ localization mechanism is overridden by conflicting _____.
    a. visual; auditory
    b. auditory; visual
    c. auditory; auditory
    d. visual; visual
    (page 119)

19. Motion sickness is one result of conflict between _____ and _____ information.
    A. visual; muscular
    b. vestibular; muscular
    c. auditory; visual
    d. visual; vestibular
    (page 119)

20. Agreement between the two perceptual systems in conflict in motion sickness can be restored by visually fixating on:
    a. the horizon
    b. an nearby object on the ship
    c. your feet
    d. your nose
    (page 120)

ANSWER KEY

EXERCISES

Exercise 1

1. sensation
2. perception
3. physical
4. psysiological
5. performance

6. experiential
7. transduces
8. photo
9. mechano
10. chemo

Exercise 2

1. quanta (or photons)
2. wavelength
3. 400 to 700 nm
4. light intensity

5. wavelength distribution
6. transparent
7. opaque
8. reflectance

Exercise 3

1. b   2. e   3. d   4. a   5. c

Exercise 4

1. photoreceptors
2. sensitivity
3. rods
4. scotopic
5. photopic

6. R-, G-, and B-type rods
7. fovea
8. periphery
9. ganglion

10. receptive
11. center/surround
12. visual
13. mapping

Exercise 5

1. b   4. i   7. f
2. d   5. c   8. g
3. h   6. a   9. e

Exercise 6

In this case, convicting the guilty person is a "hit," and releasing the innocent person is a "correct rejection." On the other hand, convicting the innocent person is a "false alarm," and releasing the guilty person is a "miss." The conservative criterion tilts the decision process so that if an error occurs, it more than likely will be a miss rather than a false alarm.

Exercise 7

This may seem like a contradiction--but it is not. The important point to remember is that the rods are located more peripherally in the retina, whereas the cones are located more densely in the central, or foveal region. The foveal cones are more directly connected to the ganglion cells which carry the visual signal to the brain. Thus, although it is easier to excite a single rod than it is to excite a single cone, you must excite many, many more rods than cones to produce the visual signal.

Exercise 8

1.	blue	4.	orange	7.	red-orange
2.	white	5.	green	8.	violet
3.	yellow	6.	blue-green	9.	red

Exercise 9

1. We experience brightness constancy because of the center versus the surround relationship of receptive fields in ganglion cells in the retina. The important factor is the RATIO of light intensity in the center-surround positions. That is, even though luminance may increase or decrease, the relative intensity of light in center versus surround remains a constant.

2. In the Hermann grid, what you should see are gray spots wherever four black corners meet a white area. These spots are a creation of your sensory system and occur because of the opposite light intensities hitting the center versus surround regions of the receptive fields in the ganglion cells.

Exercise 10

1.	feature detectors	8.	cell	
2.	constructed	9.	phase	
3.	hierarchy	10.	set	
4.	image	11.	context	
5.	feature	12.	schema	
6.	cognitive	13.	category	
7.	decision			

Exercise 11

1. If kittens are reared in restricted visual environments (such as with only vertical lines), and this is done within an early critical interval (4 to 5 months after birth), they will develop additional (vertical-line) detector cells. In other words, the genetic prewiring seems flexible enough to be modified by environmental experience.

2. The notion of direct perception states that something like depth is inherent in the stimulus (such as texture gradients). The notion of construction suggests that bits and pieces of information from the two retinas are fed to the cortex, which in turn literally builds, or constructs, the perception.

Exercise 12

1. proximity
2. similarity
3. closure
4. Pragnanz

Exercise 13

1. depth
2. monocular
3. linear perspective
4. texture gradients
5. motion parallax
6. accommodation
7. convergence
8. impossible
9. binocular
10. retinal disparity

Exercise 14

1. Size constancy is the ability of our perceptual processes to represent an object's constant size, even though the image of this object may vary in size on our retinas. Differences in the size of the retinal image (process 1) are constantly compared with the distance of the object (process 2). Thus, a smaller retinal image is offset by an increase in distance, and a larger retinal image is offset by a decrease in distance.

2. Illusions based on size occur when we are tricked with respect to the distance process. For example, the moon looks larger on the horizon than overhead because we think the moon is closer when it is on the horizon (when it fact it is not). Tricks involving distance cues are also apparent in the Herring-Helmholtz, Muller-Lyer, Ponzo, and Zollner illusions.

Exercise 15

1. e
2. f
3. d
4. a
5. j
6. c
7. g
8. i
9. h
10. b

Exercise 16

1. eardrum
2. bones
3. cochlea
4. basilar
5. hair
6. nerve
7. frequency
8. loudness
9. pitch
10. timbre
11. spatial

Exercise 17

1. The receptors for kinesthesis are located in muscles, tendons, and joints throughout the body. For this reason, it is called a *diffuse* system. Stretching and contracting the receptors provides the brain with information regarding body position.

2. The receptors for the vestibular sense are located in the semicircular canals and vestibular sacs of the inner ear. Hair cells in the sac respond to gravity, whereas hair cells in the canal respond to movement of fluid. Body movement is perceived because head movements produce changes in both gravitational forces and fluid movement.

Exercise 18

1. endings
2. pressure
3. warmth and cold
4. free
5. enkephalins and endorphins
6. inhibiting
7. substance P
8. acupuncture
9. gate
10. close
11. passive
12. active
13. Braille
14. visual

Exercise 19

1. molecules
2. buds
3. sour
4. salty
5. sweet
6. bitter
7. shape
8. primary and secondary
9. food
10. communication
11. pheromones
12. sexual
13. humans

Exercise 20

1. Sensory stimulation occurs from all modalities at all times. We are incapable of processing all of this information. Thus, we must be selective in what is perceived, given the multiplicity of things that are sensed.

2. On a peripheral level, we can determine what will be sensed. For example, we have some control over what our eyes will see. On a central level we are more likely to attend to those things that have meaning relative to our past experiences (think of the cognitive "demons").

3. Attentional splitting is difficult when the different tasks require the same modality. For example, it is difficult to hear two messages simultaneously. However, if we become skilled at one task, such as driving, it is possible to carry on other tasks, such as conversation, at the same time. This is called automatization and is limited to tasks that can be carried out with limited attentional monitoring.

Exercise 21

1. g
2. a
3. f
4. c
5. b
6. e
7. d
8. h

MULTIPLE-CHOICE

Self-Test 1

1.	b	6.	a	11.	b	16.	c	21.	d	26.	d
2.	d	7.	a	12.	a	17.	b	22.	a	27.	d
3.	a	8.	b	13.	d	18.	a	23.	a	28.	b
4.	c	9.	a	14.	b	19.	a	24.	c	29.	a
5.	d	10.	c	15.	a	20.	c	25.	d	30.	c

Self-Test 2

1.	c	6.	b	11.	b	16.	a	21.	d	26.	b
2.	a	7.	a	12.	d	17.	c	22.	b	27.	c
3.	c	8.	c	13.	a	18.	c	23.	d	28.	c
4.	c	9.	c	14.	d	19.	a	24.	c	29.	c
5.	a	10.	c	15.	b	20.	b	25.	a	30.	a

WHAT DOES IT MEAN?

Self-Test

1.	a	6.	c	11.	b	16.	c
2.	a	7.	a	12.	c	17.	a
3.	d	8.	b	13.	c	18.	b
4.	b	9.	a	14.	b	19.	d
5.	d	10.	b	15.	a	20.	a

4 Basic Principles of Learning

OBJECTIVES

1. What is the definition of learning, and why, by this definition, is learning an intervening variable?
2. What are the stimuli and responses in classical conditioning, and what are the important temporal considerations for these events?
3. What are the contingencies and consequences in instrumental (or operant) conditioning, and what principles and procedures have been derived from these contingencies?
4. What is the proposed interaction between classical and instrumental conditioning in two-process theory?
5. What are the various aspects of classical and instrumental conditioning?
6. What effects are obtained when pleasant and unpleasant events are presented independently of behavior, and what are the implications of these effects?
7. What important factors determine how causality is perceived in classical and instrumental conditioning procedures?
8. What is cognitive learning, and when does it occur?

SYNOPSIS

Learning is operationally defined as a relatively permanent change in behavior as a result of practice (or experience). Thus, learning has the status of an intervening variable--something assumed to occur between an objective environmental stimulus and the resulting performance by the subject. This chapter deals with three types of learning: classical, conditioning, instrumental (or operant) conditioning, and cognitive (or observational) learning.

From a procedural standpoint, classical conditioning requires a contingency between a CS and UCS. The subject responds reflexively to the UCS with a UCR, but in time, it also develops a CR to the CS. The CS-UCS interval should be short for optimum conditioning (the law of contiguity), but there are exceptions (prepared learning).

In instrumental conditioning, the contingency is between behavior (which often needs to be shaped) and consequences. These contingencies may be arranged to increase (positive and negative reinforcement) or decrease (omission and punishment) the frequency of behavior, and each of these types of conditioning may be cued. The Premack principle has been used to identify primary positive reinforcers, but the manipulation of Premack contingencies may produce unexpected results (see Allison's principle of behavioral conservation).

Two-process theory has been applied primarily to avoidance learning. Specifically, classical conditioning of fear (process 1) is presumed to motivate the instrumental response, which is negatively reinforced by fear reduction (process 2).

There are a number of aspects common to both classical and instrumental conditioning, including acquisition, extinction, spontaneous recovery, generalization, and discrimination. In addition, partial reinforcement increases resistance to extinction primarily in instrumental conditioning. Events may be presented according to four types of schedules of partial reinforcement. Counterconditioning appears more effective in eliminating unwanted behavior than simple extinction does.

Autoshaping and superstitious behavior are two of the phenomena obtained when pleasant events are presented independently of behavior. Both phenomena imply that organisms are biologically prepared to find causes for such events. Learned helplessness occurs when unpleasant events are presented independently of behavior. This phenomenon has both behavioral (associative and motivational) and physiological (pain and stress) implications.

In general, inferences of causality are influenced by both spatial contiguity and similarity of intensity pattern. However, it is also important to know the degree to which stimuli (in classical conditioning) and responses (in instrumental conditioning) predict stimulus consequences. The greater the predictability (or correlation) is, the greater the validity of the cue or response will be.

Finally, learning may occur without explicit classical or instrumental contingencies. Such learning is based on our ability to perceive, imagine, and reason while observing others in various situations.

KEY WORDS AND PHRASES

OBJECTIVE 1

learning
performance
intervening variable

OBJECTIVE 2

classical conditioning
conditioned stimulus (CS)
unconditioned stimulus (UCS)
conditioned response (CR)
unconditioned response (UCR)
CS-UCS interval
law of contiguity
prepared learning

OBJECTIVE 3

instrumental (operant) conditioning
contingency
consequences
law of effect
functional analysis
behavior modification
positive reinforcer (or reward)

negative reinforcer
primary reinforcer
secondary reinforcer
Premack principle
behavioral conservation
omission training (punishment by time out)
punishment
stimulus control
discriminative stimulus (or cue)
discriminated operant training
active avoidance training
discriminated omission training
discriminated punishment training
shaping

OBJECT 4

two-process theory
    process 1 = fear
    process 2 = avoidance

OBJECTIVE 5

acquisition
extinction
spontaneous recovery
continuous reinforcement
partial reinforcement
schedules of reinforcement
    fixed ratio (FR)
    fixed interval (FI)
    variable ratio (VR)
    variable interval (VI)
counterconditioning
stimulus generalization
stimulus discrimination
response generalization
response discrimination
gradient of generalization

OBJECTIVE 6

response independence
superstition
autoshaping
learned helplessness
cognitive effect
motivational effect
emotional effect
analgesia
stress reaction
controllability (inescapability)
neurotransmitters

OBJECTIVE 7

causality detector
spatial contiguity
intensity pattern
predictability (correlation)

OBJECTIVE 8

cognitive (observational) learning
perceiving, imaging, and reasoning
active versus passive learning

EXERCISES

EXERCISE 1: Objective 2

TITLE: CLASSICAL CONDITIONING
TASK: Fill in the blanks

    Smith lives in the upstairs apartment of a two-family dwelling. When-
ever his downstairs neighbor, Jones, turns on the hot water in his shower,
Smith loses the hot water in his shower. Fortunately, Smith does have a
warning signal--the pipes rattle whenever Jones turns on the hot water. It
is understandable that Smith would scream and howl whenever his water
turned from hot to cold. However, Smith also begins to scream whenever he
hears the pipes rattle (before the water actually turns cold).

1.   Having the water turn from hot to cold is the _____.
2.   The rattling of the pipes is the _____.
3.   The interval of the time between the rattling and the turning from
     hot to cold is the _____.
4.   Screaming when the water turns cold is the _____.
5.   Screaming when the pipes rattle is the _____.
6.   According to the law of _____, the shorter the interval is between
     rattling and coldness, the stronger the conditioning will be.
7.   One clear-cut exception to this law is _____ learning

EXERCISE 2: Objective 3

TITLE: INSTRUMENTAL CONDITIONING
TASK: Short Essays

1.   What is the difference between positive and negative reinforcement?
2.   What is the difference between negative reinforcement and punishment?
3.   What is the difference between punishment and omission?
4.   What is the difference between primary and secondary reinforcers?

EXERCISE 3: Objective 3

TITLE: TYPES OF INSTRUMENTAL CONDITIONING
TASK: Match letters to numbers

_____1. Spanking a child for misbehaving.
_____2. Spanking for misbehavior occurs only when visitors are present.
_____3. Depriving the child of allowance for misbehaving.
_____4. Depriving the child of allowance only when misbehavior occurs in
         the presence of visitors.
_____5. The rat will increase its response rate in order to turn off a
         painful electric shock.
_____6. If given a warning signal, the rat will perform the same response
         in order to prevent the shock from being turned on.
_____7. The dog performs tricks for dog yummies.
_____8. The dog will perform tricks for dog yummies, but only when its
         master is present.

A.   Positive reinforcement (or reward training)
B.   Negative reinforcement (or escape training)
C.   Punishment by time out
D.   Punishment training
E.   Discriminated operant training
F.   Active avoidance training
G.   Discriminated omission training
H.   Discriminated punishment training

EXERCISE 4: Objective 3

TITLE: LAWS, PRINCIPLES, THEORIES, AND CONCEPTS
TASK: Fill in the blanks

1. Historically, the precursor to the modern-day version of the principle
    of reinforcement was the law of _____.
2. The end product of functional analysis is _____.
3. All types of instrumental contingencies are based on the _____ of
    behavior.
4. We will engage in low-probability behaviors in order to engage in
    high-probability behaviors--so says the _____ principle.
5. However, according to the principle of behavioral _____, time spent
    in either behavior reduces time spent in the other behavior.
6. Unlike the CR in classical conditioning, which is elicited, the response
    in instrumental conditioning is often _____, by reinforcing
    successive approximations to the desired behavior.
7. A stimulus that signals that reward or punishment will take place
    contingent on behavior is called a _____ cue.
8. The process represented by such cues is called stimulus _____.

81

EXERCISE 5: Objective 4

TITLE: A CASE STUDY IN ANXIETY
TASK: Essay

A month ago, Charlie was bitten by a vicious dog. The incident has made him tense and anxious whenever he sees a dog. Now, whenever a dog is present, Charlie sneaks away, and when he is far enough away, he feels safe and begins to relax. How would two-process theory explain Charlie's behavior?

EXERCIES 6: Objective 5

TITLE: ASPECTS OF CONDITIONING
TASK: Fill in the blanks

1.   The _____ of a conditioned response is typically gradual, taking place over a series of trials or experiences.
2.   When the UCS no longer follows the CS or when the reinforcer no longer follows the learned response, the result is _____.
3.   But with a rest period after extinction, the conditioned or learned response will _____ recover.
4.   Reinforcement on 100 percent of the trials is called _____ reinforcement.
5.   Reinforcement on less that 100 percent of the trials is called _____ reinforcement.
6.   A habit learned under partial reinforcement is more difficult to _____ than is one learned under continuous reinforcement.
7.   This is particularly true for _____ conditioning.
8.   Replacing one habit with another one is termed _____.

EXERCISE 7: Objective 5

TITLE: SCHEDULES OF REINFORCEMENT
TASK: Match letters to numbers

____ 1. Reinforcing every tenth response.
____ 2. Reinforcing on the average of every tenth response.
____ 3. Reinforcing a response every twenty seconds.
____ 4. Reinforcing a response on the average of every twenty seconds.
____ 5. The kind of reinforcement you receive in a gambling casino.
____ 6. Garment workers are paid by the number of garments produced.
____ 7. Consultants are paid by the hour.
____ 8. Hitchhiking.

A.   fixed interval
B.   variable interval
C.   fixed ratio
D.   variable ratio

EXERCISE 8:   Objective 5

TITLE: GENERALIZATION VERSUS DISCRIMINATION
TASK: Match letters to numbers

_____1. Little children tend to behave differently in church compared with
         school.
_____2. We tend to stop at red and go at green.
_____3. We tend to stop at red lights that look sort of orange.
_____4. Swinging a baseball bat is different from swinging a golf club.
_____5. Steering a boat is different from steering a car.
_____6. We can eat certain foods with a knife or fork.
_____7. We can eat in the kitchen or the dining room.
_____8. We can chew gum as well as tobacco.

A.   stimulus generalization
B.   response generalization
C.   stimulus discrimination
D.   response discrimination

EXERCISE 9:   Objective 6

TITLE: SUPERSTITION, AUTOSHAPING, AND LEARNED HELPLESSNESS
TASK: Fill in the blanks

1.   Superstition, autoshaping, and learned helplesness have one thing in
     common, that the important events happening to the organism are
     response _____.
2.   In the case of superstition and autoshaping, these events are _____.
3.   In the case of learned helplessness, these events are _____.
4.   _____ occurs with "chance reinforcers."
5.   _____ involves classical conditioning through pairings of key light
     and food.
6.   It is possible that the autoshaped key peck is _____ reinforced
     after it is made.
7.   Both superstition and autoshaping imply that organisms are predisposed
     to find _____ for their behaviors.
8.   Learned helplessness is exemplified by a dog's failure to _____
     from shock after earlier exposure to response-independent shock.
9.   One component of this effect involves the loss of _____ even to
     try to escape.
10. A second component involves a failure to learn an _____ between the
     escape response and shock termination.
11. However, earlier exposure to escapable shock produces an _____
     effect.
12. The _____ for learned helplessness is literally to force the dog
     to make the escape response.
13. In addition to the motivational and cognitive effects above, there are
     also _____ effects such as the loss of dominance.
14. Physiologically, uncontrollable aversive events lead to reduced pain
     perception, or _____.
15. There is also evidence of an increase in the _____ reaction, as
     indicated by increases in stomach ulcers.
16. Finally, _____ such as norepinephrine and dopamine are disturbed by
     uncontrollable aversive events.

EXERCISE 10: Objective 7

TITLE: THE CAUSALITY DETECTOR
TASK: Fill in the blanks

1. The most important function of conditioning is to allow the organism to learn relationships among events so as to anticipate _____ important stimuli.
2. It makes sense that _____ should select a mechanism that prompts such attempts at detecting causality.
3. In classical conditioning, there is more than mere contiguity. Indeed, the CS _____ the occurence of the UCS.
4. A variety of findings indicate that conditioning serves to internalize the _____ structure of the environment and to isolate the best predictors of important events.
5. One important determining factor of this internalizing and predicting process is similarity in point in space, or spatial _____.
6. A second factor of this process refers to changes in events as time passes, or changes in _____ pattern.
7. In general, conditioning will be greatest to the best predictor, or the most _____ cue.
8. With respect to instrumental conditioning, the effects are greater when reinforcers/punishers have similar _____ characteristics.
9. Stimulus control varies with the extent to which cues _____ reinforcers/punishers.
10. It is suggested that in terms of causality, classical and instrumental conditioning may have the same underlying _____.

EXERCISE 11: Objective 8

TITLE: COGNITIVE LEARNING
TASK: Essay

What makes cognitive learning different from either classical or instrumental conditioning?

EXERCISE 12:

TITLE: IMPORTANT NAMES
TASK: Match letters to numbers

_____1. behavioral conservation
_____2. prepared conditioned aversions
_____3. learned helplessness
_____4. classical conditioning
_____5. signs and expectations
_____6. high-probability behaviors reinforce low-probability behaviors
_____7. operant conditioning
_____8. the law of effect

A.   Pavlov
B.   Revusky
C.   Thorndike
D.   Skinner

E. Premack
F. Allison
G. Tolman
H. Maier and Seligman

MULTIPLE-CHOICE TESTS

SELF-TEST 1

1. Because learning is inferred from performance, learning is called:
   a. an independent variable
   b. a dependent variable
   c. an intervening variable
   d. an empirical variable
   (page 122)

2. Classical conditioning is said to have taken place when:
   a. two stimuli are paired together
   b. the UCS elicits the UCR
   c. the CS elicits the CR
   d. the UCS and the CS have been paired several times

3. When two events overlap in time, these events are said to be:
   a. contiguous
   b. contingent
   c. dependent
   d. operational
   (page 125)

4. If you were to become nauseaous at midnight, the chances are good that you would associate this illness with something that you ate hours earlier. Such learning would be called:
   a. contiguous
   b. prepared
   c. uncorrelated
   d. discriminative
   (page 126)

5. Instrumental action is exemplified by:
   a. intention and achievement
   b. reaction
   c. use of implements
   d. active rather than passive behavior
   (page 127)

6. The basic instrumental learning situation is characterized behavior --stimulus interactions that involve:
   a. contiguity
   b. contingency
   c. superstition
   d. autoshaping
   (page 127)

7. The termination of an ongoing aversive stimulus by a response leads
   to an increase in such escape behavior. Clearly, this phenomenon
   represents:
   a. positive reinforcement
   b. negative reinforcement
   c. punishment
   d. discriminated omission training
   (page 129)

8. The basic difference between punishment and reinforcement boils down to
   a difference between:
   a. stimuli and responses
   b. presenting and removing stimuli
   c. increasing and decreasing response rate
   d. conditioned and unconditioned stimuli
   (page 129)

9. Which of the following statements about secondary reinforcers is
   correct?
   a. secondary reinforcers can be established only for adults
   b. sexual interactions are clear examples of secondary reinforcers
   c. secondary reinforcers established in laboratory situations tend to
      extinguish readily
   d. attention is a fairly weak secondary reinforcer
   (page 129)

10. According to a sociobiological analysis, socially based rewards would
    be considered to be examples of:
    a. primary reinforcers
    b. secondary reinforcers
    c. conditioned stimuli
    d. stimulus generalization
    (page 130)

11. If you party more than you study when the opportunity for both is
    available, then partying should serve as a reinforcer for studying
    according to:
    a. the concept of prepared learning
    b. the law of effect
    c. the law of contiguity
    d. the Premack principle
    (page 130)

12. If a reward is contingent on a particular response not being made, the
    procedure is called:
    a. punishment by time out
    b. omission training
    c. negative reinforcement
    d. reward training
    (page 132)

13. A child asks his father for money when his father is smiling but not when his father is frowning. The boy's behavior shows good:
a. avoidance
b. superstition
c. stimulus control
d. generalization
(page 133)

14. With responses that are uncommon or difficult, the training method for response acquisition in instrumental conditioning is:
a. generalization
b. discrimination
c. autoshaping
d. shaping
(page 133)

15. Classical conditioning of fear will lead to an instrumental avoidance response according to:
a. the Premack principle
b. two-process theory
c. learned-helplessness theory
d. the law of contiguity
(page 134)

16. In avoidance learning, the avoidance response is:
a. punished
b. positively reinforced
c. negatively reinforced
d. extinguished
(page 134)

17. The curve that describes the acquisition of conditioned responses is:
a. linear
b. positively accelerated
c. negatively accelerated
d. first increasing, then decreasing
(page 135)

18. When the CS is presented in the absence of the UCS, the procedure is called:
a. conditioning
b. extinction
c. acquisition
d. forgetting
(page 135)

19. Partial reinforcement is most effective:
a. before conditioning has occurred
b. at the very beginning of conditioning
c. just before the organism is performing well
d. after the organism has learned the response quite well
(page 136)

20. If you wanted to stop smoking, perhaps the most effective technique
    would be a form of:
    a. punishment
    b. extinction
    c. negative reinforcement
    d. counterconditioning
    (page 136)

21. A salesperson who gets an increase in salary for every 100 policies he
    or she sells is being reinforced according to what schedule of
    reinforcement?
    a. fixed ratio
    b. fixed interval
    c. variable ratio
    d. variable interval
    (page 137)

22. A begger's approach behaviors on a city street are reinforced according
    to what schedule of reinforcement?
    a. fixed ratio
    b. fixed interval
    c. variable ratio
    d. variable interval
    (page 137)

23. If a rat were rewarded initially for depressing a lever with its right
    paw and if it later began to press with either paw as well as with
    its tail, we would have the phenomenon called:
    a. stimulus generalization
    b. stimulus discrimination
    c. response generalization
    d. response discrimination
    (page 138)

24. Many people eat differently when at home than when in a restaurant. We
    would say that this illustrates
    a. stimulus generalization
    b. response generalization
    c. stimulus discrimination
    d. response discrimination
    (page 138)

25. Response independent reinforcers are thought to be the precursors to:
    a. response-dependent reinforcers
    b. superstitions
    c. learned helplessness
    d. depression
    (page 139)

26. In the learned-helplessness procedure, it is thought that the subject
    learns that his or her behavior and the aversive stimulus are independent
    events. Which component of learned helplessness does this represent?
    a. cognitive
    b. motivational
    c. emotional
    d. behavioral
    (page 140)

27. The most important characteristic of stimulus occurrence in the learned-helplessness procedure is that it is:
a. unpredictable
b. intolerable
c. stressful
d. uncontrollable
    (page 140)

28. If a subject in a learned-helplessness experiment is first exposed to escapable shock, the helplessness effect will be blocked. What is this manipulation called?
a. inhibitory management
b. analgesia
c. immunization
c. therapy
    (page 140)

29. Location in space and similarity in intensity pattern are two factors that contribute to:
a. conditioning
b. assumptions of causal relationships
c. autoshaping
d. avoidance extinction
    (page 141)

30. In instances of cognitive learning:
a. the learner is passive cognitively
b. the learner need not be aware of the environment
c. the learner's responses must be reinforced
d. the learner actively processes information from the environment
    (page 143)

SELF-TEST 2

1. With respect to learning:
a. performance is not always an adequate measure of learning
b. learning is an independent variable
c. conditioning is a special form of learning
d. there are three types, classical, instrumental, and cognitive
    (page 122)

2. Salivation in response to food in the mouth is an example of a:
a. UCS
b. UCR
c. CS
d. CR
    (page 124)

3. Before being associated with a puff of air to the eye, a bell is a(n) _____ stimulus.
a. conditioned
b. unconditioned
c. neutral
d. discriminative
    (page 124)

4. Some psychologists have suggested that fear conditioned to specific neutral stimuli is the essence of:
a. depression
b. unhappiness
c. anxiety
d. cognitive learning
   (page 124)

5. A bell rings, and twenty minutes later a puff of air is directed at the cornea of a rabbit's eye.
a. conditioning is not likely to occur
b. conditioning will occur within five trials
c. the rabbit will begin to blink continuously
d. conditioning will not be complete until after about thirty trials
   (page 125)

6. Prepared learning serves as an exception to:
a. the law of effect
b. the law of contiguity
c. the Premack principle
d. two-process theory
   (page 126)

7. The temporal relationship of stimuli and responses in instrumental conditioning is:
a. response follows stimulus
b. stimulus follows response
c. stimulus follows stimulus
d. response follows response
   (page 127)

8. If studying for an exam serves to reduce your anxiety and if anxiety is an aversive event, then studying is being:
a. positively reinforced
b. negatively reinforced
c. negatively discriminated
d. positively punished
   (page 129)

9. Secondary reinforcers gain their power by association with primary reinforcers. An example of a secondary reinforcer is:
a. food
b. sex
c. water
d. money
   (page 129)

10. the concept of sociobiology:
a. describes principles of classical conditioning
b. describes principles of social relationships
c. puts constraints on laws of learning
d. has been used to describe the phenomenon of discrimination
   (page 130)

11. A child must study for 60 minutes in order to be able to watch 30
minutes of television. Her parents decide this is too strict and change
the contingency so that 30 minutes of studying earns 60 minutes of television
viewing. Allison's principle of conservation predicts that the:
a. amount of studying will increase gradually
b. amount of studying will increase suddenly
c. amount of studying will decrease
d. amount of studying will not change
    (page 131)

12. Decreasing the rate of response by using a pleasant stimulus describes:
a. reward training
b. escape training
c. punishment training
d. omission training
    (page 132)

13. If a parent sends a child to his room as a consequence of misbehaving,
we might suspect that the parent is trying to control the boy's behavior
through:
a. learned helplessness
b. punishment
c. escape
d. punishment by time-out training
    (page 132)

14. A stimulus-control situation is one in which:
a. there are cues about whether a response will be reinforced or punished
b. there is total generalization of responses to all stimuli
c. discriminations have not yet been formed
d. only one response is possible, and that response is cued
    (page 133)

15. The procedure of differentially reinforcing successive approximations to
a target behavior is called:
a. shaping
b. discrimination
c. counterconditioning
d. generalization
    (page 133)

16. A man who is afraid of dogs runs away as soon as he sees a dog nearby.
This behavior could best be explained by:
a. the Premack principle
b. learned-helplessness theory
c. two-process theory
d. the law of contiguity
    (page 134)

17. According to two-process theory, the initial fear that motivates the
avoidance response is:
a. classically conditioned
b. negatively reinforced
c. due to uncontrollability
d. due to prepared learning
    (page 134)

18. Two-process theory suggests that a large portion of human behavior occurs in order to:
a. produce rewards
b. avoid unpleasant emotional states
c. pass on the genes to the next generation
d. engage in social situations
   (page 135)

19. A fourth-grade teacher realized that one of his students was acting out in order to receive attention. The teacher decided to ignore the acting-out behavior. Technically this tactic would be called:
a. the Premack principle
b. extinction
c. response discrimination
d. escape
   (page 135)

20. When a response occurs to a previously extinguished CS, the process is called:
a. generalization
b. differentiation
c. spontaneous recovery
d. internalization
   (page 135)

21. Conditioned behavior will be most resistant to extinction if:
a. it has been partially reinforced
b. it has been continuously reinforced
c. alternatives to it have been punished
d. it was learned in childhood
   (page 136)

22. When one habit is conditioned to take the place of another habit, the procedure is called:
a. escape
b. avoidance
c. differentiation
d. counterconditioning
   (page 136)

23. If a person is paid at the end of each workday, the reinforcement schedule would be:
a. fixed ratio
b. fixed interval
c. variable ratio
d. variable interval
   (page 137)

24. The training that athletes go through to refine their skills exemplifies:
a. stimulus generalization
b. response generalization
c. stimulus discrimination
d. response discrimination
   (page 138)

25. Concept formation is based on the process of:
a. discrimination
b. generalization
c. superstition
d. autoshaping
   (page 138)

26. The notion of gradient of generalization relates to:
a. perceived similarity of stimulus objects
b. extinction of instrumental responses
c. autoshaping of prepared responses
d. cognitive learning
   (page 138)

27. Attribution of cause to environmental events is an example of:
a. classical conditioning
b. generalization
c. autoshaping
d. law of contiguity
   (page 139)

28 Dragging dogs over barriers between chambers of an experimental box
was used as therapy for:
a. learned helplessness
b. incomplete avoidance learning
c. extinction
d. superstitious behavior
   (page 140)

29. An example of an emotional by-product of learned helplessness would be:
a. learning that shock and behavior are unrelated
b. depression
c. lack of desire to escape
d. ulcers
   (page 140)

30. Perceiving, imaging, and reasoning are basic abilities that are seen
to underlie:
a. classical conditioning
b. instrumental conditioning
c. cognitive learning
d. learned helplessness
   (page 142)

WHAT DOES IT MEAN?

LEARNING OBJECTIVES

1. How do theorists use the principles of classical conditioning to
   account for morphine tolerance and for asthma?
2. How have the principles of classical conditioning been applied to such
   diverse problems as bed-wetting, coyotes killing sheep, early
   detection of physical problems in infants, deviant behavior, and
   taste aversions of chemotherapy patients?

3. How has biofeedback been used in conjunction with instrumental conditioning of physiological responses?
4. What is behavior modification, and how does it use tokens and contracts?
5. How can individuals manage self-control through techniques of instrumental conditioning?
6. How does learned-helplessness theory explain depression and instances of chronic failure in school?
7. What is the partial reinforcement extinction effect, and how does it apply to patients in therapy and to spoiling children?
8. Under what circumstances can punishment effectively control behavior, and what side effects can be expected during its use?

SELF-TEST

1. The tendency for the effect of a given quantity of a drug to have less and less of an effect with repeated usage is termed:
a. preparedness
b. tolerance
c. addiction
d. extinction
   (page 146)

2. According to Siegal, tolerance to morphine develops because:
a. morphine binds with certain receptor sites to make them inactive
b. morphine causes the body to produce its own "natural morphine"
c. a CS for morphine causes the body to make the opposite reaction
d. we are biologically prepared to tolerate morphine after several injections
   (page 146)

3. A treatment for asthma that involves the substitution of a different response for the anxiety CR is technically called:
a. counterconditioning
b. extinction
c. omission
d. generalization
   (page 147)

4. The main reason that classical conditioning can be used to diagnose and understand why infants do things is:
a. infants are essentially animals
b. infants have no true perceptual systems
c. infants have no true verbal fluency, and these procedures require none
d. instrumental conditioning procedures are not effective
   (page 147)

5. In classical conditioning procedures designed to stop bed-wetting, the UCS is:
a. bed-wetting itself
b. bladder tension
c. waking up
d. a very loud noise
   (page 148)

6. The desired conditioned response in the classical conditioning treatment of bed-wetting is:
a. sleeping through the entire night
b. waking up as the bladder tension increases
c. changing the sheets immediately after wetting the bed
d. relaxation and a resulting decrease in anxiety
   (page 148)

7. In the taste aversion procedure developed to keep coyotes from attacking and killing sheep, the CS is:
a. approaching the sheep
b. tasting sheep meat
c. becoming sick
d. killing the sheep
   (page 149)

8. About how many trials are necessary to condition coyotes not to eat sheep?
a. very few--just one or two
b. about five to ten
c. typically about twenty
d. conditioning has never been shown with less than thirty trials
   (page 149)

9. Treatment of child molesters according to classical conditioning principles usually involves:
a. substitution of fraternal for erotic love
b. redirection of sexual targets from children to adults
c. associating nude children with nausea or aversive electric shocks
d. procedures of self-management whereby the patients give themselves strong shocks every time they think about touching children
   (page 149)

10. In which area has the use of classical conditioning principles been the most controversial?
a. treatment of homosexuality
b. diagnosis of infants
c. conditioning of coyotes to avoid sheep
d. treatment of alcoholics with nausea-inducing drugs
   (page 149)

11. How would you minimize the general loss of appetite in chemotherapy patients who tend to become nauseous after treatment?
a. deprive them of all food before chemotherapy sessions
b. feed them a variety of foods before the sessions
c. deprive them of food after the sessions
d. feed them the same food before all sessions and make it one they don't like
   (page 150)

12. Which of the following is NOT an application of instrumental conditioning via biofeedback?
a. control of brain waves for treating epilepsy
b. modification of blood circulation
c. relaxation training
d. changing the appetites of chemotherapy patients
   (page 151)

13. Treatment of epilepsy has been accomplished through the use of:
a. biofeedback
b. time out from punishment procedures
c. appetite suppression through taste aversion therapy
d. the A-B-A design
   (page 151)

14. The sequence of extinction, implementation of some instrumental procedure such as reinforcement, and extinction once again, describes:
a. multiple treatment designs
b. shaping
c. the A-B-A design
d. the typical token economy
   (page 152)

15. Treating behavior defects by using operant conditioning procedures is termed:
a. shaping
b. applied instrumental conditioning
c. behavioral contracting
d. behavior modification
   (page 152)

16. In a token economy, the tokens serve as:
a. primary reinforcers
b. secondary reinforcers
c. conditioned stimuli
d. unconditioned stimuli
   (page 153)

17. You would be most likely to find a token economy in use in:
a. a prison
b. a city hall
c. a mental hospital
d. a general hospital
   (page 153)

18. Which of the following typifies the behavioral contract?
a. use of biofeedback to reduce blood pressure
b. the A-B-A design
c. use of a token economy
d. setting well-defined goals at the outset of therapy
   (page 154)

19. Someone who was interested in developing better self-control could profit from:
a. a knowledge of instrumental conditioning principles
b. a knowledge of classical conditioning principles
c. a knowledge of prepared learning
d. a knowledge of insight-oriented literature
   (page 155)

20. According to the theory of learned helplessness, depression is brought on by:
a. lack of positive reinforcement
b. too much extinction
c. too much punishment
d. too many uncontrollable aversive events
   (page 156)

96

21. In Seligman's reformulated view of learned helplessness, a very important concept has been added. It is:
a. attribution
b. prepared learning
c. depression
d. lack of positive reinforcement
   (page 157)

22. The theory of learned helplessness has been used to account for all of the following EXCEPT:
a. chronic failure in school
b. depression
c. hysteria
d. stress response in urban environments
   (page 157)

23. According to Jack Nation, therapists make a big mistake in:
a. using punishment with their clients
b. reinforcing continuously when teaching patients new responses
c. reinforcing partially when teaching patients new responses
d. using extinction too frequently
   (page 158)

24. Which of the following is NOT a typical side effect of punishment?
a. the effect generalizes to other, nonpunished responses, causing them to decline
b. the punished response can never be reconditioned
c. the punished response may decrease only in the presence of punishment-associated cues
d. the person punished may learn to use punishment with others
   (page 159)

25. Which of the following is NOT a principle for the effective use of punishment?
a. avoid strong punishing stimuli
b. avoid rewards after punishment
c. always provide an acceptable alternative to the punished response
d. punish immediately after the undesirable behavior
   (page 159)

ANSWER KEY

EXERCISES

Exercise 1

1. unconditioned stimulus
2. conditioned stimulus
3. CS-UCS interval
4. unconditioned response
5. conditioned response
6. contiguity
7. prepared

Exercise 2

1. A reinforcer always increases response rate or strength. With positive reinforcement, the rate increases because something pleasant is presented. With negative reinforcement, the rate increases because something unpleasant is removed.

2. Negative reinforcement and punishment both involve unpleasant events. With negative reinforcement, the unpleasant event is removed (thus the increasing rate). With punishment, the unpleasant event is presented (thus the decreasing rate).

3. Punishment and omission both decrease the response rate. However, punishment does so because unpleasant events are presented, whereas omission does so because pleasant events are presented if the response does not occur.

4. Primary reinforcers are innate, whereas secondary reinforcers require learning. For example, food for a hungry animal is an example of a primary reinforcer, whereas money is an example of a secondary reinforcer.

Exercise 3

1.	D	3.	C	5.	B	7.	A
2.	H	4.	G	6.	F	8.	E

Exercise 4

1. effect
2. behavior modification
3. consequences
4. Premack
5. conservation
6. shaped
7. discriminative
8. control

Exercise 5

   According to two-factor theory, Charles has associated dogs with dog bites--that is, the bite has produced classical conditioning of fear of dogs. This fear, in turn, has motivated Charlie's escape behavior, which is negatively reinforcing, as the fear is reduced by the act of escaping.

Exercise 6

1. acquisition
2. extinction
3. spontaneously
4. continuous
5. partial
6. extinguish
7. instrumental (or operant)
8. counterconditioning

Exercise 7

1.	c	3.	A	5.	D	7.	A
2.	D	4.	B	6.	C	8.	D

Exercise 8

1.	C	3.	A	5.	D	7.	A
2.	C	4.	D	6.	B	8.	B

Exercise 9

1.	independent	6.	instrumentally	11.	immunization
2.	pleasant	7.	causes	12.	therapy
3.	unpleasant	8.	escape	13.	emotional
4.	superstition	9.	motivation	14.	analgesia
5.	autoshaping	10.	association	15.	stress
				16.	neurotransmitters

Exercise 10

1.	brilogically	6.	intensity
2.	evolution	7.	valid
3.	predicts	8.	spatial/temporal
4.	causal	9.	predict
5.	contiguity	lo.	mechanism

Exercise 11

Classical conditioning involves explicit contingencies between stimuli. Instrumental conditioning involves explicit contingencies between behaviors and consequences. In comparison, with cognitive learning, the learner is presumed to use cognitive abilities (such as perceiving, imaging, and reasoning) to reorganize knowledge. This reorganization is based on observations that do not necessarily depend on explicit contingencies. Finally, the cognitive learner is presumed to be an active, as opposed to being a passive, recipient of contingencies.

Exercise 12

1.	F	5.	G
2.	B	6.	E
3.	H	7.	D
4.	A	8.	C

MULTIPLE-CHOICE TESTS

Self-Test 1

1.	c	6.	b	11.	d	16.	c	21.	a	26.	a
2.	c	7.	c	12.	b	17.	c	22.	c	27.	d
3.	a	8.	c	13.	c	18.	b	23.	c	28.	c
4.	b	9.	c	14.	d	19.	d	24.	c	29.	b
5.	a	10.	a	15.	b	20.	d	25.	b	30.	d

Self-Test 2

1.	a	6.	b	11.	c	16.	c	21.	a	26.	a
2.	b	7.	b	12.	d	17.	a	22.	d	27.	c
3.	c	8.	b	13.	d	18.	b	23.	b	28.	a
4.	c	9.	d	14.	a	19.	b	24.	d	29.	b
5.	a	10.	c	15.	a	20.	c	25.	b	30.	c

WHAT DOES IT MEAN?

Self-Test

1.	b	6.	b	11.	d	16.	b	21.	a
2.	c	7.	b	12.	d	17.	c	22.	c
3.	a	8.	a	13.	a	18.	d	23.	b
4.	c	9.	c	14.	c	19.	a	24.	b
5.	d	10.	a	15.	d	20.	d	25.	a

5   Human Learning, Memory, and Language

OBJECTIVES

1.   What are the four assumptions made in the information-processing model?
2.   What are the characteristics of the three stages in the fundamental memory system?
3.   What is required for information in short-term memory to be encoded into long-term memory, and what factors facilitate this encoding?
4.   What are the various ways in which knowledge may be represented in long-term memory, and how are such representations organized?
5.   What are the four theories of forgetting, and how does distortion contribute to forgetting, at both the time of storage and the time of retrieval?
6.   What factors allow us to understand language and to process discourse?

SYNOPSIS

You will recall from Chapter 1 that the human information-processing model is one of the two contemporary trends in psychology. This model makes four assumptions: the existence of stages and processes, limitations in capacity, the existence of control mechanism, and a two-way flow of information. The most important of these assumptions is stages and processes.

The three stages are sensory memory (SM), short-term memory (STM), and long-term memory (LTM). Information first enters SM and either fades or, with continued attention, is passed onto STM. STM has a limited capacity, thus forcing new information to bump out existing information. In (availability) does not automatically imply retrieval (accessibility).

Encoding is the process whereby information is stored or represented in memory. Mere repetition of information (that is, maintenance or Type I rehearsal) is not sufficient for encoding information from STM into LTM. That process requires elaborative (or Type II) rehearsal. Factors facilitating encoding into LTM are deep rather than shallow processing, elaboration, distinctiveness, and effort. Imagery is an effective encoding strategy but is difficult to apply to abstract concepts. Organizing material is another effective encoding strategy.

Knowledge may be represented as a procedure (knowing how) versus a declaration (knowing that) and as a proposition (with a predicate and arguments). Another important distinction is between episodic (that is, autobiographical) and semantic (meaning) memory. Regarding this retrieval of these representations, the network model (a hierarchy with nodes and connections) is postulated for semantic memories, whereas schemata are postulated for stereotyped episodic memories.

Currently, there are four theories of memory, and they attribute forgetting to some form of trace dependency (Gestalt and consolidation theory), cue dependency (for example, encoding specificity theory), or combination of the two (interference theory). It is important to recognize that our LTM represents more than a photocopy of our experiences. Clearly, distortion can occur at both the point of storage (that is, construction) and the point of retrieval (that is, reconstruction).

The understanding of language is based on both structural considerations (syntax) and meaning (semantics). Sentences convey meaning at the level of the word, the proposition, and the whole sentence itself. When processing a sentence, we combine what the sentence contains with our preexisting knowledge and, as a result, make inferences (for example, presuppositions, elaborations, and pragmatics). At the level of a story, we try to grasp the gist, or the "whole idea." To do this, we need to know the grammar of the story, which consists of a setting, theme, plot, and resolution.

KEY WORDS AND PHRASES

OBJECTIVE 1

stages and processes
capacity
control mechanism
two-way flow

OBJECTIVE 2

sensory memory (SM)
short-term memory (STM)
long-term memory (LTM)
primary versus secondary memory
iconic memory
echoic memory
cued partial report procedure
limited capacity
veridical versus nonveridical representation
trace duration
fading of the trace
pattern recognition
feature extraction
bottom-up versus top-down influences
verbal representation
immediate (read-out) memory
working memory
encoding
decoding
memory-span task
serial-position effect
    primacy
    recency
chunks of information
availability versus accessibility

OBJECTIVE 3

encoding from STM into LTM
maintenance (Type I) rehearsal
elaborative (Type II) rehearsal
levels of processing
     shallow
     deep
distinctiveness
elaboration
effort
imagery
dual coding
organization
chunking as an encoding strategy
digit-span task

OBJECTIVE 4

procedure
declaration
knowing how versus knowing that
all-or-none versus partial knowledge
sudden versus gradual acquisition
communication versus demonstration
practice
feedback
proposition
predicate
argument
serial processing
parallel processing
digital versus analogical form
episodic knowledge
semantic knowledge
contextual arguments
networks
nodes
connections
hierarchy
speed of retrieval
schemata
stereotyped information
default knowledge

OBJECTIVE 5

trace dependency
cue dependency
Gestalt theory
consolidation theory
encoding specificity theory
interference theory
leveling

sharpening
assimilation
recall versus recognition
tip-of-tongue phenomenon
ECS and convulsive drugs
retrograde amnesia
hypermnesia
state dependency
reminder cues
reinstatement
proactive interference
retroactive interference
unlearning
response competition
transfer of training
reconstruction model
constructive processing
reconstructive processing

OBJECTIVE 6

language
semantics
syntax
words, propositions, and sentences
discourse processing
inferences
presupposition
elaboration
pragmatics
gist
story grammar

EXERCISES

EXERCISE 1: Objective 1

TITLE: THE INFORMATION-PROCESSING MODEL
TASK: Fill in the blanks

1. A major assumption of the information-processing model is that there
    are three _____ of memory (that is, SM, STM, and LTM).
2. Operating at the various stages are _____, including encoding,
    storage, and retrieval.
3. A second major assumption of the information-processing model is that
    the system is _____ in terms of capacity or space.
4. A third major assumption is the existence of a _____ mechanism
    to oversee the flow and analysis of all data in the system.
5. The _____ control mechanism allows you to tune in and tune out
    information.
6. The last major assumption of the information-processing model is that
    of _____ flow.

7. This last assumption involves new data entering the system via the receptors, or _____ processing.

8. This last assumption also involves knowledge-driven information, or _____ processing.

EXERCISE 2: Objective 2

TITLE: COMPARISON OF THE STAGES OF MEMORY
TASK: Essay

1. What are the three key points regarding information entering sensory memory?

2. What are the four ways in which short-term memory differs from sensory memory?

3. What are the three ways in which long-term memory differs from sensory and short-term memory?

EXERCISE 3: Objective 2

TITLE: FOCUS ON SENSORY MEMORY
TASK: Match letters to numbers

____ 1. This is the process by which new information in SM makes contact with the information in LTM

____ 2. The auditory component of SM.

____ 3. The visual component of SM.

____ 4. The procedure used by Sperling (Highlight 5-2 in the text) to demonstrate that the visual trace fades in less than a second.

____ 5. The bottom-up process that begins the comparison of information in SM with knowledge in LTM.

A. iconic memory
B. echoic memory
C. pattern recognition
D. feature extraction
E. cued partial report

EXERCISE 4: Objective 2

TITLE: FOCUS ON SHORT-TERM AND LONG-TERM MEMORY
TASK: Fill in the blanks

1. Primary and secondary memory are additional names used for _____.

2. The _____ memory component of STM contains information that can be directly read out.

3. This read-out component has been implicated in the _____ effect in the serial-position curve.

4. The _____ memory component of STM processes and changes the encoding of incoming information.

5. _____ experiments show that STM can hold seven (plus or minus two) chunks, or items of information.

6. The opposite of chunking is _____.

7. The _____ effect in the serial-position curve is attributed to information entering LTM.
8. In general, in LTM, some information is never stored to begin with and is thus not _____.
9. Stored information in LTM that cannot be retrieved is said to be _____.

EXERCISE 5: Objective 3

TITLE: MAINTENANCE (TYPE I) AND ELABORATIVE (TYPE II) REHEARSAL
TASK: Essay

What is encoding, and what are the roles of maintenance and elaborative rehearsal with respect to encoding information from STM into LTM?

EXERCISE 6: Objective 3

TITLE: REAL-WORLD MEMORY
TASK: Fill in the blanks

You are at a party and meet someone nice. This person is so nice that you do not want to forget his or her name under any circumstances. What do you do?

1. If you repeat the name over and over again, this is _____ rehearsal --it won't lead to encoding into LTM.
2. If the name is Jack it rhymes with track--but that's an example of very _____ processing, and it may not be very effective.
3. If the name is June, and June reminds you of a lovely time of the year, then you are dealing with semantic meaning, which is much _____ processing than simply a rhyme.
4. Another good strategy would be to think of the _____ features of the name. For example, in the case of Xavier, it is one of the few names beginning with the letter x.
5. In general, deeper processing requires extra _____.
6. Thus, do not _____ your attention--concentrate solely on what the name means.
7. You can take advantage of _____ coding theory and associate the name with a mental image of the person, and/or images of what the name is associated with.
8. Finally, you can place the name into some sort of _____. For example, you already know names of people who fit various categories --which one does this name fit into?
9. By the way, if you also get his or her phone number (for example 555-3701), you might organize it by _____ it into an exchange (555) and a single four-digit unit (3701).
10. The latter tactic above works quite well in the _____-span task, so it should work for remembering a phone number.

EXERCISE 7: Objective 4

TITLE: DECLARATIVE VERSUS PROCEDURAL KNOWLEDGE
TASK: Match letters to numbers

1. knowing that.
2. Knowing how.

106

3. All-or-none knowledge that is acquired suddenly and is communicated verbally.
4. It is implicated in the ability to transfer new information from STM to LTM.
5. Partially possessed knowledge that is learned gradually and is better demonstrated than communicated.
6. Requires a great deal of practice and feedback.

A. declarative knowledge
B. procedural knowledge

EXERCISE 8: Objective 4

TITLE: KNOWLEDGE AS PROPOSITIONS
TASK: Fill in the blanks

1. Discrete digital information such as words are processed one piece at a time. This is called _____ processing.
2. In comparison, imaginal, or analogue information such as pictures are processed simultaneously. This is called _____ processing.
3. A _____ reduces information in a sentence to a central relational term and a set of participating elements.
4. The central term in a proposition is called the _____ .
5. The elements in a proposition are called _____ .
6. Kintsch suggests that both analogue and digital information can be recorded into more abstract _____ representations.
7. The feasibility of Kintsch's argument is supported by the fact that _____ manipulate and store information in a propositional format and yet produce either verbal or pictorial outputs.

EXERCISE 9: Objective 4

TITLE: REPRESENTATION AND ORGANIZATION
TASK: Match letters to numbers

1. Representation of what things mean.
2. Representation of actual autobiographical events.
3. Organization of meaning into a hierarchy of nodes (locations) and connections (associations).
4. Knowledge that is more easily communicated than demonstrated.
5. Knowledge that is more easily demonstrated than communicated.
6. Organization of autobiographical knowledge, particularly stereotyped knowledge.
7. Logical structure with a predicate and arguments.

A. declarative knowledge
B. procedural knowledge
C. propositions
D. episodic memory
E. semantic memory
F. networks
G. schemata

EXERCISE 10:   Objective 4

TITLE: FOCUS ON NETWORKS
TASK: Essay

Figure 5-6 in the text illustrates a simple hierarchy in semantic memory. What are the essential features of this hierarchy, and what are the implications for such an organization for retrieving information from memory?

EXERCISE 11:   Objective 5

TITLE: THEORIES OF FORGETTING
TASK: Fill in the blanks

1.   _____ theory attributes forgetting to the changing of the memory trace over time.
2.   In the Gestalt theory of forgetting, the memory trace may lose detail, or _____.
3.   The trace may _____, in which case certain features are accentuated and take on more importance.
4.   Or the trace may _____ in the direction of something already familiar to us.
5.   Another view of forgetting is that the trace is all or partially destroyed before it is _____.
6.   This latter view mentioned above is illustrated by research with ECS and electroconvulsive drugs which induce retrograde _____.
7.   However, an alternative account of these ECS effects is inaccessibility, as is evidenced by the ability to restore memories with _____.
8.   According to _____ theory, forgetting is due to differences in cues present at recall, versus those present at the original learning.
9.   Thus, according to the theory above, to facilitate memory, at recall, we must _____ the original encoding cues.
10. _____ theory incorporates both trace and cue dependency.
11. The _____ dependency component of interference theory is evidenced by proactive and retroactive interference and response competition.
12. The _____ dependency component of interference theory is evidenced by the fact that unlearning may alter the previous memory.

EXERCISE 12:   Objective 5

TITLE: CONCEPTS IN MEMORY AND FORGETTING
TASK: Identify each of the following

1.   Forgetting based on the fading or alteration of stored memories.
2.   Foregtting based on the inaccessibility of stored memories.
3.   Loss of detail alters the trace.
4.   Accentuation alters the trace.
5.   Distortion to the already-known information alters the trace.
6.   Illustrated by a fill-in-the-blank test.
7.   Illustrated by multiple-choice test.
8.   Induced by ECS and convulsive drugs.
9.   Reinstatement due to cues present during original learning.

10. "Mood" dependency.
11. New memory interferes with old memory.
12. Old memory interferes with new memory.
13. New learning retroactively alters the old trace.
14. A given cue is associated with more than one response.
15. A test which shows whether new learning is helped, hindered, or unaffected by previous knowledge.
16. Memory improves when you try harder to recall.

EXERCISE 13:   Objective 5

TITLE: STATE DEPENDENCY AND STUDY HABITS
TASK: Essay

The encoding specificity principle suggests that for the best retrieval, we should reinstate the original learning cues at the time of retrieval. The principle of state dependency suggests that our "mood" (among other things) is one of those cues. What are the implications of encoding specificity and state dependency for study habits?

EXERCISE 14:   Objective 5

TITLE: RECONSTRUCTION
TASK: Essays

1. Why isn't the brain a copy machine?

2. What kinds of memory distortion occur at the time of storage?

3. What kinds of memory distortion occur at the time of retrieval?

EXERCISE 15:   Objective 6

TITLE: UNDERSTANDING LANGUAGE
TASK: Fill in the blanks

1. _____ deals with the formal structure of strings of symbols that make up sentences.
2. In comparison, _____ refers to the meaning of a message.
3. Meaning is extracted at three levels, the first of which is the _____ level.
4. The second level of meaning is the atomic _____.
5. The third and final level of meaning is the _____.

EXERCISE 16:   Objective 6

TITLE: DISCOURSE PROCESSING
TASK: Fill in the blanks

1. The sentence we read interacts with preexisting knowledge and results in our making _____.
2. For example, in _____, the sentence conveys information that implies that other information must be true.
3. Also, we may construct _____, which may or may not be true.

4. Finally, there are _____, that is, inferences regarding the speaker's intentions.
5. When processing a story, we attempt to extract the _____, or "whole idea."
6. Stories have a _____ consisting of four components.
7. There is the context, or _____ of the story.
8. There is a goal, or _____.
9. There are episodes, or the _____.
10. And finally, there is an outcome, or _____.

EXERCISE 17

TITLE: KEY NAMES
TASK: Match letters to numbers

1. Levels of processing.
2. Cued partial report and sensory memory.
3. Distortion at the point of storage (construction).
4. The network model.
5. Principle of encoding specificity.
6. Primary versus secondary memory.
7. Analogy--working memory and the carpenter's workbench.
8. Distortion at the point of retrieval (reconstruction).
9. The gist of the story.
10. State ("mood") dependency.
11. First to point out that LTM is more than a photocopy.
12. Effort and divided attention.
13. Hippocampal effect is limited to declarative knowledge.
16. Organization and the digit-span task.
17. Dual-coding theory.

A. James
B. Millner
C. Sperling
D. Klatzky
E. Glanzer and Cunitz
F. Craik and Lockhart
G. Ellis
H. Pavio
I. Chase and Ericsson

J. Cohen, Squire, and Moscovitz
K. Collins and Quillian
L. Tulving
M. Bower
N. Bartlett
O. Johnson, Bransford, and Solomon
P. Hanwalt and Demerest
Q. Bransford and Franks

MULTIPLE-CHOICE TESTS

SELF-TEST 1

1. Which of the following is NOT one of the three broad classes of learning and memory processes?
a. attention
b. encoding
c. storage
d. retrieval
    (page 162)

2. In which case below would the limited-capacity assumption of processing predict ineffective learning?
a. studying while listening to instrumental music
b. studying while riding on a train
c. studying while "watching" TV
d. studying while in the bath
    (page 162)

3. Damage to the hippocampus appears to:
a. cause an impairment in short-term memory
b. interfere with the transfer from short-term to long-term memory
c. disrupt memories of childhood
d. block sensory images from short-term memory
    (page 163)

4. All incoming data are available in:
a. sensory memory
b. short-term memory
c. long-term memory
d. episodic memory
    (page 164)

5. When information in sensory memory is lost, the most probable cause is:
a. consolidation failure
b. proactive interference
c. retrieval failure
d. a faded trace
    (page 164)

6. Which memory stage or process seems to have the most limited capacity?
a. sensory memory
b. short-term memory
c. long-term memory
d. semantic memory
    (page 164)

7. If you attended a football game and afterwards could only recall well the plays at the very beginning and end of the game, you would be demonstrating the:
a. primacy effect
b. recency effect
c. serial-position effect
d. immediate memory effect
    (page 166)

8. Availability is to accessibility as
a. STM is to LTM
b. encoding is to storage
c. decoding is to retrieval
d. storage is to retrieval
    (page 167)

9. Suppose that it was late at night and your car broke down. There was no directory in the phone booth so you had to remember the number of the towing service after calling directory assistance. To keep from forgetting the number you would probably employ:
a. maintenance rehearsal
b. elaborative rehearsal
c. deep processing
d. an analogue process
    (page 168)

10. What is needed for information to pass from STM to LTM?
a. maintenance rehearsal
b. elaborative rehearsal
c. episodic rehearsal
d. immediate rehearsal
    (page 168)

11. When particular meanings are attached to stimuli to be remembered, what kind of processing becomes involved?
a. shallow
b. deep
c. short-term
d. episodic
    (page 169)

12. Investigations of children who listened to nursery rhymes as opposed to prose narratives showed that:
a. there was better recall of content of the rhymes
b. there was better recall of content with prose
c. the children ignored the similarity in sound in the rhymes and attended to the meaning
d. the phrasing of the rhymes controlled how well the children recalled the meaning
    (page 170)

13. The use of visual imagery during learning:
a. seems to have little effect on learning words but greatly affects learning pictures
b. has little effect generally on learning
c. is easier with concrete than with abstract words
d. is easier with abstract than with concrete words
    (page 171)

14. It is believed that short-term memory can hold between five and nine units of information. However, what fits into each of these units can be enlarged through the process of:
a. maintenance rehearsal
b. pattern recognition
c. feature extraction
d. chunking
    (page 173)

15. The difference between a declaration and a procedure is like the difference between:
a. events and meanings
b. knowing what and knowing how
c. images and replicas
d. stereotyped and nonstereotyped information
   (page 174)

16. The statement, "you have to learn by doing" exemplifies:
a. semantic memory
b. maintenance rehearsal
c. procedural knowledge
d. proactive interference
   (page 174)

17. A central relational term and a set of elements that participate in that relationship defines:
a. declaration
b. syntax
c. schema
d. proposition
   (page 175)

18. What you had for breakfast this morning would be represented in:
a. semantic memory
b. episodic memory
c. networks
d. schemas
   (page 175)

19. According to the network model of memory representation to which of the following would we answer the fastest?
a. is a canary yellow?
b. are canaries found in New York?
c. does a canary have skin?
d. do canaries like worms?
   (page 176)

20 Routine matters (eating out, going to baseball games, the theater, and so on) are represented in memory as:
a. semantic memory
b. networks
c. chunks
d. schemas
   (page 177)

21. When an original memory is not available for remembering, the phenomenon is called:
a. trace-dependent forgetting
b. cue-dependent forgetting
c. retroactive interference
d. negative transfer
   (page 178)

22. In the Gestalt theory of forgetting, the loss of detail by decay of the memory trace is referred to as:
a. assimilation
b. sharpening
c. leveling
d. hypermnesia
   (page 178)

23. This test that you are currently taking is a test of:
a. recall
b. recognition
c. primacy
d. episodic memory
   (page 178)

24. Those of us who have grown up in the United States have learned to drive our cars on the right side of the road. Consequently, when we visit a country such as England, where people drive on the left side of the road, we have a difficult time adjusting, at least initially. This is an example of:
a. retroactive interference
b. zero transfer
c. positive transfer
d. negative transfer
   (page 178)

25. If you were knocked unconscious by a blow to the head, chances are that you would lose your memory for events just before the blow. Such memory loss would be called:
a. proactive interference
b. negative transfer
c. retrograde amnesia
d. trace-dependent forgetting
   (page 179)

26. If you overheard an assassination plot when you were intoxicated and didn't recall the conversation until you were intoxicated again, you would be experiencing:
a. state-dependent learning
b. cue-dependent learning
c. trace-dependent forgetting
d. proactive interference
   (page 180)

27. When we store information in long-term memory, we usually change that information as we are encoding it. In other words, we are:
a. constructing
b. reconstructing
c. unlearning
d. elaborating
   (page 181)

28. The basic mechanism for congnitve learning in human beings is:
a.   attention
b.   association
c.   observation
d.   culture
     (page 183)

29. Meaning is to structure as:
a.   syntax is to semantics
b.   semantics is to syntax
c.   abstract is to concrete
d.   presupposition is to inference
     (page 183)

30. In discourse processing, a sentence may contain information that implies
that other information is true. Such an inference is called:
a.   presupposition
b.   pragmatic
c.   elaboration
d.   denotation
     (page 186)

SELF-TEST 2

1.   Much human learning is observational, and most observational learning
is:
a.   a form of classical conditioning
b.   an imprecise representation of reality
c.   encoded verbally
d.   more difficult to remember than is learning accomplished through
     instrumental conditioning
     (page 161)

2.   In the information-processing theory of human menory, when the system
is mostly processing incoming information from the environment, we would say
that the system is:
a.   knowledge driven
b.   data driven
c.   memory driven
d.   externally driven
     (page 162)

3.   Sensory memory traces typically last for:
a.   less than one-thousandth of a second
b.   between one-half to four seconds
c.   about ninety seconds
d.   periods that can reach several days if rehearsal is constant
     (page 162)

4.   Sensory memory interacts with long-term memory through the process of:
a.   pattern recognition
b.   episodic memory
c.   chunking
d.   primacy
     (page 164)

5. The available evidence suggests that we can hold between five and nine "units" of information in STM. For this reason, we say that STM:
a. is hierarchical
b. has limited capacity
c. is schematic
d. lacks accessibility
(page 166)

6. As you read this question you are encoding it. This involves:
a. immediate memory
b. working memory
c. episodic memory
d. sensory memory
(page 165)

7. In serial-position learning, the primacy effect refers to better recall for:
a. items at the beginning of the list
b. items at the end of the list
c. isolated items
d. grouped items
(page 166)

8. Which of the following is necessary for information to be encoded into long-term memory?
a. elaborative rehearsal
b. maintenance rehearsal
c. shallow processing
d. pattern recognition
(page 168)

9. According to the levels of processing theory developed by Craik and Lockhart, one advantage of deep processing is that it:
a. makes us attend to the semantic aspects of information
b. allows us to use a rote (maintenance) process
c. allows us to focus in on the sensory aspects of information
d. prevents us from elaborating on the information
(page 168)

10. Shallow processing involves mainly the _____ aspects of information.
a. semantic
b. categorical
c. sensory
d. abstract
(page 169)

11. Deep processing is a form of:
a. decoding rehearsal
b. schematic processing
c. maintenance rehearsal
d. elaborative rehearsal
(page 169)

12. The organizational technique that allows the greatest expansion of short-term memory capacity is:
a. elaborative rehearsal
b. imagery
c. chunking
d. feature detection
    (page 173)

13. You have read a number of articles about how to ride a horse. This knowledge would be:
a. episodic
b. declarative
c. procedural
d. elaborative
    (page 174)

14. An important characteristic of procedural knowledge is that it requires:
a. observation
b. mental rehearsal
c. positive transfer
d. practice
    (page 174)

15. The last time that I went to a Shakespearean play, I heard an actor say, "To be or not to be, that is the question." The difference between my memory of this event and my trying to figure out the meaning of the line is like the difference between:
a. a proposition and an analogy
b. episodic and semantic memory
c. pattern recognition and chunking
d. a hierarchy and a schema
    (page 175)

16. According to the network model of memory, it would take the LONGEST to respond to the question:
a. is a canary a bird?
b. does a fish swim?
c. is a robin an animal?
d. can a canary fly?
    (page 176)

17. Organizing features of LTM that contain stereotyped information and default knowledge are:
a. chunks
b. episodes
c. networks
d. schemata
    (page 177)

18. Suppose that you learned how to solve geometry problems in grade 10 and that this learning had no effect on your learning how to solve trigonometry problems in grade 11. This illustrates:
a. hypermnesia
b. negative transfer
c. proactive interference
d. zero transfer
    (page 178)

19. According to Gestalt theories of forgetting, assimilation, the distortions that occur in memory traces, usually:
a. are biased toward something familiar
b. are random with respect to meaning
c. are unaffected by context
d. happen only after a long passage of time
   (page 178)

20. An essay examination is a test of:
a. recall
b. recognition
c. schematic memory
d. hypermnesia
   (page 178)

21. According to consolidation theory, forgetting is most related to:
a. trace dependency
b. cue dependency
c. state dependency
d. analogue dependency
   (page 179)

22. Drugs, in dosages that excite the brain's electrical activity, might also:
a. cause retrograde amnesia
b. facilitate the consolidation of memory traces
c. inhibit the acquisition of learning
d. interfere with encoding
   (page 179)

23. If you learned a list of paired-associate words including the pair, "table--man," the most effective recall cue for "man" would probably be:
a. table
b. woman
c. tall
d. pan
   (page 179)

24. If a new memory interferes with the recall of an older one, then we would say that _____ has taken place.
a. negative transfer
b. positive transfer
c. retroactive interference
d. proactive interference
   (page 180)

25. Hypermnesia occurs when:
a. you forget something after a blow to the head
b. brain damage destroys previous undamaged circuits
c. you recall something under hypnosis
d. you recall something previously forgotten when you return to the original context of the learning
   (page 180)

26. The active, nonmechanistic processes involved in learning and memory are particularly important in:
a.   the construction-reconstruction model
b.   interference theory
c.   maintenance rehearsal
d.   levels of processing theory
      (page 181)

27. If a defendant was said to have killed the victim, I would probably assume that the victim had been alive previously. This kind of inference is called a(n):
a.   elaboration
b.   presupposition
c.   proposition
d.   declaration
      (page 186)

28. In question 27 above, I also inferred that a weapon was used to kill the victim. In this case, my inference would be called a(n):
a.   elaboration
b.   presupposition
c.   proposition
d.   declaration
      (page 186)

29. Particularly important to understanding and learning material in stories are:
a.   networks
b.   retrieval cues
c.   schemata
d.   inferences
      (page 188)

30. Probably the most important aspect of a story that aids understanding and recall is the story's:
a.   length
b.   setting
c.   imagery
d.   structure
      (page 188)

WHAT DOES IT MEAN?

OBJECTIVES

1.   How can earlier organization of information coupled with retrieval cues improve study habits and memory?
2.   What are five common mnemonic methods that facilitate learning and recall of information?
3.   How can the method of chunking enlarge the memory system's capacity?
4.   What is the relationship between depth of processing and motivation in learning and memory?

5. How do the reconstructive processes of memory account for the variability in eyewitness testimony?
6. What is the relationship between reading speed and comprehension?

SELF-TEST

1. The first prerequisite for reliable memory of material is:
a. establishing retrieval cues
b. maximizing the degree of original learning
c. using memory hooks
d. avoiding any preorganization of the material
    (page 190)

2. All other things being equal, recall will be best when:
a. the encoding was distinctive and the same or similar cues are present at recall
b. the person learning has had a good night's sleep
c. retrieval cues and other crutches are not used
d. the material is verbal rather than pictorial
    (page 191)

3. Memory hooks are:
a. state dependent
b. comprehension aids
c. retrieval cues
d. unwanted side effects of learning
    (page 191)

4. Which of the following is not included in the SQ3R method?
a. preview
b. careful reading
c. use of chapter outlines as retrieval cues
d. try to use the words written rather than your own reconstructions
    (page 191)

5. Mnemonics are basically of help in:
a. initial comprehension
b. encoding
c. retrieval
d. inference
    (page 191)

6. A combination of numbers and words that rhyme is called:
a. a memory peg
b. a natural language device
c. the method of loci
d. the key-word method
    (page 191)

7. The mnemonic called *natural language mediation* involves:
a. transformation of unfamiliar words into familiar words or phrases
b. substitution of numbers for words
c. formation of new words from the first letters of words to be memorized
d. forming rhymes between the words to be memorized
    (page 191)

8.   Tying items to be learned and remembered to real locations that are commonly seen is called:
a.   natural language mediation
b.   the method of loci
c.   mnesia
d.   acronym assignment
     (page 191)

9.   The knowledge possessed by an expert in a field can probably be best differentiated from the knowledge of a novice by way of its:
a.   organizational hierarchy
b.   reconstruction
c.   lack of distortion
d.   mnemonic devices
     (page 193)

10. Intention to learn:
a.   is more important than depth of processing
b.   is relatively unimportant if deep processing occurs
c.   must occur concurrently with deep processing for learning to be achieved
d.   results in elaborative encoding
     (page 193)

11. The results of the eyewitness testimony studies are consistent with the view of memory as a(n) _____ process.
a.   consolidative
b.   elaborative
c.   schematic
d.   reconstructive
     (page 194)

12. In eyewitness testimony, a key factor in determining whether the witness will recite or agree to wrong information is:
a.   what exactly was seen to begin with
b.   the emotional state at the time the crime was committed
c.   how the interrogator phrases the questions
d.   the facts themselves
     (page 194)

13. The relationship between the speed of reading and the level of comprehension is:
a.   inverse
b.   positive
c.   increasing and then decreasing
d.   zero
     (page 195)

14. The upper limit on reading speed is a function of:
a.   the capacity of the nervous system to process individual words
b.   the language in which the person is reading
c.   the manner in which the eye fixates
d.   there is no upper limit on reading speed
     (page 195)

15. Two factors that tend to decrease most people's reading speed are:
a. reading too far ahead and saying each word to oneself
b. looking back too frequently and saying each word to oneself
c. reading too far ahead and reading every word aloud
d. fixating too long on individual words that are unfamiliar and looking back too frequently
(page 196)

ANSWER KEY

EXERCISES

Exercise 1

1.	stages	5.	attentional
2.	processes	6.	two-way
3.	limited	7.	bottom-up
4.	control	8.	top-down

Exercise 2

1. First, SM is a high-capacity system registering virtually all incoming data available at a given moment. Second, at the point of registration, there is no top-down influence. Third, the SM trace is verdical and fades in less than a second for visual data and in one to four seconds for auditory data.

2. The first difference between STM and SM is that STM has a limited capacity (about seven items). Second, because there is top-down influence, the representation of information in STM is not usually verdical. Third, representation is verbal rather than visual or auditory. Fourth, fading in STM takes longer (about 20 to 30 seconds) than it does in SM.

3. Relative to SM and STM, LTM has (functionally) an unlimited capacity. Second, information in LTM has been deeply processed, thus allowing for considerable bias and distortion. Third, information in LTM is far more resistant to forgetting that that in either SM and STM is,

Exercise 3

1. C   2. B   3. A   4. E   5. D

Exercise 4

1.	STM and LTM	6.	decoding
2.	immediate	7.	primacy
3.	recency	8.	available
4.	working	9.	inaccessible
5.	memory-span		

Exercise 5

Encoding is the process whereby information is put into, or represented, in memory. Maintenance rehearsal is a process in which information is simply repeated. This prevents information from leaving STM but does not lead to encoding into LTM. In comparison, elaborative rehearsal is a process in which information in STM is related to information in LTM. The evidence suggests that some sort of elaboration (for example, categorizing and mental images) is required to encode information in STM into LTM.

Exercise 6

1.	maintenance (or Type I)	6.	divide
2.	shallow	7.	dual
3.	deeper	8.	organization
4.	distinctiveness	9.	chunk
5.	effort	10.	digit

Exercise 7

1.	A	4.	A
2.	B	5.	B
c.	A	6.	B

Exercise 8

1.	serial	5.	arguments
2.	parallel	6.	propositional
3.	proposition	7.	computers
4.	predicate		

Exercise 9

1.	E	5.	B
2.	D	6.	G
3.	F	7.	C
4.	A		

Exercise 10

This figure illustrates the network model, the essential features of which are nodes and connections. Nodes (or places) higher in the hierarchy are for more general information (for example, animals), whereas nodes lower in the hierarchy are for more specific information (for example birds, canaries). The connections store information about the various concepts (for example, aminals eat, birds have wings, canaries are yellow). Given such an organization, it follows that retrieval is faster when a concept is retrieved from the level at which it is stored. Thus, "animals eat" and "canaries are yellow" are quickly retrieved, whereas "canary eats" takes longer. In general, the more levels that have to be crossed, the slower the retrieval. Thus, "canaries fly" is more quickly retrieved than "canaries eat," because the former crosses only one level, whereas the latter crosses two levels.

Exercise 11

1. Gestalt
2. level
3. sharpen
4. assimilate
5. consolidated
6. ~~animals~~ amnesia
7. reminder
8. encoding specificity
9. reinstate
10. interference
11. cue
12. trace

Exercise 12

1. trace-dependent forgetting
2. cue-dependent forgetting
3. leveling
4. sharpening
5. assimilation
6. test of recall
7. test of recognition
8. retrograde amnesia
9. encoding specificity principle
10. state dependency
11. retroactive interference
12. proactive interference
13. unlearning
14. response competition
15. transfer of training procedure
16. hypermnesia

Exercise 13

First of all, a good organization at the point of original learning will provide many cues for retrieval. But in addition to that, you should not study while relaxing in the sun, while tired, drugged, or whatever, because these all are conditions that are unlikely to be present in the classroom at the time of testing. In general, try to compile a set of internal and external conditions at the time of original learning that you expect to be most similar to those conditions present at the time of testing.

Exercise 14

1.   According to the reconstruction model, we do not simply copy events to and from memory. Instead, we construct representations of events for storage, and we reconstruct the event from the representation that was stored.

2.   When we listen to a message, we try to abstract the gist of it. In so doing, distortion may by adding default knowledge on the basis of schemata already present in LTM.

3.   At the time of retrieval, distortions may occur because of trace-dependent effects (such as leveling, sharpening, and assimilation of the representation), or cue-dependent effects (such as the presence of different cues at recall relative to original learning).

Exercise 15

1. syntax
2. semantics
3. word
4. proposition
5. sentence

Exercise 16

1. inferences
2. presuppositions
3. elaborations
4. pragmatics
5. gist
6. grammar
7. setting
8. theme
9. plot
10. resolution

Exercise 17

1.	F	7.	D	13.	B
2.	C	8.	P	14.	E
3.	O	9.	Q	15.	J
4.	K	10.	M	16.	I
5.	L	11.	N	17.	H
6.	A	12.	6		

MULTIPLE-CHOICE

Self-Test 1

1.	a	6.	b	11.	b	16.	c	21.	a	26.	a
2.	c	7.	c	12.	b	17.	d	22.	c	27.	a
3.	b	8.	d	13.	c	18.	b	23.	b	29.	c
4.	a	9.	a	14.	d	19.	a	24.	d	29.	b
5.	d	10.	b	15.	b	20.	d	25.	c	30.	a

Self-Test 2

1.	c	6.	b	11.	d	16.	c	21.	a	26.	a
2.	b	7.	a	12.	c	17.	d	22.	b	27.	b
3.	b	8.	a	13.	b	18.	d	23.	a	28.	a
4.	a	9.	a	14.	d	19.	a	24.	c	29.	c
5.	b	10.	c	15.	b	20.	a	25.	c	30.	d

WHAT DOES IT MEAN?

Self-Test

1.	b	6.	a	11.	d
2.	a	7.	a	12.	c
3.	c	8.	b	13.	a
4.	d	9.	a	14.	c
5.	c	10.	b	15.	b

6 Cognitive Processes

OBJECTIVES

1. How do the Gestalt and information-processing frameworks differ in their analyses of problem solving?
2. What is a concept, and how have studies of process and structure contributed to our knowledge of logical and natural concepts?
3. What differentiates formal logic from natural reasoning, and why are we so prone to making reasoning errors?
4. Which heuristics contribute to decision making?
5. What is intelligence, what are its historical roots, and what have the modern-day information-processing theorists contributed to the concept?
6. What is creativity, how is it measured, and how does it correlate with intelligence?

SYNOPSIS

The cognitive processes are those activities that are considered to be mental. These include the topics of learning and memory already discussed in Chapters 4 and 5. In the present chapter, emphasis will be on problem solving, concept formation, reasoning, judgment and decision making, intelligence, and creativity.

Problem solving consists of preparation, production of ideas, and judgment. Currently, this area is dominated by Gestalt theory and information-processing theory. Gestalt theorists are proponents of insight as a solution strategy. They have discovered interesting effects such as functional fixedness and mental set, both of which can retard the solution process. The information processors have given us the computer approach to problem solving, with its emphasis on logic rather than insight. These logical strategies use algorithms and heuristics.

A concept is the most basic unit of knowledge and is often called a *mental quantum*. There are two types. Well-defined concepts are logical and have clearly defined boundaries between instances and noninstances. In comparison, ill-defined (or natural) concepts have fuzzy boundaries and better and worse examples (for example, superordinate, basic, and subordinate levels of the concept).

We can conceive of reasoning as the process of analyzing arguments and reaching conclusions, and formal logic as the criterion for proper reasoning. However, we are not perfectly logical and instead are given to a natural logic that is prone to error. Factors responsible for errors include emotional arousal and commitment, preexisting knowledge, invalid conversions of premises, decisions based on surface structure (atmosphere), and faulty premises.

Ideally, formal logic could be used to make rational judgments, but unfortunately, we are not always rational--witness the "gambler's fallacy."

Instead, we tend to use intuitive decision-making heuristics, which rely on the availability of information in memory at the time of the decision and on the outcome that is most representative (that is, probable) given the available evidence.

Intelligence refers to the ability to perform cognitive tasks, and there are some who believe in a single ability and others who believe in a collection of separable abilities. Either way, intelligence is closely tied to intelligence tests. Historically, Binet's test was designed to compare individual performance at a given age with average performance at that age. Although similar in principle, Wechsler's tests are designed to distinguish verbal abilities from performance. Subsequent research (via factor analysis) led Cattell to distinguish between fluid (insightful) and crystallized (already learned skills) intelligence and led Guilford to postulate as many as 120 different abilities. Most recently, information processors have attempted to analyze intelligence into its component cognitive processes: verbal and spatial abilities.

Lastly, it should be noted that intelligence and creativity are not the same. Creativity refers to solutions to problems that are new and practical. The correlation between IQ and intelligence is positive up to IQs of about 110, but at higher levels, there is no relationship. Also, factors such as social and physical environment and personality are also related to creativity.

KEY WORDS AND PHRASES

OBJECTIVE 1

problem solving
Gestalt theory
information-processing theory
insight
functional fixedness
incubation effect
mental set
task analysis
General Problem Solver (GPS)
initial, intermediate, and goal states
operators
algorithms
heuristics
means-end analysis
current versus new state
planning ahead (subgoals)
preparation, production, and judgment

OBJECTIVE 2

concept formation
well-defined concepts
ill-defined concepts
fuzzy versus clear boundaries
examples versus nonexamples
better versus worse examples
hypothesis testing

conservative focusing
conjunctive versus disjunctive rule
prototype
superordinate, basic, and subordinate categories
stereotypy

OBJECTIVE 3

reasoning
logical analysis
emotional arousal
emotional commitment
preexisting knowledge
formal logic
syllogisms
invalid conversions
atmosphere
faulty premises
discourse
cooperative principle

OBJECTIVE 4

judgment
decision making
probabilities
gambler's fallacy
decision-making heuristics
availability heuristic
representativeness heuristic

OBJECTIVE 5

intelligence
measurement
ability versus achievement
Stanford Binet tests
mental versus chronological age
intelligence quotient
Weschler tests
    WAIS
    WISC
    WISC-R
    WPPSI
verbal versus performance IQ
    gifted versus retarded
    urban versus rural intelligence
retardation
    profound
    severe
    moderate
    mild
factor analysis
g-factors
s-factors

fluid versus crystallized intelligence
structure-of-intellect model
mental rotation
high and low verbals
high and low spatials

OBJECTIVE 6

creativity
novel solutions
practical solutions
divergent production
convergent thinking
physical and social environment
personality factors

EXERCISES

EXERCISE 1: Objective 1

TITLE: PROBLEM SOLVING
TASK: Fill in the blanks

1. According to Gestalt theory, problem solving is achieved by suddenly perceiving the solution, a process known as _insight_ .
2. Gestalt theorists have discovered that earlier experience with objects tends to prevent us from using those objects in a different way, a phenomenon known as _func. fixedness_ .
3. The _incubation_ effect describes the lessening of interference with delays between initial learning and problem solving.
4. When we are overpracticed using a given strategy, it is hard to develop a new strategy--this is called _mental set_
5. The information-processing approach is illustrated by _task analysis_ , as is used in the General Problem Solver (GPS).
6. In the GPS, there is an initial state, goal state, intermediate states, and _operators_ that are applied to move across the states.
7. One operator in the GPS is an _algorithm_ which samples all possibilities and thus guarantees the solution.
8. In comparison with algorithms, _heuristic_ can yield a quicker solution, but they are not guaranteed to succeed.
9. The heuristic used by GPS that constantly compares the current with the goal state is _means-end analysis_.
10. Because heuristics often fail when rigidly applied, it is wise to plan ahead and use _subgoals_ rather than a single goal.
11. In general, there are three stages in problem solving, the first of which is understanding the problem, or _prepar._ .
12. The second stage in problem solving is generating possible solutions, or _produc._.
13. The third stage in problem solving is evaluating solutions, or _judgment_.

EXERCISE 2: Objective 1

TITLE: EXAMPLES IN PROBLEM SOLVING
TASK: Match letters to numbers

_____1. Given that some pairwise combination of A,B,C,D is needed to solve the problem, one could use AB, AC, AD, BC, BD, and CD.
_____2. Failure to solve the two-string problem.
_____3. Means-end analysis.
_____4. Using a rote-learning studying strategy all the time might hurt you when learning abstract concepts.
_____5. An inability to use an object in a way different from its intended or learned use.
_____6. The process of seeking short-cut solutions by trying out higher-probability hypotheses.
_____7. It's the long way, but because it samples every possible outcome it is guaranteed to work.
_____8. Not all problems can be solved using the same old solutions.

A. functional fixedness
B. mental set
C. algorithm
D. heuristics

EXERCISE 3: Objective 2

TITLE: CONCEPT FORMATION
TASK: Fill in the blanks

1. The _____ is defined as the basic unit of knowledge, or the mental quantum.
2. Well-defined or _____ concepts are rigorously defined and have clear-cut boundaries.
3. Formulating well-defined concepts appears to involve _____ formulation and testing.
4. One strategy for well-defined concepts involves selecting and varying only one attribute at a time. This is called _____.
5. The strategy of conservative focusing will work only for _____(and rule) and not disjunctive concepts (and/or rule).
6. Ill-defined or _____ concepts have fuzzy boundaries and better and worse examples.
7. The single best example of a natural concept, or its reference point, is the _____.
8. A concept such as furniture includes things like chairs and tables. This concept is considered _____.
9. Concepts may be described as simple, subordinate, or superordinate. The concepts, tables and chairs, are considered _____ relative to the concept of furniture.
10. Card table and dining room table are _____ relative to table.
11. For a number of reasons, _____-level concepts are the most important ones in our daily lives.
12. A general problem with categorization is that we sometimes tend to treat all examples of a concept in the same way. This problem is called _____.

EXERCISE 4:   Objective 2

TITLE: HYPOTHESIS TESTING
TASK: Find the solution

1.	large, black, triangle	==>	incorrect
2.	large, black, square	==>	correct
3.	large, blue, square	==>	incorrect
4.	small , black, square	==>	correct
5.	medium, black, square	==>	correct

Given the above information, what kind of concept are we dealing with, what is the strategy used, what is the correct answer, and what rule does that answer illustrate?

EXERCISE 5:   Objective 2

TITLE: BASIC-LEVEL CONCEPTS
TASK: Essay

What are the four reasons that basic-level concepts are the most important natural concepts for our everyday lives?

EXERCISE 6:   Objective 3

TITLE: REASONING AND LOGICAL ANALYSIS
TASK: Fill in the blanks

1. _____ logic consists of a set of rules for anlayzing an argument and deciding whether it is internally consistent.
2. One factor that may prevent logical thinking is emotional _____.
3. A second emotional hindrance is _____, because it is hard to reason logically about things we are attached to.
4. In addition to emotional factors, _____ knowledge can lead us to invalid conclusions.
5. A _____ is a three-step argument having two premises, both of which are believed true.
6. When the premises of a syllogism are indeed true, then the syllogism is said to be _____.
7. One error in syllogistic reasoning stems from misunderstanding the premises, and it is termed a(n) _____.
8. A second syllogistic error stems from surface similarities among premises which creates a false _____.
9. Reasoning is particularly difficult during _____ because much of the information must be inferred.
10. Discourse appears to follow the principle of _____, which states that the speaker (or writer) attempts to maximize the effectiveness of the communication to the listener (or reader).

EXERCISE 7:   Objective 3

TITLE: SYLLOGISMS
TASK: True or false?

1.   All A's are B's; all B's are C's; therefore, all A's are C's.

2.   No A's are B's; all B's are C's; therefore, no A's are C's.

3.   All A's are B's; all C's are B's; therefore, all A's are C's.

4.   Some A's are B's; some B's are C's; therefore, some A's are C's.

EXERCISE 8:   Objective 3

TITLE: THE COOPERATIVE PRINCIPLE
TASK: Essay

     What are the four parts of the cooperative principle as they apply to reasoning during discourse?

EXERCISE 9:   Objective 4

TITLE: JUDGMENT AND DECISION MAKING
TASK: Match letters to numbers

_____1.   The general concept of which the gambler's fallacy is an example.
_____2.   The general concept of which availability and representativeness are components.
_____3.   The belief that after ten heads in a row, the next toss must come out to be tails.
_____4.   The only person in the vicinity of the crime was the little old lady, and we all know that little old ladies do not commit crimes.
_____5.   Although becoming a lawyer sounds like a good idea, you met one last week who is clearly a crook.
_____6.   Decisions are based on the contents of memory at the time of decision.
_____7.   The decision maker who relies on knowledge of past events that, according to a rational model, has nothing to do with the future.
_____8.   Decisions that are biased by the available evidence.

A.   gambler's fallacy
B.   decision-making heuristics
C.   availability heuristic
D.   representativeness heuristic

EXERCISE 10:   Objective 5

TITLE: ACHIEVEMENT AND ABILITY IN IQ TESTING
TASK: Essay

     What is the distinction between achievement and ability, and what implications does it have for intelligence testing?

EXERCISE 11:   Objective 5

TITLE: MEASURING INTELLIGENCE
TASK: Fill in the blanks

1. For the original Binet test, Binet and Simon made two assumptions.
    The first was that intelligence is a composite of many _____.
2. The second assumption was that intelligence changes with _____.
3. By comparing the performance of an individual child at a given age with
    the average performance of children of that age group, Binet and Simon
    developed the concept of _____.
4. The _____ equals the ratio of mental age divided by chronological
    age, multiplied by 100.
5. If MA = 8 and CA = 5, then the quotient = _____.
6. The revised version of the original Binet and Simon test is called the
    _____ test.
7. Wechsler designed the WAIS test for _____.
8. Wechsler designed the WISC (of which WISC-R is a revision) for _____.
9. A third Wechsler test called SPPSI is used with _____.
10. Unlike the Binet Tests, the Wechsler tests are organized into _____
    which measure different abilities.
11. About half the questions on Wechsler tests measure _____ abilities
    (for example, similarities and differences among words), and the other
    half assesses _____ (for example, object assembly and picture
    arrangement).
13. In general, Binet tests tend to emphasize _____ abilities more than
    Wechsler tests do.

EXERCISE 12:   Objective 5

TITLE: MENTAL RETARDATION
TASK: Match letters to numbers

____ 1. Marked delay in motor development between 0 and 5 years (although
         may self-feed), some understanding of speech between 6 and 21 and
         can conform to daily routines as an adult, but needs continuing
         direction in a protective environment.
____ 2. Noticeable delays in motor development between 0 and 5 (although
         may respond to training in various self-help activities), can learn
         simple communications, but does not progress in function reading and
         math between 6 and 21, can perform simple tasks as adult, but is
         incapable of self-maintenance.
____ 3. Gross retardation requiring nursing care between 0 and 5, obvious
         delays in all areas between 6 and 21, and may need nursing care
         throughout adulthood.
____ 4. Between 0 and 5, often not noticeably retarded to casual observer,
         can acquire third to sixth grade reading and math skills between
         6 and 21, and can usually achieve social and vocational skills
         adequate for self-maintenance as an adult.

A.   profoundly retarded
B.   severely retarded
C.   moderately retarded
D.   mildly retarded

EXERCISE 13: Objective 5

TITLE: RESEARCH ON INTELLIGENCE
TASK: Fill in the blanks

1. Research into the components of intelligence has benefited from a
    statistical procedure called _____.
2. Spearman, who first used factor analysis, discovered a _____ for
    general abilities.
3. Spearman also discovered an _____ for specific abilities.
4. Cattell conceptualized _____ intelligence, which is insightful
    performance independent of experience.
5. Cattel also conceptualized _____ intelligence, which requires
    already-learned skills.
6. Guilford developed a structure-of-intellect model that contains as many
    as _____ separate abilities.
7. Recently, information processors such as Hunt have found differences
    between low and high _____ in tasks testing the retrieval of
    information from short- and long-term memory.
8. Similarly, Just and Carpenter have found differences in complex mental
    rotation tasks between low and high _____.

EXERCISE 14: Objective 6

TITLE: CREATIVITY
TASK: Fill in the blanks

1. The term _____ is used to describe coming up with an original and
    practical solution to a problem.
2. _____ production refers to an ability to produce a number of
    different yet relevant responses to an open-ended item.
3. In comparison, _____ thinking involves selecting the most appropriate
    solution out of many possible ones.
4. Creativity and intelligence are positively correlated for IQs up to
    _____, but there is no relationship thereafter.
5. Thus, a certain level of intelligence is required for creativity, but
    _____ intelligence does not guarantee it.
6. It is also evident that creative individuals come from special social
    and physical _____.
7. Creative individuals also have unique _____ characteristics.

EXERCISE 15

TITLE: IMPORTANT NAMES
TASK: Match letters to numbers

_____1. Basic level versus superordinate versus subordinate concepts.
_____2. Fluid versus crystallized intelligence.
_____3. Insight in chimpanzees.
_____4. Environmental and personality factors in creativity.
_____5. The cooperative principle.
_____6. Demonstration of mental set with water jar problem.
_____7. Means-end analysis with water jar problems.

_____8. Structure-of-intellect model.
_____9. Urban versus rural intelligence
_____10. The General Problem Solver (GPS)
_____11. High versus low verbals.
_____12. High versus low spatials.
_____13. The prototype of modern intelligence tests.
_____14. Modification of the first intelligence test.
_____15. The g-factor and s-factor.
_____16. Methods for overcoming processing capacity.
_____17. WAIS, WISC, WISC-R, and WPPSI.

A.	Luchins	G.	Grice	M.	Cattell
B.	Kohler	H.	Binet and Simon	N.	Guilford
C.	Newell and Simon	I.	Stanford	O.	Hunt
D.	Neisser	J.	Wechsler	P.	Carpenter and Just
E.	Attwood and Polson	K.	Shimberg	Q.	Amabile
F.	Rosch	L.	Spearman		

MULTIPLE CHOICE TESTS

SELF-TEST 1

1. Problem solving requires:
a. the solver to supply new knowledge
b. appeal for assistance from others
c. well-learned behaviors
d. good knowledge of previous solutions
    (page 199)

2. Goal-oriented changes in the setup of a problem are characteristic of the _____ approach to problem solving.
a. Gestalt
b. information-processing
c. behavioral
d. knowledge
    (page 199)

3. The ability to conceptualize new uses for objects is lacking in the phenomenon called:
a. convergence
b. divergence
c. functional fixedness
d. mental set
    (page 200)

4. When the solution to a problem that you have been working on to no avail suddenly comes to you after you have taken a break, the phenomenon called _____ has been demonstrated.
a. mental set
b. functional fixedness
c. insight
d. incubation effect
    (page 200)

5.   Being unable to play good chess after playing checkers is most probably attributable to:
a.   functional fixedness
b.   mental set
c.   invalid conversions
d.   atmosphere
     (page 201)

6.   A difference between insight and the incubation effect is that in insight:
a.   old solutions are tried continuously
b.   physical objects must be present
c.   components of the problem are reconfigured
d.   some amount of time must pass between initial solution attempts and the successful solution
     (page 203)

7.   According to the information-processing approach to problem solving:
a.   we are constantly planning and testing hypotheses
b.   we are in search of sudden new solutions
c.   information flows through a series of internal stages
d.   we think out those things that mediate stimuli and responses
     (page 203)

8.   In task analysis, _____ are processes that can be applied to move from one state to another:
a.   operators
b.   algorithms
c.   prototypes
d.   conversions
     (page 204)

9.   Which of the following terms is out of place?
a.   problem space
b.   insight
c.   operators
d.   constraints
     (page 204)

10. In an algorithm:
a.   we sample all possibilities
b.   we sample long shots
c.   we sample the most likely possibilities
d.   we sample randomly
     (page 205)

11. Intermediate states in means-end analysis that tend to maintain motivation are called:
a.   incentives
b.   heuristics
c.   subgoals
d.   operators
     (page 205)

12. If you decided simply to look at a problem until the solution became clear to you, you would be applying a _____ solution strategy.
a. Gestalt
b. means-end
c. information-proce sing
d. task-orientation
   (page 207)

13. "Basic unit of knowledge" defines:
a. information
b. insight
c. Gestalt
d. concept
   (page 209)

14. Well-defined and ill-defined are two types of:
a. logic
b. concept
c. constraints
d. memory

15. Testing hypotheses seems to be an extremely important aspect for:
a. forming well-defined concepts
b. solving problems through insight
c. task analysis through algorithms
d. abstract thinking
   (page 211)

16. Concepts based on the conjunctive rule are amenable to solution through the method called:
a. abstraction
b. algorithm
c. conservative focusing
d. refocus analysis
   (page 211)

17. According to Rosch, which are the three levels of abstraction in natural categories?
a. basic, subordinate, and superordinate
b. basic, contrived, and natural
c. object, concept, and person
d. first level, second level, and third level
   (page 213)

18. The most important concepts in everyday life are:
a. basic concepts
b. subordinate concepts
c. superordinate concepts
d. nonspecific
   (page 213)

19. Clear and logical thinking would probably be disrupted most by:
a. a low level of emotion
b. a low level of arousal
c. a high level of arousal
d. a reliance on formal logical processes
   (page 214)

20. All wild boars are sleazy.
    All sleazy animals are sickening.
    All wild boars are sickening.
This is a(n):
a. invalid conversion
b. a valid conversion
c. an instance of poor natural reasoning
d. an example of the atmosphere effect
    (page 215)

21. Some dogs are ferocious.
    Some cats are ferocious.
    Some dogs are cats.
This is a(n):
a. algorithm
b. a valid conversion
c. atmosphere effect
d. heuristic
    (page 216)

22. Which of the following would NOT be a typical cause of invalid reasoning?
a. atmosphere effects
b. high arousal
c. social conformity
d. influence of preexisting knowledge
    (page 216)

23. Reasoning errors that undermine self-confidence are frequently seen in people who would be described as:
a. schizophrenic
b. paranoid personalities
c. overreactive
d. depressive personalities
    (page 217)

24. Ability is to achievement as:
a. accomplishment is to potential
b. potential is to accomplishment
c. success is to accomplishment
d. accomplishment is to success
    (page 219)

25. Binet wanted to measure:
a. pure ability
b. as many as 120 different abilities
c. fluid and crystallized intelligence
d. creativity
    (page 220)

26. If your mental age is 12 and your chronological age is 8, your IQ is:
a. 60
b. 120
c. 150
d. 200
    (page 221)

27. Which of the following tests would most likely be used to measure intellectual ability in adults?
a.   WISC
b.   Stanford-Binet
c.   WPPSI
d.   WAIS
     (page 221)

28. The statistical method used to determine which sets of tests display consistent individual differences is called:
a.   correlation
b.   factor analysis
c.   g-factor
d.   Spearman test
     (page 224)

29. According to Cattell, fluid intelligence involves:
a.   achievement
b.   already-learned skills
c.   future accomplishments
d.   insightful solutions
     (page 224)

30. New, correct solutions or approaches to problems are the hallmark of:
a.   crystallized intelligence
b.   rural intelligence
c.   creativity
d.   trial-and-error learning
     (page 229)

SELF-TEST 2

1. According to Gestalt theory, solutions to problems are obtained via:
a.   mediation
b.   insight
c.   trial and error
d.   task analysis
     (page 199)

2. Being able to see beyond an object's intended use is needed to overcome:
a.   functional fixedness
b.   mental set
c.   divergent production
d.   mental stagnation
     (page 200)

4. Our unwillingness to try different methods to solve new problems characterizes:
a.   functional fixedness
b.   mental set
c.   divergent production
d.   the atmosphere effect
     (page 201)

The opposite of insight is:
a.   mediation
b.   task analysis
c.   trial and error
d.   divergent production
     (page 203)

6.   Which of the following is NOT one of the basic features of the information-processing approach?
a.   information flow is analyzed into processes and stages
b.   the system has an unlimited capacity for processing information
c.   there are control mechanisms for overseeing the flow and analysis of information
d.   there is a two-way flow of information
     (page 204)

7.   According to Newell and Simon, the first stage in the solution to a problem is:
a.   creating an internal representation of the problem
b.   establishing constraints on problem states
c.   creating a series of alogrithms
d.   creating a series of heuristics
     (page 204)

8.   Performance of two similar tasks in parallel is:
a.   impossible because of the system's limited capacity
b.   possible only for individuals whose IQ is above 135
c.   impossible because one task requires too much of the problem space
d.   possible but only after considerable practice
     (page 205)

9.   Which does not fit?
a.   algorithm
b.   heuristic
c.   inefficient combinations
d.   all possible solutions
     (page 206)

11. Which does not fit ?
a.   efficient strategies
b.   not necessarily leading to a solution
c.   inefficient combinations
d.   means-end analysis
     (page 206)

12. When the solution to a problem is simple, _____ theory seems best able to explain the outcome processes.
a.   information-processing
b.   means-end
c.   Gestalt
d.   task-analysis
     (page 207)

13. *Quanta, basic units,* and *packets* all are terms used to connote:
a.   intelligence
b.   creativity
c.   reasoning
d.   concepts
     (page 209)

14. Having expert knowledge seems to depend on all of the following EXCEPT:
a.   accumulating many facts
b.   gaining extensive experience
c.   storing facts in an efficient memory network
d.   being able to perceive relationships between the facts in one part of
     a network and another
     (page 209)

15. Most of the concepts that we use in ordinary, everyday life are:
a.   ill defined
b.   contrived
c.   logical
d.   well defined
     (page 210)

16. The single best example of a natural concept is referred to as a(n):
a.   archetype
b.   basic unit
c.   prototype
d.   model
     (page 213)

17. Which of the following would exemplify a basic concept?
a.   chair
b.   furniture
c.   arms
c.   red
     (page 213)

18. Which of the following is out of place?
a.   syllogism
b.   concept
c.   premise
d.   argument
     (page 214)

19. _____ stems from misunderstanding a basic premise.
a.   Functional fixedness
b.   Mental set
c.   Invalid conversion
d.   Divergent production
     (page 215)

20. Atmosphere effects lead to:
a.   correct solutions to problems
b.   errors in reasoning
c.   lack of creativity
d.   an inability to form concepts
     (page 216)

21. The gambler's fallacy exemplifies the effect that _____ can have on causing bias in decision making.
a.   superstition
b.   emotion
c.   ill-defined concepts
d.   prior knowledge
    (page 218)

22. Which of the following tests would be considered culture-free?
a.   Stanford-Binet
b.   WAIS
c.   WPPSI
d.   none of the above
    (page 220)

23. Shimberg's work on urban and rural intelligence shows that:
a.   rural people are more likely to be mentally retarded
b.   rural people are slightly more intelligent than urban people
c.   IQ tests are biased in favor of urban people
d.   IQ tests can be biased in favor of either urban or rural populations
    (page 220)

24. Gross retardation and absolute minimal capacity for functioning in even sensory-motor areas characterize:
a.   profound retardation
b.   severe retardation
c.   moderate retardation
d.   mild retardation
    (page 224)

25. Ability is like:
a.   crystallized intelligence
b.   fluid intelligence
c.   creative accomplishments
d.   performance
    (page 225)

26. Achievement is like:
a.   one's actual potential
b.   fluid intelligence
c.   crystallized intelligence
d.   creative ability
    (page 225)

27. Compared with people who are low in verbal ability, people who are high in verbal ability:
a.   can retrieve familiar information from long-term memory faster
b.   can engage in fewer mental rotations
c.   take longer to scan short-term memory
d.   tend to make more errors in recalling the order of words in lists
    (page 226)

28. Being able to create many relevant solutions to an open-ended problem is a characteristic of:
a.   convergent thinking
b.   convergent production
c.   divergent thinking
d.   divergent production
    (page 229)

29. Creativity and intelligence are related so that:
a. there is a positive correlation up to IQs equaling about 110
b. there is a negative correlation up to IQs equaling 110
c. there is no correlation up to IQs equaling 110
d. there is no relationship at any IQ level
   (page 229)

30. At extremely high levels of measured intelligence (that is, 140 or more), there is:
a. little or no evidence of creativity
b. a very large positive correlation between intelligence and creativity
c. a very large negative correlation between intelligence and creativity
d. no relationship between intelligence and creativity
   (page 229)

WHAT DOES IT MEAN?

OBJECTIVES

1. What are the relative advantages and disadvantages of formal versus general training?
2. How has artificial intelligence been applied to chess and problems of medical diagnosis?
3. How can heuristics such as means-end analysis, planning, and working backwards help in the solution of everyday problems?
4. What are some of the skills that can aid in creative problem solving?
5. What are the relationships between birth order and intelligence, and how can these relationships be explained?
6. What methods have been used to improve creativity?
7. Why is it difficult to determine the relative roles of heredity and environment in intelligence?

SELF-TEST

1. Formula-trained students do better than generally trained students on:
a. math problems
b. verbal problems
c. new problems
d. familiar problems
   (page 232)

2. Generally trained students do better than formula-trained students on:
a. math problems
b. verbal problems
c. new problems
d. familiar problems
   (page 232)

3. Research on animal intelligence has shown that:
a. animal intelligence seems qualitatively different from human intelligence
b. animal intelligence seems qualitatively similar to human intelligence
c. animal intelligence can be explained by principles of behavioral conditioning
d. mammals but not birds have been shown to have intelligence
   (page 233)

4. Computer simulations of chess play have taught us that:
a. complex human thought involves more than just algorithms
b. the computer cannot simulate human thought processes
c. humans rarely use heuristics when playing chess
d. humans are not very good chess players
    (page 234)

5. The purpose of artificial intelligence in the medical setting is to:
a. perform medical tests
b. reduce the need for physicians in small communities
c. assist the physician in making diagnoses
d. collate medical information from library and other sources
    (page 234)

6. Suppose that one wanted to be a lawyer and began the process by first
figuring out what it is that lawyers must do to be successful. This heuristic
would be called:
a. GPS
b. means-end analysis
c. working backwards
d. task definition
    (page 235)

7. Breaking down complex problems into attainable, smaller steps, with a
plan for achieving each:
a. is the method of problem solving called working backwards
b. usually results in less overall accomplishment
c. tends to increase motivation toward the overall goal
d. decreases the overall probability of success
    (page 236)

8. According to research by Seligman and Beck, depression can be treated
effectively by:
a. cognitive behavior therapy
b. psychoanalysis
c. drugs
d. a change in environment
    (page 237)

9. Inhibition of problem solving by mental set can be remedied by the
method called:
a. working backwards
b. planning ahead
c. forgetting
d. brainstorming
    (page 238)

10. Brainstorming approaches to problem solving typically work best in:
a. combination with psychotherapy
b. groups of people
c. individual settings
d. evening rather than daytime sessions
    (page 238)

11. According to Zajonc's data, who is likely to be most intelligent?
a. the first born
b. the second born
c. the third born
d. the last born
   (page 238)

12. The relationship between birth order and intelligence seems to depend on:
a. the gender of the children
b. the socioeconomic status of the parents
c. the spacing between the ages of the children
d. the spacing between the ages of the parents
   (page 239)

13. According to Zajonc, a firstborn child tends to be more intelligent than other children in the family because of:
a. genetic factors
b. greater attention from other family members
c. biochemical factors
d. greater competition between parent and child
   (page 239)

14. Zajonc's confluence model of birth order and intelligence has been challenged by Galbraith on the grounds that:
a. the sample was too small
b. the sample was based on misleading national data sets rather that on individual sibling data
c. the sample was collected with homogeneous populations rather than diverse ethnic groups
d. the family size in the sample was too small on the average
   (page 239)

15. Increases in SAT scores of students following attendance at special "coaching schools":
a. is thought to be due to changes in motivation
b. disproves the premise that SAT tests measure basic abilities
c. were found to be due to cheating
d. have resulted in widespread changes in the theory and development of the SAT
   (page 241)

16. The extent to which differences in some measured trait are due to differences in genetic makeup is called:
a. nurture
b. heritability
c. heterosis
d. retrenchment
   (page 119)

17. Leon Kamin rejects the relationship proposed by Jensen and Shockley (that is, that differences in intelligence are due mostly to heredity) on the grounds that:
a. it is basically impossible to study the influence of genetics
b. fraternal twins show just as high concordance rates as identical twins do
c. identical twins show a higher concordance rate than fraternal twins do
d. the available twin data are simply not trustworthy enough to justify analysis of heritability
   (page 121)

18. High heritability of a trait in one setting means:
a.   it is likely to be high in another setting
b.   it is likely to be low in another setting
c.   the trait is inherited
d.   very little when it comes to predicting to another setting
     (page 121)

19. Recent studies of IQ levels and school achievement scores of black and white adopted children:
a.   support the notion that race is an important determinant of intelligence
b.   suggest that genetic background is an important determinant of intelligence
c.   suggest that adopted children are duller than other children are, regardless of race
d.   suggest that black adopted children are more likely to be adopted by white families than by black families
     (page 124)

20. Sandra Scarr's study of adopted children's race, intelligence, and family background revealed that genetic background probably controlled about _____ of the variance in intelligence.
a.   10 percent
b.   30 percent
c.   50 percent
d.   70 percent
     (page 124)

ANSWER KEY

EXERCISES

Exercise 1

1.   insight
2.   functional fixedness
3.   incubation
4.   mental set
5.   task analysis
6.   operators
7.   algorithm
8.   heuristics
9.   means-end analysis
10. subgoals
11. preparation
12. production
13. judgment

Exercise 2

1.   c   5.   a
2.   a   6.   d
3.   d   7.   c
4.   b   8.   b

Exercise 3

1.   concept
2.   logical
3.   hypothesis
4.   conservative focusing
5.   conjunctive
6.   natural
7.   prototype
8.   superordinate
9.   basic
10. subordinate
11. basic
12. stereotypy

Exercise 4

The example illustrates well-defined, or logical, concepts. The strategy used is called conservative focusing, because only one attribute is varied at a time. The correct answer is black and square, which illustrates the conjunctive ("and") rule.

Exercise 5

1. There is evidence that children learn basic-level concepts before they learn either superordinate or subordinate concepts.

2. It is easier to imagine a prototype such as a table than to envision a prototypical piece of furniture.

3. You behave the same way with respect to all basic-level concepts (for example, you sit next to all tables).

4. Basic-level concepts share the most properties (for example, tables have more in common than furniture in general does).

Exercise 6

1. formal
2. arousal
3. commitment
4. preexisting
5. syllogism
6. valid
7. invlaid conversion
8. atmosphere
9. discourse
10. cooperativeness

Exercise 7

The only correct syllogism is choice 1. For each of the others, incorrect conclusions are possible. For example:

2. No chickens are turkeys; all turkeys are edible; therefore, no chickens are edible.

3. All professors are human; all children are human; therefore, all professors are children.

4. Some men are gifted; some gifted people are women; therefore, some men are women.

Exercise 8

1. The structure of the discourse is no more or less informative that is required.
2. What is said is only what is believed by the speaker and for which the speaker has adequate evidence.
3. The utterance is relevant.
4. The structure of the utterance is such that it is easy to understand.

Exercise 9

1. b   5. c
2. b   6. c
3. a   7. a
4. d   8. d

Exercise 10

Achievement refers to existing knowledge and skills, whereas ability refers to potential for future achievement. Clearly, intelligence tests are designed to measure ability, but this is a difficult task. The individual with more ability may score only as well or less well than will an individual with less ability, because of factors that retard achievement or because certain items on tests favor different parts of the population (see Highlight 6-3 on Urban Versus Rural Intelligence).

Exercise 11

1. abilities
2. age
3. mental
4. intelligence quotient
5. 160
6. Stanford-Binet

7. adults
8. children
9. preschool children
10. subscales
11. verbal; performance
12. verbal

Exercise 12

1. B   2. C   3. A   4. D

Exercise 13

1. factor analysis
2. g-factor
3. s-factor
4. fluid

5. crystallized
6. 120
7. verbals
8. sapatials

Exercise 14

1. creativity
2. divergent
3. convergent
4. 110

5. high
6. environments
7. personality

Exercise 15

1. F   7. E   13. H
2. M   8. N   14. I
3. B   9. K   15. L
4. Q   10. C   16. D
5. G   11. O   17. J
6. A   12. P

MULTIPLE-CHOICE

Self-Test 1

1. a   6. c   11. c   16. c   21. c   26. c
2. b   7. a   12. a   17. a   22. c   27. d
3. c   8. a   13. d   18. a   23. d   28. b
4. d   9. b   14. b   19. c   24. b   29. d
5. b   10. a   15. a   20. b.   25. b   30. c

Self-Test 2

1.	b	6.	b	11.	c	16.	c	21.	d	26.	c
2.	a	7.	a	12.	c	17.	a	22.	d	27.	a
3.	a	8.	d	13.	d	18.	b	23.	d	28.	d
4.	b	9.	b	14.	b	19.	c	24.	a	29.	a
5.	c	10.	a	15.	a	20.	b	25.	b	30.	d

WHAT DOES IT MEAN?

Self-Test

1.	d	6.	c	11.	a	16.	b
2.	c	7.	c	12.	c	17.	d
3.	b	8.	a	13.	b	18	d
4.	a	9.	d	14.	b	19.	b
5.	c	10.	b	15.	a	20.	c

7 Motivation and Emotion

OBJECTIVES

1. How is motivation used as an explanatory concept, and under what conditions is it misused?
2. What are needs, drives, and incentives, and what kinds of motivational conflicts emerge when two or more of these are operating at the same time?
3. What is homeostasis, and how do homeostatic mechanisms operate to control eating?
4. How do homeostatic mechanisms operate to control drinking?
5. How do homeostatic mechanisms operate to control arousal?
6. What are instincts, and how are they used to account for feeding, reproductive, and defensive behaviors?
7. What is the usefulness of combining motivational concepts with concepts from personality theory?
8. How do cognitive processes such as attribution and utility influence motivation?
9. How are biological, learning, social-personality, and cognitive factors thought to influence sexual behavior?
10. What are the various dimensions of and perspectives on emotion, and how are they represented in the various theories of emotion?
11. What are anxiety and anger, and why are they of particular interest to psychologists?

SYNOPSIS

Motivation is a concept used to explain variability within and among individuals. This concept is viewed from three major perspectives, namely, biological, social-personality, and cognitive.

Three important unobservable factors in motivational theories are needs, drives, and incentives. Needs are the internal biological states of deprivation that provide the basis for drive. Drive is the energy that pushes us toward goals. Incentives are goals that pull or attract us. When these pushes and pulls operate simultaneously and in opposition, we suffer approach-approach, avoidance-avoidance, or approach-avoidance conflicts.

Biologically, our body tries to maintain a steady state, a concept called *homeostasis*. Hunger and thirst are sensed by detector cells in the body and brain. Glucose is the major short-term energy source, and glucose regulatory systems in the liver and hypothalamus appear to control day-to-day variations in food intake. The long-term regulation of feeding and weight appears to be dependent on the amount of fat cells in relation to set-weight level detectors in the hypothalamus.

In thirst, the kidneys and hypothalamus seem to share responsibility for maintaining proper fluid levels. In addition to hunger and thirst, there appears to be a diffuse homeostatic system that regulates arousal.

The optimal level of arousal varies across individuals, across situations (in the same individual), and as a function of environmental variables such as task complexity (compare the Yerkes-Dodson law).

Instincts are inherited mechanisms of behavior that occur in response to specific stimuli. As such, there is little variation among members of a given species from situation to situation. The behaviors that make up the instinct are called *fixed-action patterns*, and the stimuli that elicit them are called *releasing*, or *sign stimuli*. According to a recent formulation called *sociobiology*, all behavior has one overriding motivation--to preserve one's own genes into the next generation.

Social-personality theorists treat motivation as a personality characteristic. For example, Murray has defined twenty psychogenic needs. Of these, the need for achievement has received the most attention. More recently, attention has shifted to needs such as social approval, power, cognition, and fear of success.

The cognitive perspective emphasizes attribution and utility. Attribution theory asserts that we determine why behavior occurs on the basis of perceived needs. Utility theory combines perceived incentives and needs with the probability of success to gauge the expected utility of a goal object or a course of action.

Sexual motivation is influenced by factors from a variety of perspectives. For example, the biological perspective emphasizes sociobiology, instinct, and hormonal control. The learning perspective emphasizes early learning and subsequent generalization and discrimination. The personality perspective emphasizes psychogenic needs, self-actualization, and the interaction between needs and learning. Finally, the cognitive perspective emphasizes thinking, knowledge, inference, and attribution.

Emotions are related to motivations in that they are frequently used to explain why a behavior occurred (for example, the slammed door because he was angry). Emotions may be viewed from qualitative, quantitative, and activity dimensions, and they contain biological, motivational, experimental, and behavioral aspects. Historically, the field was dominated by the James-Lange and the Cannon-Bard theories. The more recent theories have either continued the arousal versus cognition battle established by the earlier theorists (for example, the juke-box theory and its variation) or have concentrated solely on homeostatic mechanisms (for example, opponent-process theory).

Finally, two emotions, anxiety and anger, have received the lion's share of attention. Both have stimulated considerable research, and both have implications for pathological behavior.

KEY WORDS AND PHRASES

OBJECTIVE 1

variability among people
variability within people
circularity
independent definitions of motivation

OBJECTIVE 2

need
drive

incentive
approach-approach conflict
avoidance-avoidance conflict
approach-avoidance conflict

OBJECTIVE 3

biological perspective
homeostasis
eating
set-weight level
lont-term regulation
glycerol
hypothalamus
ventromedial versus lateral hypothalamus
hyperphagia versus aphagia
free fatty acids
glucoreceptors
short-term regulation
glucose
insulin
enterogastrone
cholecystokinin (CCK)
satiety signal
liver
free fatty acids
ketones
obesity
external regulators

OBJECTIVE 4

drinking
urine formation
osmoreceptors
blood volume
kidneys
antidiuretic hormone (ADH)
angiotensin

OBJECTIVE 5

arousal
optimal level
brain stimulation
sensory deprivation
Yerkes-Dodson law
inverted U-shaped function
task complexity

OBJECTIVE 6

instinct
libido
ethology
fixed-action patterns

sign stimuli (releasers)
biological readiness

OBJECTIVE 7

personality perspective
psychogenic versus viscerogenic needs
need versus press
Thematic Apperception Test (TAT)
hierarchy of needs
need for affiliation
need for succorance
need for achievement
need to succeed versus fear of failure
fear of success
need for social approval
social desirability
conformity

OBJECTIVE 8

cognitive perspective
inference and attribution
self-attribution
need versus incentive value
utility theory
subjective utility
subjective probability of success
expected utility

OBJECTIVE 9

sexual motivation
sociobiology
instinctual and hormonal contributions
learning perspective
observation and conditioning
generalization and discrimination
needs, self-actualization, and positive expectations
thinking, knowledge, inference, and attribution

OBJECTIVE 10

emotion
qualitative (pleasant versus unpleasant) dimension of emotion
quantitative (intensity) dimension of emotion
activity
biological, motivational, experiential, and behavioral aspects of emotion
James-Lange theory
fear versus running
Cannon-Bard theory
fight versus flight
qualitative differences in physiological states
situational control of emotional expression
cognitive aspects of emotion

general arousal versus cognitive appraisal
juke-box theory
Zajonc's theory
opponent-process theory
a-process versus b-process

OBJECTIVE 11

anxiety (anticipatory fear)
free-floating (diffuse) anxiety
anger
frustration-aggression hypothesis

EXERCISES

EXERCISE 1: Objective 1

TITLE: MOTIVATION AS AN EXPLANATORY CONCEPT
TASK: Fill in the blanks

1. Motivation raises the question of _____ people behave as they do.
2. Motivation seeks to explain _____ both within the same person and across different individuals.
3. We should avoid _____ in motivational explanations (for example, he eats because he is hungry).
4. The best way to avoid such circular reasoning is to find _____ ways of defining motivation.
5. Motivational concepts are powerful _____ devices because they can account for a variety of behaviors without having to create a new principle for each new behavior.
6. Motivational concepts are not the only ones that account for variability in behaviors. For example, _____ and heredity are also used the same way, and it is important to separate these concepts from one another.

EXERCISE 2: Objective 2

TITLE: NEEDS, DRIVES, AND INCENTIVES
TASK: Match letters to numbers

_____ 1. what energizes and directs behavior toward a goal
_____ 2. an internal biological state that requires correction
_____ 3. what attracts or pulls behavior
_____ 4. it increases as the hours of food deprivation increase
_____ 5. it pushes behavior toward the goal
_____ 6. objects that attract people
_____ 7. seeking food when you are hungry
_____ 8. eating food because it's there
_____ 9. lack of glucose in the cells

A. need
B. drive
C. incentive

EXERCISE 3: Objective 2

TITLE: MOTIVATIONAL CONFLICTS
TASK: Match letters to numbers

_____ 1. You want steak and you want seafood, and you cannot have both.
_____ 2. You would like to party, but you have a test on Monday.
_____ 3. The choice is between extreme heat and extreme cold.
_____ 4. The conflict in which the negative aspect does not seem so bad from a distance.
_____ 5. The conflict in which we try to avoid making a decision.
_____ 6. The conflict that is readily resolved by putting off one of the choices until later.

A.   approach-approach
B.   avoidance-avoidance
C.   approach-avoidance

EXERCISE 4: Objective 3

TITLE: FOCUS ON HUNGER
TASK: Fill in the blanks

1.   From the biological perspective, the system strives for a steady state, of _____ .
2.   Like a thermostat, the body may have a _____ weight level.
3.   A person can be overweight because there are too many _____ cells, and/or because these cells are overfilled.
4.   The _____ is sensitive to changes in glycerol, which in turn changes in proportion to fat storage.
5.   Destruction of the ventromedial nucleus of the hypothalamus produces overeating, or _____ .
6.   Destruction of the lateral nucleus of the hypothalamus produces the failure to eat, or _____ .
7.   The short-term fluctuations around set-weight level are a function of changes in blood _____ level.
8.   Glucose is the body's basic store of _____ .
9.   _____ will reduce blood sugar levels and promote eating.
10. The general belief is that _____ in blood sugar between arteries and veins provides the short-term feeding signal.
11. Peripherally, the hormone enterogastrone contains CCK, which is a potent _____ signal that inhibits feeding.
12. _____ is involved in regulating what we eat.
13. The lack of a needed nutrient creates a specific _____ .
14. Regarding nutrients, the _____ converts amino acids into glucose, free fatty acids into ketones, and glucose into energy.
15. Some obese people are unduly influenced by _____ regulators.

EXERCISE 5: Objective 4

TITLE: FOCUS ON DRINKING
TASK: Fill in the blanks

1.   As with the control of eating, there is a sophisticated _____ system for drinking.

155

2. The critical brain structure for regulating drinking is the _____.
3. Thirst regulation involves control of both drinking and _____ formation.
4. The rate of urine formation is controlled by the _____.
5. In the hypothalamus, there are cells called _____ which shrink in size as water levels decline.
6. Also, the hypothalamus detects changes in _____ volume on the basis of information from the kidneys and heart.
7. The hypothalamus regulates urine formation by signaling the pituitary to secrete _____. This hormone, in turn, inhibits urine formation, and by forming less urine, water is conserved.
8. _____ is the hormone that signals the hypothalamus and pituitary that fluid levels are low.

EXERCISE 6: Objective 5

TITLE: FOCUS ON AROUSAL
TASK: Essays

1. What are the two pieces of evidence that support the notion of an optimal level of arousal?

2. How is the Yerkes-Dodson law related to the optimal level of arousal?

EXERCISE 7: Objective 6

TITLE: INSTINCT
TASK: Fill in the blanks

1. An _____ is a predisposition to behave in a genetically determined (that is, hard-wired) way.
2. The concept of instinct had its origins in Darwin's theory of _____.
3. The theory of evolution stressed _____ value of instincts, especially as they related to aggression, feeding, and reproduction.
4. There was also an instinctual component in Freud's theory called _____.
5. Although it enjoyed early success with McDougall and James, learning theorists influenced by Pavlov and Watson shifted their emphasis from instinct to _____.
6. More recently, the _____, such as Lorenz, Frisch, and Tinbergen have resurrected the concept of instinct.
7. In ethology and other contemporary treatments, the concept of instinct is referred to as _____.
8. For such patterns, behavior is first of all _____.
9. Second, behavior is _____ from one time to the next.
10. Third, the pattern is found in all members of the _____.
11. Finally, the pattern is _____ to a given species.
12. In general, fixed-action patterns are triggered by _____ stimuli.
13. Fixed-action patterns will be released only when the animal is biologically _____.
14. On the negative side, a major concern with ethological theory comes from several recent attempts to generalize notions from animals to _____.

EXERCISE 8: Objective 7

TITLE: FOCUS ON HENRY MURRAY'S WORK
TASK: Match letters to numbers

____1. We arrange our needs according to priorities--some needs must be
        satisfied before others are.
____2. You are given a picture and asked to make up a story.
____3. The survival needs such as for food, water, and oxygen.
____4. Learned needs such as affiliation, succorance, and achievement.
____5. Particular situations bring out or suppress various needs.

A.   TAT
B.   psychogenic needs
C.   viscerogenic needs
D.   hierarchy of needs
E.   press

EXERCISE 9: Objective 7

TITLE: SOME SAMPLE NEEDS ACCORDING TO MURRAY
TASK: Fill in the blanks

1.   The need for _____ is the need to be with others.
2.   The need to be nurtured and loved is the need for _____.
3.   The need to excel is the need for _____.
4.   The need for achievement may be broken down further into a need to
     _____, and . . . .
5.   a fear of _____.
6.   More recently, it has been suggested that women, more than men, have a
     fear of _____.
7.   The need for social _____ is perhaps the most fundamental need; indeed,
     it can be argued that the need to achieve is a need to win recognition
     from others.
8.   The need to achieve has been measured by using the _____.
9.   The need for social approval can be measured with the social _____
     scale.
10. If you have a low need for approval, it is unlikely that you will
     _____ to social pressures.
11. The need to dominate is the need for _____.
12. Interestingly, suppressing this need to dominate seems to raise the
     _____.
13. The need to understand, analyze, abstract, and, in general, process
     information, is the need for _____.
14. Interestingly, those with high versus low needs to process information
     differ with respect to their preference for complex _____ tasks.
15. Each of the needs discussed above would be classified by Murray as
     being _____.

EXERCISE 10: Objective 7

TITLE: MASLOW'S HIERARCHY OF NEEDS
TASK: Identify each of the following needs

1.   The need to feel safe from others.

157

2. The need for basic things like food and water.
3. The need for spiritual identity.
4. The need to feel good about oneself.
5. The need to be cared for.
6. The need to fulfill oneself.

EXERCISE 11: Objective 8

TITLE: ATTRIBUTION AND UTILITY
TASK: Fill in the blanks

1. Attribution entails the establishment of incentive values through the process of _____.
2. Attribution theory is concerned with the question of _____ behavior occurs.
3. When we try to explain our own behavior, this is called _____.
4. A ploy of advertisers is to create a perceived _____ for a product so as to raise its incentive value.
5. Utility theory combines incentive and _____ into a single concept.
6. In other words, _____ utility is a function of how much you need something and how attractive that something is.
7. A second critical aspect in utility theory is the subjective probability of _____.
8. When subjective utility is combined with subjective probability of success, we emerge with a(n) _____ utility of a particular goal object or course of action.

EXERCISE 12: Objective 9

TITLE: SEXUAL MOTIVATION
TASK: Essay

Compare and contrast the biological, learning, personality, and cognitive view points of sexual motivation.

EXERCISE 13: Objective 10

TITLE: CLASSIFYING EMOTIONS
TASK: Match letters to numbers

____1. The difference between anger and rage is one of intensity.
____2. The difference between anger and joy is one of direction.
____3. Two emotions can be unpleasant and intense and yet still differ.
____4. Positive and negative incentive states.
____5. Both sadness and anger are unpleasant and intense, but sadness is more passive.
____6. The degree of motivation will depend on the strength of the anticipated or experienced state.

A. qualitative dimension
B. quantitative dimension
c. activity dimension

EXERCISE 14: Objective 10

TITLE: ASPECTS OF EMOTION
TASK: Essay

What are the four aspects that any theory of emotion must integrate?

EXERCISE 15: Objective 10

TITLE: JAMES-LANGE VERSUS CANNON-BARD THEORY
TASK: Fill in the blanks

1. According to _____ theory, when we see a bear, first we run, and then we experience fear.
2. This theory implies that we experience different emotions because of the body's _____ changes.
3. It also implies that physiological activity is _____ different during different emotions.
4. In comparison, _____ theory makes the common-sense argument that first we fear, and then we run.
5. According to this theory, the autonomic nervous system produces a state of _____, which prepares the organism for "flight or fight."
6. In accord with the James-Lange theory, A. F. Ax has found physiological differences corresponding to different emotional states. For example, epinephrine seems to dominate during a _____ state.
7. In comparison, both epinephrine and norepinephrine are implicated in the emotion of _____.
8. Additional evidence comes from Ekman, Levenson, and Wallace. These researchers either induced _____ configurations, or . . . .
9. . . . had subjects _____ emotional experiences.
10. In the above study, different _____ states were associated with different emotions.

EXERCISE 16: Objective 10

TITLE: THE MORE MODERN THEORIES OF EMOTION
TASK: Fill in the blanks

1. From the cognitive aspect, first there is emotional arousal, and then there is cognitive _____.
2. The cognitive aspect comes from _____ theory.
3. The arousal and cognitive aspects together comprise what is known as _____ theory.
4. In support of the cognitive component, Schachter and Singer tricked their subjects into thinking they were receiving _____ shots, when in fact, they were getting adrenalin shots.
5. Subsequently, the emotion expressed by these subjects depended on the _____ they were in.
6. Valins demonstrated the same type of effect by using false _____ as feedback for males viewing nudes.
7. Contrary to the juke-box theory, Zajonc contends that arousal and appraisal occur in _____.

8. More recently, Solomon and Corbit have proposed a theory based on
    _____ processes.
9. Specifically, an emotional experience first triggers an _____,
    which remains constant.
10. The opponent, or _____, grows with each experience of the original
    emotional experience, and eventually outweighs the original emotion.
11. The net emotional effect is a function of the _____ between these
    two processes.
12. Thus, for drug addiction, the a-state is a "high," and the b-state is
    _____.
13. Consequently, after many highs, the drug user is no longer motivated by
    the high but instead tries to avoid _____ pain.

EXERCISE 17: Objective 11

TITLE: ANXIETY AND ANGER
TASK: Essays

1. What is anxiety, and how may it lead to pathological behavior?

2. What is the frustration-aggression hypothesis, and what are the
    alternative explanations of aggression?

EXERCISE 18

TITLE: KEY NAMES
TASK: Match letters to numbers

_____ 1. fear then run
_____ 2. run then fear
_____ 3. electrical brain stimulation
_____ 4. transcendence and self-actualization tops the hierarchy
_____ 5. adrenalin shots when vitamins were expected
_____ 6. sensory deprivation study
_____ 7. frustration-aggression hypothesis
_____ 8. experiment on rats escaping from cue associated with shock
_____ 9. experiments on social approval and desirability
_____ 10. use of nude pictures to study emotion
_____ 11. ethologists
_____ 12. psychogenic needs versus press
_____ 13. opponent processes
_____ 14. activity dimension of emotion
_____ 15. cross-cultural study of sexual behavior
_____ 16. early psychologists who favored instincts
_____ 17. theorists who led psychology away from instinct
_____ 18. neurotransmitters and fear versus anger
_____ 19. experiments on need for achievement
_____ 20. fear of success, particularly in women
_____ 21. arousal and appraisal occur in parallel
_____ 22. muscle configuration versus reliving an emotion

A. Olds and Milner
B. Bexton, Heron, and Scott
C. McDougall and James
D. Pavlov and Watson
E. Lorentz, von Frisch, Tinbergen, and so forth
F. Murray
G. Maslow
H. McClelland and Atkinson
I. Horner
J. Crowne and Marlowe
K. Ford and Beach
L. Daly, Lancee, and Polivy
M. James-Lange
N. Cannon-Bard
O. A. F. Ax
P. Ekman, Levenson, and Wallace
Q. Schacter and Singer
R. Valins
S. Zajonc
T. Solomon and Corbit
U. Miller
V. Dollard and his collegues

MULTIPLE-CHOICE TESTS

SELF-TEST 1

1. One common problem in using motivation to explain behavior is:
a. circularity of reasoning
b. there are too many concepts in motivation
c. motivation and emotion are identical
d. it can account for the differences in behavior across people
    (page 246)

2. Questions about why people behave in different ways when in the same situation are approached in the study of:
a. emotion
b. developmental psychology
c. motivation
d. personality
    (page 246)

3. The motivational push that is given to behavior and that results from the individual being in a biological state of need is called:
a. incentive
b. psychogenic need
c. press
d. drive
    (page 248)

4. An internal biological or cognitive state of deviance from the normal that requires correction defines:
a. drive
b. need
c. incentive
d. motivation
    (page 248)

5. The effects of goal objects on behavior refers to:
a. drive
b. need
c. incentive
d. motivation
    (page 248)

6. The fact that human beings do things such as go to movies, read mystery stories, and streak naked across football fields all seem to favor a(n) _____ notion rather than a(n) _____ of motivation.
a. need; incentive
b. incentive; drive
c. drive; incentive
d. drive; need
    (page 249)

7. When a goal object has both positive and negative aspects, an individual is faced with a(n):
a. approach-approach conflict
b. approach-avoidance conflict
c. avoidance-avoidance conflict
d. no conflict at all
    (page 251)

8. Which of the following is NOT one of the three perspectives that psychologists use in understanding motivation?
a. biological
b. social-personality
c. cultural
d. cognitive
    (page 251)

9. The three important examples of homeostatic systems with respect to motivation are:
a. sex, eating, and drinking
b. sex, drinking, and arousal
c. drinking, arousal, and eating
d. arousal, sex, and eating
    (page 251)

10. The weight at which we maintain ourselves appears to be controlled by:
a. the amount of glucose in the blood
b. the amount of glucose in the liver
c. the number of fat cells in the body
d. the number of fat cells in the hypothalamus
    (page 252)

11. Electrical stimulation of the hypothalamus's ventromedial nucleus would cause an animal to:
a. start drinking
b. stop drinking
c. start eating
d. stop eating
   (page 253)

12. A rat is fed a diet lacking in salt for several weeks. When given the choice between a salty food and a sweet food, which would the rat more likely eat?
a. the salty food
b. the sweet food
c. no difference in likelihood between the two
d. the rat would have lost the desire to eat because of changes in the hypothalamus
   (page 253)

13. The central processor of nutrients in the body is the:
a. stomach
b. brain
c. liver
d. hypothalamus
   (page 254)

14. Which two organs provide the hypothalamus with information about changes in blood volume?
a. heart and lungs
b. liver and kidneys
c. kidneys and heart
d. intestine and bladder
   (page 255)

15. The homeostatic system of arousal:
a. stimulates the organism to produce high levels of excitement
b. motivates the organism to seek very low levels of arousal
c. motivates the organism to maintain an optimal level of arousal
d. causes the brain to be more active when asleep than when awake
   (page 255)

16. If you were engaged in a very complex task, it would be desirable to maintain a _____ level of arousal.
a. low
b. moderate
c. high
d. very high
   (page 257)

17. The instinct conception of human motivation can be traced back to:
a. Freud
b. Lorenz
c. Darwin
d. James
   (page 258)

18. A major problem with using instincts to explain behavior is:
a. it is very difficult to identify all the instincts
b. it is too easy to postulate just the right instinct for a behavior so that we end up naming rather than explaining
c. it eliminates the contribution of biology to motivation
d. the way in which instincts are said to control behavior is never specified
   (page 258)

19. Which of the following is NOT one of the crucial aspects of fixed-action patterns?
a. they are innate
b. they can change from one time to the next
c. the pattern is unique to all members of the species
d. the pattern is exhibited by all members of the species
   (page 258)

20. The TAT has been used successfully by _____ to identify various psychogenic needs.
a. Stanley Schacter
b. Frank Beach
c. Sigmund Freud
d. Henry Murray
   (page 261)

21. People who perform well in school are likely to be:
a. high in need for affiliation
b. high in need for approval
c. high in need for achievement
d. high in need for power
   (page 263)

22. Atkinson has broken down the concept of need for achievement into two components:
a. need for approval and need for success
b. fear of success and fear of failure
c. need for power and fear of failure
d. fear of failure and need for success
   (page 263)

23. Perhaps the most basic of all the purely psychological needs is:
a. fear of failure
b. need for social approval
c. need for affiliation
d. need for achievement
   (page 264)

24. Personality-based theories of motivation suggest that motivation is at least partly determined by:
a. instinct
b. stable predispositions of the person
c. self-attribution
d. cognitive style
   (page 265)

25. A major problem in the assignment of various psychogenic needs to account for instances of behavior is the same problem faced by _____ theories.
a. instinct
b. learning
c. incentive
d. homeostatic
    (page 265)

26. When we ask ourselves "Why did I do that?" we are engaged in the process called:
a. self-analysis
b. self-motivation
c. self-attribution
d. self-explanation
    (page 266)

27. The concept that combines the two major aspects of motivation (drive and incentive) into one is called:
a. utility theory
b. attribution theory
c. sociobiology
d. homeostatic theory
    (page 266)

28. The notion that sexual behaviors are motivated by a need to reproduce one's own genes is a postulate of:
a. sociobiology
b. self-attribution theory
c. need theory
d. psychodynamic theory
    (page 267)

29. All of the following are probably instinctual sexual behaviors among primates (according to Ford and Beach) except:
a. homosexual activity
b. masturbation
c. coitus
d. love
    (page 267)

30. According to contemporary research on emotions, the two major dimensions of love are:
a. love and hate
b. pleasure and pain
c. intensity and pleasantness
d. arousal and attribution
    (page 270)

SELF-TEST 2

1. What are the three basic components of motivation?
a. reward, punishment, and need
b. need, drive, and incentive
c. goal, reinforcement, and direction
d. discrimination, incentive, and pull
    (page 248)

2.   The study of the types of objects that people want to acquire would be a study of:
a.   drives
b.   needs
c.   incentives
d.   attributions
     (page 248)

3.   Incentives are seen as consequences of behavior that produces them. As such, incentives are very similar to:
a.   reinforcers
b.   drives
c.   conditioned stimuli
d.   unconditioned stimuli
     (page 248)

4.   We typically think of motivation as the joint effect of two concepts:
a.   learning and heredity
b.   drive and incentive
c.   personality and sociality
d.   instinct and personality
     (page 248)

5.   Wanting to eat a piece of pizza but at the same time wanting to lose weight would result in:
a.   eating pizza
b.   a motivational conflict
c.   an avoidance-avoidance conflict
d.   losing weight
     (page 250)

6.   With respect to the set-weight theory, which of the following is out of place?
a.   number of fat cells
b.   amount of blood glucose
c.   blood levels of glycerol
d.   size of fat cells
     (page 252)

7.   The peptide cholecystokinin (CCK) has what effect on the body?
a.   inhibits eating
b.   inhibits drinking
c.   causes eating
d.   causes drinking
     (page 253)

8.   Probably the most important regulatory mechanism for the short-term control of eating is:
a.   level of fat in fat cells
b.   difference between levels of glucose in veins and arteries
c.   amount of fluid passing through the kidneys
d.   amount of food present in the stomach
     (page 253)

9. People who are obese are most likely to be overcontrolled by _____ precipitators of eating.
a. nutritious
b. internal
c. external
d. pleasant
   (page 254)

10. The hypothalamus is extremely important to the overall control of eating. Which brain structure is very important to the overall control of drinking?
a. hippocampus
b. thalamus
c. hypothalamus
d. medulla
   (page 254)

11. Antidiuretic hormone (ADH) is released by:
a. the liver
b. the kidney
c. the bladder
d. the pituitary gland
   (page 255)

12. Sensory deprivation experiments have caused the subjects to hallucinate and report bizarre experiences. A major conclusion of these types of experiments is that:
a. people generally do not try to maintain low levels of stimulation
b. sensory deprivation activates the same mechanisms as LSD does
c. schizophrenia may be caused by low sensory input from the environment
d. high levels of stimulation are necessary for proper conscious functions
   (page 256)

13. According to the Yerkes-Dodson law, as task complexity increases, the arousal level should _____ for the best performance.
a. increase
b. decrease
c. remain the same
d. first increase and then decrease
   (page 257)

14. The optimum level of arousal is unlike an instinct in that:
a. it varies from one person to the next
b. it is low for all humans
c. it is high for all humans
d. there is little variability among humans
   (page 257)

15. Which of the following terms is out of place?
a. species specific
b. fixed-action pattern
c. sign stimulus
d. incentive
   (page 259)

16. According to Henry Murray, individuals have needs that can be arranged in a hierarchy. When two incompatible needs arise, the one that will be satisfied first will be:
a. the need that is higher in the hierarchy
b. the need that is lower in the hierarchy
c. they will both be satisfied simultaneously
d. neither will be satisfied
   (page 261)

17. We would expect that people who are high in their need for social approval would also show a great amount of:
a. anxiety
b. achievement
c. conformity
d. abnormal behavior
   (page 264)

18. Differences in people in terms of their preferred activities, such as preferring *Princess Daisy* to *War and Peace*, and *Sherrif Lobo* to *Star Trek* are conceptualized as reflecting differences in their:
a. need for achievement
b. need for social approval
c. need for cognition
d. need for power
   (page 265)

19. A major goal of advertising that follows the principles of self-attribution theory is to:
a. raise the product's incentive value in the consumer's mind
b. cause the consumer to feel emotion
c. cause the consumer to think about the product
d. cause the consumer to laugh at the commercial
   (page 266)

20. According to utility theory, a critical aspect of overall motivation is:
a. probability of success
b. fear of success
c. usefulness of the object
d. fear of failure
   (page 267)

21. Although the data are not very convincing, it seems that women may be most likely to initiate sexual behavior:
a. equally often throughout the menstrual cycle
b. about at the time of ovulation
c. just before menstruation
d. just after menstruation
   (page 268)

22. According to Eleanor Daly, emotional experience can be described by assigning points on three dimensions:
a. love, hate, and anger
b. need, drive, and incentive
c. pleasantness, intensity, and activity
d. arousal, attribution, and perception
   (page 271)

23. According to the James-Lange theory of emotion:
a. physiological arousal precedes behavior
b. behavior precedes feeling
c. attribution is necessary for emotion to be felt
d. fear and anger are identical
   (page 271)

24. Which theorist(s) argued that emotions are similar rather than qualitatively different physiological states?
a. James and Lange
b. Ax
c. Freud
d. Cannon and Bard
   (page 272)

25. Cross-cultural analysis of facial expression while smiling led Ekman to conclude that:
a. Asians and Westerners differ in their expression of negative emotions
b. Latins and Scandinavians smile more than Africans do
c. human faces the world over use the same expressions to show the same emotions
d. each culture learns its own emotional expression, based mostly on environmental uniqueness
   (page 272)

26. The key element that attribution theory contributed to modern conceptualizations of emotion is:
a. cognitive appraisal of the situation
b. specificity of arousal
c. utility of the right emotion at the right time
d. incentive value of showing emotion in different contexts
   (page 273)

27. Theories of addiction are well accounted for by the _____ theory of motivation.
a. incentive
b. drive
c. self-attribution
d. opponent-process
   (page 276)

28. An emotional state that seems to play a large part in the motivation of abnormal behavior is:
a. anxiety
b. anger
c. fear
d. hate
   (page 276)

29. Someone who was very hesitant to go anywhere or do anything, who felt jumpy and on edge, and who really couldn't point to any reason for such feelings would be said to be suffering from:
a. a delusional state
b. nonspecific phobia
c. free-floating anxiety
d. fear of failure
   (page 276)

30. Research that has investigated frustration and anger has shown clearly that:
a. aggressive acts are not actually products of anger
b. frustration sometimes, but not always, produces aggression
c. frustration necessarily produces anger
d. most aggressive acts are unlearned
   (page 278)

WHAT DOES IT MEAN?

OBJECTIVES

1. How can behavioral variables be manipulated to increase motivation and improve performance?
2. How does extrinsic versus intrinsic motivation affect performance?
3. In what ways can the personality aspects of motivation be changed?
4. How have motivational analyses contributed to methods of weight control?
5. In what ways does emotion contribute to psychological disorders, and how can emotional control alleviate some disorders?

SELF-TEST

1. With regard to motivation and performance in industrial settings:
a. all motivational change can be boiled down to one incentive: money
b. increased performance may sometimes depend more on praise and recognition than on more money
c. giving praise frequently reduces the efficiency of performance
d. drive seems more important than incentive
   (page 280)

2. It seems that extrinsic reinforcement:
a. always facilitates performance
b. always inhibits performance
c. never suppresses performance
d. sometimes inhibits performance
   (page 281)

3. The basis for the facilitating effect of intrinsic as compared with extrinsic motivation may well be:
a. the competence motive
b. anticapitalistic cultures
c. the need for social approval
d. the activity of the libido
   (page 281)

4. It seems that the need for _____ plays a crucial role in the personality of alcholics.
a. social approval
b. affiliation
c. power
d. achievement
   (page 282)

5. People who are described as having the imperial power syndrome:
a. have high affiliation needs
b. have low power needs but high approval needs
c. are very effective managers
d. are most likely to be only children
    (page 283)

6. In selecting someone for a job selling toasters, it would be a good idea to:
a. find people with the imperial power syndrome
b. find people who exhibit behaviors that are known to be important to selling
c. find people who really want to work hard
d. find people with a high need for achievement
    (page 283)

7. With respect to people's attempts to control their weight:
a. only 50 percent of dieters are successful in keeping off lost weight
b. most dieters spend their entire lives gaining and losing the same ten pounds
c. we currently have very effective techniques for controlling weight
d. dieting is not very profitable, as it goes against biologically set mechanisms
    (page 283)

8. Which factor has Schachter's experiments on eating behavior isolated as particularly important to controlling the tendency of obese people to eat?
a. they cannot differentiate tastes
b. they eat mainly in response to external cues
c. they eat mainly in response to internal cues
d. they have preset "obesity" levels in their hypothalamus
    (page 283)

9. Causing oneself to vomit after "pigging out" is a disorder called:
a. anorexia
b. hypothalamic insufficiency
c. bulimia
d. weight anxiety
    (page 283)

10. Judith Rodin's suggestion for losing weight is based mostly on metabolic mechanisms and recommends:
a. eat several small meals per day
b. alternate periods of normal eating with starvation diets
c. surgical removal of detectorless fat cells
d. injection with insulin three times per day
    (page 284)

11. Many psychologists believe that the inability to control emotions and express them appropriately is a major cause of:
a. aggression
b. automobile accidents
c. psychopathology
d. suicide
    (page 284)

12. Probably one of the best and maybe easiest ways to improve performance or make behavior more natural is to:
a. reduce the level of emotional arousal
b. take a tranquilizer
c. increase your natural aggression
d. increase the general level of arousal
    (page 286)

13. Lie detector tests:
a. are 99 percent accurate
b. tend to err most often by indicating a lie by a person telling the truth
c. are being used less and less frequently
d. detect only the abnormal physical arousal that accompanies lying
    (page 287)

14. Which of the following is not one of Selye's three stages of the general adaptation syndrome?
a. alarm reaction
b. resistance to stress
c. exhaustion
d. spontaneous recovery
    (page 288)

15. According to Benson, which of the following should NOT be conducive to achieving the relaxation response?
a. assuming a comfortable position
b. maintaining a passive attitude
c. repeating a phrase over and over
d. keeping an uncomfortable posture to avoid going to sleep
    (page 289)

ANSWER KEY

EXERCISES

Exercise 1

1. why
2. variability
3. circularity

4. independent
5. explanatory
6. learning

Exercise 2

1.	B	4.	A	7.	B
2.	A	5.	B	8.	C
3.	C	6.	C	9.	A

Exercise 3

1.	A	4.	C
2.	C	5.	B
3.	B	6.	A

Exercise 4

1.	homeostasis	6.	aphagia	11.	satiety
2.	set	7.	glucose	12.	taste
3.	fat	8.	energy	13.	need
4.	hypothalamus	9.	insulin	14.	liver
5.	hyperphagia	10.	differences	15.	external

Exercise 5

1.	homeostatic	5.	osmoreceptors
2.	hypothalamus	b.	blood
3.	urine	7.	ADH
4.	kidneys	8.	angiotensin

Exercise 6

1.   The term *optimal* implies neither minimal nor maximal arousal. In support of the optimal level, there is evidence opposed to a need for either minimal or maximal stimulation. Regarding maximal stimulation, Olds and Milner, the researchers who found the pleasure centers, also found "unpleasurable" centers, or brain areas whose stimulation rats would work to terminate. Regarding minimal stimulation, Bexton, Heron, and Scott found that human subjects could not tolerate sensory deprivation very long, even though they were being paid $25 per day to do so.

2.   In general, it is believed that efficiency of performance is an inverted U-shaped function of level of arousal. In other words, we perform poorly at high and low levels and efficiently somewhere in between (that is, at some optimal level). According to the Yerkes-Dodson law, the optimal level is an inverted U-shaped function, whose peak varies with task difficulty. More specifically, as task difficulty increases from easy to moderate to difficult, the optimal level of arousal in the inverted U-function moves closer to the low end (see Figure 7-6).

Exercise 7

1.	instinct	6.	ethologists	11.	unique
2.	evolution	7.	fixed-action pattern	12.	releasing
3.	survival	8.	innate	13.	ready
4.	libido	9.	invariant	14.	humans
5.	drive	10.	species		

Exercise 8

1.   D   2.   A   3.   C   4.   B   5.   E

Exercise 9

1.	affiliation	6.	success	11.	power
2.	succorance	7.	approval	12.	blood pressure
3.	achievement	8.	Tat	13.	cognition
4.	succeed	9.	desirability	14.	cognitive
5.	failure	10.	conform	15.	psychogenic

Exercise 10

1.   safety and security
2.   physiological needs
3.   transcendence
4.   self-esteem
5.   love and belongingness
6.   self-actualization

Exercise 11

1.   interference
2.   why
3.   self-attribution
4.   need
5.   drive
6.   subjective
7.   success
8.   expected

Exercise 12

The biological perspective considers both the species and the individual organism. At the level of the species, sociobiology theory maintains that organisms are driven to pass on their genes to the succeeding generation. At the individual level, there is evidence of instinctual control, particularly in lower animals, and hormonal control, both in animals and humans. Some theorists view common behaviors (for example, coitus, masturbation, homosexual acts) in animals and humans as being genetically based.

There is no single learning theory of sexual behavior, but the learning approach emphasizes conditioning and observation in early childhood and changes throughout life that result as a function of generalization and discrimination.

From a personality perspective, sexual motivation may be viewed according to selected needs (for example, achievement, affiliation, social approval, and power). It may also be viewed according to the need for self-actualization (that is, Maslow's hierarchy). Some theorists combine learning and personality factors (for example, we engage in sexual behavior because we have learned to expect positive changes in our lives as a result).

Finally, the cognitive perspective emphasizes thinking, knowledge, inference, and attribution. For example, we make attributions about potential sexual partners in social situations, and our decision to proceed may be based on a utility analysis (that is, the subjective utility combined with the probability of success).

Exercise 13

1. B   2. A   3. C   4. A   5. C   6. B

Exercise 14

The first aspect is biological activation, which is related to the fact that the autonomic nervous system and associated hormones act to fire us up for action. The second aspect is motivation, which is related to the fact that emotions can act as incentives that push us to seek certain emotional states. The third aspect is experiential, which involves private feelings that are difficult to investigate scientifically. The final aspect is behavioral, which relates to emotional gestures and responses that are subject to conditioning.

Exercise 15

1.	James-Lange	6.	fear
2.	physiological	7.	anger
3.	qualitatively	8.	muscle
4.	Cannon-Bard	9.	relive
5.	arousal	10.	physiological

Exercise 16

1.	appraisal	8.	opponent
2.	attribution	9.	a-process
3.	juke-box	10.	b-process
4.	vitamin	11.	difference
5.	situation	12.	withdrawal
6.	situation	13.	withdrawal
7.	parallel		

Exercise 17

1. Anxiety is anticipatory fear. When a stimulus elicits anxiety, we try to escape it (for example, Miller's experiments with rats escaping stimuli associated with shock). The potential for pathology comes from the prospect that escape from anxiety is itself reinforcing. Thus, anxiety may produce habitual (inappropriate) escape patterns that are difficult to break (for example, reducing fear of an exam by habitually developing ailments).

2. Having a goal blocked leads to frustration and anger. The frustration-aggression hypothesis suggests that frustration will produce an aggressive reaction (for example, the frustrated pigeon who attacks the innocent bystander pigeon). Alternatively, the ethologists have suggested that we have an aggressive instinct. More recently, learning theorists have suggested that aggressive behavior is often motivated by positive rather than negative incentives (for example, pushing someone out of the way to get what you want).

Exercise 18

1. N	4. G	7. V	10. R	13. T	16. C	19. H
2. M	5. Q	8. U	11. E	14. L	17. D	20. I
3. A	6. B	9. J	12. F	15. K	18. O	21. S
						22. P

MULTIPLE-CHOICE

Self-Test 1

1. a	6. b	11. d	16. a	21. c	26. c
2. c	7. b	12. a	17. c	22. d	27. a
3. d	8. c	13. c	18. b	23. b	28. a
4. b	9. c	14. c	19. b	24. b	29. d
5. c	10. c	15. c	20. d	25. a	30. c

Self-Test 2

1.	b	6.	b	11.	d	16.	a	21.	b	26.	a
2.	c	7.	a	12.	a	17.	c	22.	c	27.	d
3.	a	8.	b	13.	b	18.	c	23.	b	28.	a
4.	b	9.	c	14.	a	19.	a	24.	d	29.	c
5.	b	10.	c	15.	d	20.	a	25.	c	30.	b

WHAT DOES IT MEAN?

Self-Test

1.	b	6.	b	11.	c
2.	d	7.	b	12.	a
3.	a	8.	b	13.	b
4.	c	9.	c	14.	c
5.	c	10.	a	15.	d

8 Developmental Psychology

OBJECTIVES

1. What is the definition of developmental psychology, and what are its four theoretical perspectives?
2. What are the two major research methods in developmental psychology, and how can they be combined?
3. What are the features of infant perceptual development in the visual system, and what changes occur with continued development in the visual and other sensory systems?
4. What is the evidence favoring active learning in neonates, and what is Piaget's general theory with respect to cognitive development from neonate to adolescent?
5. What are the steps from initial speech through linguistic transformations, and what are the three hypothesized relationships between language and thought?
6. What are the processes of integration and differentiation, and how do they affect infants' social and emotional development?
7. What factors affect peer relations, morality, relations with parents, and sex roles in children?
8. What factors affect peer relations, morality, and psychosocial development in adolescents?
9. What are the varying viewpoints with respect to development from adulthood through old age, and what are some of the commonly held myths about the aged?

SYNOPSIS

Developmental psychologists study changes throughout the entire life span (infancy, childhood, adolescence, and adulthood), which are influenced by four theoretical perspectives. The psychoanalytic perspective emphasizes internal influences (that is, Freud's dynamic forces, sequential stages, and mental structures), whereas the behavioral-learning perspective emphasizes both conditioning (classical and instrumental) and "mental" operations such as memory and perception. The cognitive perspective favors a more active interaction between organism and environment and sees development as a function of imbalances, or states of disequilibrium. Finally, the most recent perspective, information processing, treats the organism like a computer, with emphasis on the brain's "hardware," "software," and processing capabilities.

The two primary research methods used by developmental psychologists are the cross-sectional and longitudinal designs. However, the cross-sectional design is subject to "cohort differences," and the longitudinal requires considerable follow-up on many individual subjects. A solution to the weaknesses of both is to combine them into the cross-sequential panel design.

In this chapter, the theoretical perspectives and research methods serve as a framework for understanding two major topical areas in developmental psychology, namely, intellectual development and social/emotional development.

The section on intellectual development is organized topically into perception, learning, cognition, and language. In perception, most of the research is on the infant's visual system (with emphasis on preference, depth perception, and size, color, and shape perception), but there is also discussion of the remaining sensory systems, organized search patterns in older children, and changes that can occur with aging. Research in learning reveals that classical and instrumental conditioning, and modeling can occur within the first few days of life. The developmental study of cognition is dominated by Piaget's four-state theory: the sensorimotor, preoperational, concrete operational, and formal operational stages. In understanding these stages, pay attention to factors that both characterize a given stage and lead to transition from one stage to the next.

Finally, the development of language can be charted from the point of initial speech to adultlike syntax and grammar. Also, there are currently three viewpoints regarding the relationship between language and thought: Piaget's which suggests that thought shapes language; Whorf's, which suggests that language shapes thought; and Vygotsky's and Luria's, which adopts a middle position on the issue.

The treatment of social/emotional development is organized according to age periods, including infancy, childhood, adolescence, and adulthood. The major issue in infancy is attachment and its impact on the subsequent differentiation of the infant from the parents. In childhood, differentiation is expressed in terms of friendships, and these friendships lead to issues such as role taking and morality. The parent-child relationship is still important and is viewed according to three types of parenting: authoritarian, authoritative, or permissive. Also, the parents play an important role in the child's development of sex roles. In adolescence, the basis of friendships become less self-serving and more intimate and "cliquish." Indeed, friendships evolve into various stages of "crowd" behavior, which are viewed as important to the development of sexual relationships. Morality is still an important issue during adolescence.

Finally, there are several issues that emerge in adulthood. Erikson's eight stages of psychosocial development cover birth through death, and at each stage, the motivational basis for behavior is seen as a crisis that must be resolved. Some psychologists think that Erikson postulates too few stages for adulthood, and others favor a different (life-span) viewpoint that focuses on a number of key issues rather than stages (for example, is the personality stable throughout life? Life-span psychologists have taught us that there are a number of misconceptions about the aged, ranging from underestimations of sexual activity and desire to overestimations of the extent of cognitive loss.

KEY WORDS AND PHRASES

OBJECTIVE 1

psychoanalytic perspective
    dynamic, sequential, and structural aspects

        eros and thanatos
        oral, anal, phallic, latency, and genital stages
        Oedipal and Electra conflicts
        sexual versus social forces
behavioral-learning perspective
        respondent versus operant behaviors
        learning
        modeling
        applications
cognitive perspective
        passive versus active organism
        states of disequilibrium
information-processing perspective
        brain hardware versus software
        strategies for problem solving

OBJECTIVE 2

cross-sectional method
longitudinal method
cohort differences
cross-sectional panel design

OBJECTIVE 3

infant perception
innate visual preferences
learned visual preferences
depth perception
visual cliff
size, color, and shape discrimination
shape and shape constancy
later perceptual skills
organized search pattern
scanning differences
sensory deterioration

OBJECTIVE 4

classical conditioning in neonates
operant conditioning in neonates
modeling in infants
assimilation versus accommodation
equilibration
sensorimotor stage
        object permanence
        magical thinking
        symbolic thinking
preoperational stage
        egocentrism
concrete operational stage
        conservation
        compensation, reversibility, and identity
formal operational stage
        abstract thinking
dialectical operations

OBJECTIVE 5

stages in speech development
production versus comprehension of words
holophrases
duos
telegraphic speech
declarative sentences
linguistic transformations
transformational rules
the Whorfian hypothesis

OBJECTIVE 6

integration versus differentiation
infancy
attachment behaviors
strange situation
secure versus insecure attachment
separation anxiety
terrible twos
emotional states and facial expressions
self-knowledge

OBJECTIVE 7

peer relations
friends as playmates
friends as associates
role taking ("two way" and "third party")
empathy
childhood morality
Damon's five stages of fairness
Piaget's four stages of obeying rules
parent-child relations
authoritarian versus authoritative versus permissive parents
instrumental competence
technique of "induction"
sex roles
      biological factors versus learning
      sexual stereotypes

OBJECTIVE 8

"chumship"
"cliquishness"
Dunphy's five stages of adolescent friendships
Kohlberg's six stages of adolescent moral development
Erikson's first five stages of psychosocial development

OBJECTIVE 9

Erikson's last three stages of psychosocial development
life-span psychology
stability of personality

EXERCISES

EXERCISE 1: Objective 1

TITLE: FOCUS ON THE PSYCHOANALYTIC PERSPECTIVE
TASK: Fill in the blanks

1. Freud's _____ theory emphasizes three aspects of development.
2. The dynamic aspect consists of two broad and opposing classes of _____.
3. One class is called _____ and represents life (or sexual) forces.
4. The second class is called _____ and represents death (or aggressive) forces.
5. The _____ aspect of Freud's theory consists of five stages of psychosexual development.
6. In the _____ stage, pleasure is received through activities such as mouthing and sucking.
7. In the _____ stage, energy is focused on organs that control the elimination of waste from the body.
8. The critical Oedipal (males) and Electra (females) conflicts occur during the _____ stage.
9. Next, there is a period of sexual dormancy known as the _____ stage.
10. Finally, sexual energy is channeled into reproductive sexual relationships in the _____ stage.
11. It should be noted that other theorists such as Erikson emphasize _____ rather than sexual factors in their stages of development.
12. The final aspect of Freud's theory is _____.

EXERCISE 2: Objective 1

TITLE: COMPARISON OF THE FOUR THEORETICAL PERSPECTIVES
TASK: Match letters to numbers

_____ 1. An active interaction with the environment characterized by imbalances (states of disequilibrium).
_____ 2. Dynamic forces predetermine psychosexual stages.
_____ 3. Some emphasize respondent and operant conditioning, and others emphasize vicarious processes (as in modeling).
_____ 4. Emphasis on the brain's "hardware" and "software."
_____ 5. There have been many applications, particularly to therapeutic situations and software packages in education.
_____ 6. The stages in this perspective describe changes in the child's understanding of the world as a result of interactions with the environment.
_____ 7. Emphasis on minute strategies in problem solving.
_____ 8. A criticism that applies is that many heretofore sexual taboos no longer exist.

A. psychoanalytic
B. behavioral-learning
C. cognitive
D. information-processing

EXERCISE 3: Objective 2

TITLE: RESEARCH METHODS IN DEVELOPMENTAL PSYCHOLOGY
TASK: Essay

Suppose that you did a cross-sectional study in which you surveyed
sexual attitudes among people aged 25, 35, 45, 55, and 65 and you found that
as age increased, so did the tendency to disapprove of premarital sexual
relations. What would you conclude?

EXERCISE 4: Objective 3

TITLE: INFANT AND CHILDHOOD PERCEPTION
TASK: Fill in the blanks

1. The most immature sense at birth is _sight_.
2. Infants spend much time just looking around and show _interest_ for
    visual arrays that contain movement, height contrast, and interesting
    contours.
3. A one-day-old infant prefers to view a(n) _complex_ stimulus.
4. A(n) _2 Month_-old infant smiles at a picture of a human face.
5. After several months, the infant's preference is for faces that are
    real and _familiar_.
6. Infants' depth perception has been studied using an apparatus called
    the visual _cliff_.
7. The evidence shows that depth perception exists at least as early as the
    infant is able to _crawl_.
8. Infants also quickly learn to discriminate among size, color, and
    shapes and develop size and shape _constancy_.
9. They also learn to discriminate among tastes and odors and have good
    tactile sensitivity, especially around the _mouth_.
10. The later changes in perceptual development reflect changes in knowledge
    as is reflected in the organized _search_ patterns of older children
    (age 10 to 12).
11. Perceptual skills are fully developed by ages 10 to 12, but later
    changes may occur because of sensory deterioration. However, improve-
    ments are possible at any age, as is evidenced in the learning of new
    scanning strategies for improved reading.

EXERCISE 5: Objective 4

TITLE: THE FIRST SIGNS OF LEARNING
TASK: Essay

An old misconception in psychology is that infants cannot actively learn.
This is clearly untrue. In infants, there is evidence of classical
conditioning, instrumental conditioning, and learning by imitation. What is
that evidence?

EXERCISE 6:   Objective 4

TITLE: KEY CONCEPTS IN COGNITION
TASK: Match letters to numbers

_F_ 1.   The principle of conservation that acknowledges that the beaker with the lower level of water is also wider.
_I_ 2.   The individual does more than solve problems; he or she creates them because he or she does not shy away from contradictions.
_B_ 3.   Modifying an internal structure to fit the demands of reality.
_G_ 4.   The principle of conservation that acknowledges that the water may be returned to the original beaker.
_A_ 5.   Modifying incoming information to fit with what is already known or believed.
_C_ 6.   Establishing balance between assimilation and accommodation.
_E_ 7.   Having difficulty imagining a perspective other than your own.
_H_ 8.   The principle of conservation that acknowledges that no water has been added or subtracted.
_D_ 9.   An infant learns that when an object drops out of sight, it does not literally drop out of existence.

A.   assimilation   F.   compensation
B.   accommodation   G.   reversibility
C.   equilibration   H.   identity
D.   object permanence   I.   dialectical operations
E.   egocentrism

EXERCISE 7:   Objective 4

TITLE: PIAGET'S STAGES OF DEVELOPMENT
TASK: Match letters to numbers

_A_ 1.   During this stage, there is a gradual shift from pure reflexive activity to primitive thought.
_C_ 2.   The first stage in which children can take the proper perspectives in the "three mountains" experiment.
_D_ 3.   The mature logic in adolescence that leads to systematic analysis, exploration, and problem solving.
_B_ 4.   The first stage in which the child masters the ability to represent symbolically the external world (particularly through the use of language).
_B_ 5.   This stage is characterized by egocentrism.
_A_ 6.   Most of this stage is characterized by lack of object permanence.
_C_ 7.   At the beginning of this stage, the principles of conservation (compensation, identity, and reversibility) are mastered.
_D_ 8.   The ability to approach a problem (such as the chemical problem) with a logical and complete plan.

A.   sensorimotor stage
B.   preoperational stage
C.   concrete operational stage
D.   formal operational stage

EXERCISE 8: Objective 5

TITLE: THE DEVELOPMENT OF SPEECH
TASK: Fill in the blanks

1. The infant's first sounds are by-products of breathing, digestion, and
    _____ in distress.
2. Of crying, cooing and babbling, _____ begins at about 12 weeks, as
    the infant responds vocally to sights and sounds in the environment.
3. Consonants begin to emerge at about 6 months and are combined with
    vowels at about 8 months to form _____ sounds.
4. This vocal progression leads to real _____.
5. In general, in the first year of life, the production of speech lags
    behind _____ of speech.
6. In their second year, babies begin to compress the meaning of entire
    sentences into single words called _____.
7. They then begin chaining together two words into utterances called
    _____.
8. Although it used to be believed that these two-word chains were _____,
    recent evidence suggests that these utterances are unique.
9. The child then goes beyond two-word sentences to simple _____
    sentences.
10. Then, during the third year, linguistic _____ of these declarative
    sentences appear as utterances.
11. To make such utterances, the child must acquire transformational
    _____ of grammar, which develop rapidly after age 2.
12. Before the end of year 3, children's vocabulary size is up to _____
    words, and by the time they enter school, they possess language much
    like adults' in its syntactical and grammatical aspects.

EXERCISE 9: Objective 5

TITLE: LANGUAGE AND THOUGHT
TASK: Essay

    What are the three views regarding the relationship between language and
thought espoused by Piaget, Wharf, and Vygotsky and Luria?

EXERCISE 10: Objective 6

TITLE: SOCIAL AND EMOTIONAL DEVELOPMENT IN INFANCY
TASK: Fill in the blanks

1. The socialization, or _____ process, connects the individual to
    society via relationships and responsibilities.
2. The opposite process, called _____, facilitates the formation of one's
    unique social identity and personality.
3. In infancy, the integration function is seen most clearly in _____
    behaviors such as smiling, cooing, and grasping.
4. There is evidence that attachment behaviors are _____ based (for
    example, infant monkeys' need to cling and contact their mother).
5. Attachment has been studied in infants via the procedure known as the
    _____ situation.

184

6. _____-attached infants use mother as a base of exploration and are more likely (among other things) to form more positive relationships with peers in early childhood.
7. The _____ role appears to be that of playing physically with the infant.
9. By month 7, the child shows _____ anxiety when away from the care-giver, as well as wariness of strangers.
10. Infants also contact the world via their _____ expressions.
11. In general, integration is so strong that differentiation at the end of infancy is difficult, particularly in a period known as the terrible _____.
12. Judging from data collected from self-image studies, self-knowledge is first acquired at the age of about _____.

EXERCISE 11: Objective 7

TITLE: PEER RELATIONS IN CHILDHOOD
TASK: Essays

1. What are the two developmental stages in friendship in childhood?

2. What are the two developmental stages in role taking in childhood?

3. Which socially important behaviors does role taking contribute to and why?

EXERCISE 12: Objective 7

TITLE: DANNON'S FIVE STAGES IN CHILDHOOD MORALITY
TASK: Reorder the following six statements to reflect the proper develop-mental order of Danon's stages of childhood morality.

A. It is fair for everyone to get the same, regardless of special considerations such as merit or need.
B. It is best to consider who deserves the reward as a function of the specific situation.
C. What is fair is what I desire.
D. It is fair to use an objective criterion (I am the fastest runner) even if such criteria are unfair, illogical, and untrue.
E. We should compromise, particularly concerning those who are not as fortunate as we are.
F. Rewards should go to those who are the most deserving (those who have worked hardest, who are smartest, who have acted the best, and so forth).

EXERCISE 13: Objective 7

TITLE: PIAGET'S FOUR STAGES IN CHILDHOOD MORALITY
TASK: Match letters to numbers

____1. At this stage, the child takes rules quite seriously and acts as if they were sacred and unchangeable. Yet, ironically, they follow rules erratically.

_____2. At this stage, rules are changeable and are made to serve people's needs. Thus, the rationale for obeying rules becomes cooperation and reciprocity rather than constraint.

_____3. At this stage, the child plays in a private, nonsocial manner and creates his or her own rules.

_____4. At this stage, when children are capable of abstract thinking, rules tend to follow from complex political and social concepts.

A. idiosyncratic morality
B. heteronomous morality
C. autonomous morality
D. ideological morality

EXERCISE 14: Objective 7

TITLE: PARENT-CHILD RELATIONS
TASK: Fill in the blanks

1. _____ parents are strict disciplinarians, but they do not communicate well, nor are they nurturant with their children.
2. _____ are also strict, but they are fair and show warmth and nurturance.
3. _____ communicate well with their children, but they do not discipline their children, nor do they expect very much in the way of intellectual or social achievements.
4. Concerning the three styles of parenting, children of the authoritative parent are most likely to develop _____ competence (that is, social responsibility, achievement orientation, and vitality).
5. Of boys and girls, this finding is particularly true of _____, in whom self-reliance and assertiveness are greatly enhanced by authoritative parents.
6. But with authoritarian and permissive parents, _____ tend to be shy and dependent . . . .
7. . . . . whereas _____ tend to be hostile.
8. Additional research has been conducted using the method of _____ (convincing a child to engage in prosocial behavior and explaining why this should be done).
9. In general, the results with this method imply that the best parents are the ones with consistent guidelines and clear _____.
10. Moreover, the adult's socializing influence is most enduring when the child believes he or she is making his or her own _____.

EXERCISE 15: Objective 7

TITLE: SEX ROLES IN CHILDREN
TASK: Essay

Recent evidence suggests that sex roles are learned rather than inherited. View the acquisition of sex roles from the perspectives of both the parent and the child, and describe the factors that research says contribute to this conclusion.

EXERCISE 16:   Objective 8

TITLE: ADOLESCENT FRIENDSHIP
TASK: Essays

1.   What are two ways in which adolescent friendships differ from childhood
     friendships?

2.   What are Dunphy's five stages of adolescent peer-group development?

3.   Why is puberty such a challenge to the adolescent's social life?

EXERCISE 17:   Objective 8

TITLE: KOHLBERG'S SIX STAGES OF MORALITY
TASK: Match letters to numbers

____1. One should obey laws, which should be applied equally to all and
        which should serve the welfare of society.
____2. Children often do things to obtain goodies. Also, one good turn
        deserves another.
____3. If you do not obey the law, then the law will punish you.
____4. If you do not obey your parents, then they will spank you.
____5. Regardless of what anyone or any law states, I must obey my
        conscience in order to live with myself.
____6. If you do not behave yourself, it is unlikely that very many people
        will like you.

A.   premoral (step 1)
B.   premoral (step 2)
C.   conventional role conformity (step 1)
D.   conventional role conformity (step 2)
E.   self-accepted moral principles (step 1)
F.   self-accepted moral principles (step 2)

EXERCISE 18:   Objective 8 and 9

TITLE: ERICKSON'S EIGHT STAGES OF PSYCHOSOCIAL DEVELOPMENT
TASK: Match letters to numbers

____1. Can I master the skills needed to adapt?
____2. Has my life's work been satisfying?
____3. Can I control my own behavior?
____4. Can I trust the world?
____5. Can I gain independence and explore my limits?
____6. What can I offer to succeeding generations?
____7. Who am I?
____8. Can I give myself fully to another?
____9. Initiative versus guilt.
____10. Trust versus mistrust.
____11. Intimacy versus isolation.
____12. Industry versus inferiority.
____13. Identity versus confusion.
____14. Integrity versus despair
____15. Autonomy versus shame/doubt.
____16. Generativity versus stagnation.

A.	oral-sensory	E.	puberty and adolescence
B.	muscular-anal	F.	young adulthood
C.	locomotor-genital	G.	adulthood
D.	latency	H.	maturity

EXERCISE 19: Objective 9

TITLE: MISCONCEPTIONS ABOUT OLD AGE
TASK: True or false

_____ 1. Most people 65 and older are senile.
_____ 2. Most older people have no interest in or capacity for sexual relations.
_____ 3. The majority of older people feel miserable most of the time.
_____ 4. At least one-tenth of the aged are living in long-stay institutions
          (nursing homes, mental hospitals, and the like).
_____ 5. Most older workers cannot work as effectively as younger workers can.
_____ 6. Most older people are set in their ways and unable to change.
_____ 7. It is almost impossible for most older people to learn new things.
_____ 8. In general, most older people are pretty much alike.
_____ 9. The majority of older people are socially isolated and lonely.
_____ 10. Over 15 percent of the U.S. population are now 65 or over.
_____ 11. The majority of older people have incomes below the poverty level.
_____ 12. Older people tend to become more religious as they age.
_____ 13. The health and socioeconomic status of older people in the year 2000
          will probably be about the same as now.

EXERCISE 20

TITLE: KEY NAMES RELATING TO THE THEORETICAL PERSPECTIVES
TASK: Match letters to numbers

_____ 1. A behavioral-learning theorist interested in modeling.
_____ 2. A behavioral-learning theorist interested in conditioning.
_____ 3. A cognitive theorist interested in stages of cognitive development.
_____ 4. A psychoanalyst interested in dynamic forces, sequences of psycho-
          sexual development, and mental structures.

A. Freud
B. Skinner
C. Bandura
D. Piaget

EXERCISE 21

TITLE: KEY NAMES IN INTELLECTUAL DEVELOPMENT
TASK: Match letters to numbers

_____ 1. The belief that language structures thought.
_____ 2. Computer programs that simulate the conservation problem.
_____ 3. Math curricula based on concrete operational thought processes.
_____ 4. Visual cliff and organized search patterns.
_____ 5. Language and thought emerge together.
_____ 6. Supposed decline in IQ after age 35.

_____7. Far less a decline in IQ in adulthood than once thought.
_____8. Operant discrimination in neonates.
_____9. Classical conditioning in neonates.
_____10. Data showing that formal operations can be taught at an earlier age than Piaget thought possible.
_____11. Evidence of modeling in neonates.
_____12. Dialectical operations--a stage after formal operations.

A. Gibson
B. Papousek
C. DeCasper and Fifer
D. Field and colleagues
E. Klahr
F. Case
G. Siegler
H. Riegal
I. Wechsler
J. Baltes and colleagues
K. Wharf and Sapir
L. Vygotsky and Luria

EXERCISE 22

TITLE: KEY NAMES IN SOCIAL AND EMOTIONAL DEVELOPMENT
TASK: Match letters to numbers

_____1. Separation anxiety
_____2. Moral development--three levels each with two steps.
_____3. Moral development--five stages of fairness.
_____4. Belief that personality is stable throughout life.
_____5. Use of "strange situation" to study attachment in infants.
_____6. The father plays physically with the infant.
_____7. Found that child's sex roles are affected by severe accidents.
_____8. Longitudinal data relating to secure versus insecure attachment.
_____9. Chumship.
_____10. Continuing potential for growth throughout adulthood.
_____11. Five stages of adolescent "crowds."
_____12. Infants soon reserve smiles for the caregiver.
_____13. A dab on the face can show self-knowledge at about 15 months of age.
_____14. Eight stages of psychosocial development.
_____15. Children learn role taking through friendships.
_____16. Authoritarian, authoritative, and permissive parents.
_____17. Documentation of childhood social play.
_____18. The adult's socializing influence on the child is most enduring when the child feels he or she is making the choices.

A. Ainsworth   J. Baumrind
B. Sroufe   K. Lepper
C. Lamb   L. Money
D. Ende   M. Sullivan
E. Bowlby   N. Dunphy
F. Lewis and Brooks-Gunn O. Kohlberg
G. Garvey   P. Erikson
H. Selman   Q. Brim and Kagan
I. Damon   R. Block and colleagues

MULTIPLE-CHOICE TESTS

SELF-TEST 1

1.   At what stage is human development thought to be complete?
a.   adolescence
b.   young adulthood
c.   mature adulthood
d.   death
      (page 291)

2.   Which of the following is NOT one of the three aspects of development
that Freud emphasized in his psychoanalytic theory?
a.   dynamic
b.   structural
c.   cognitive
d.   sequential
      (page 292)

3.   According to the psychoanalytic perspective on development:
a.   we react to imbalances between current knowledge and environmental
      information
b.   we react to conflicts between our own pleasures and society's demands
c.   we are a function of our reinforcement history
d.   we pass through several stages of morality
      (page 292)

4.   Which psychosexual stage is coincident with elementary school age?
a.   oral
b.   genital
c.   latency
d.   phallic
      (page 293)

5.   Which theoretical perspective avoids the use of stages in characterizing
the development of the individual?
a.   behavioral-learning
b.   psychoanalytic
c.   cognitive
d.   stages are characteristic of each perspective
      (page 293)

6.   The cognitive perspective on development has been critical of both the
psychoanalytic and behavioral perspective because the latter two:
a.   treat the organism too passively
b.   treat the organism too actively
c.   rely too much on sequential processes
d.   rely too much on dynamic forces within the organism
      (page 294)

7.   The principle of active construction is most closely linked with the
_____ perspective on development.
a.   psychoanalytic
b.   behavioral-learning
c.   cognitive
d.   dispositional
      (page 294)

8.   Both Freud's psychoanalytic theory and Piaget's cognitive developmental theory rely on a stage approach. An element common to both is:
a.   energy is seen as springing from sexual desire
b.   the stages must occur in a fixed sequence
c.   the child is seen as an active constructor rather than a passive reactor
d.   conflicts that must be resolved for further development to occur at each stage
     (page 295)

9.   The Piagetian approach to the study of development in children:
a.   includes analysis of how a child visually scans a problem
b.   focuses only on the child's solution to the problem
c.   describes how well the child remembers unimportant aspects of the problem
d.   measures how long it takes the child to solve the problem

10. Measurements of changes in heart rate have been used to measure _____ in handicapped infants.
a.   performance skills
b.   attention
c.   intellectual development
d.   language development
     (page 296)

11. If a researcher selected 25 children with high IQs and studied them intensively over the next decade, the research technique would be called:
a.   a training study
b.   cross-sectional
c.   longitudinal
d.   normative
     (page 296)

12. One of the major weaknesses of longitudinal research designs to study developmental processes is:
a.   there are too few measures of each individual subject
b.   the number of subjects that must be used is excessive
c.   cohort differences are confounded with developmental changes
d.   the constant testing and retesting may alter normal development
     (page 297)

13. Which of the following is NOT one of the three major ways of knowledge acquisition that are available to us?
a.   internalization
b.   perception
c.   language
d.   cognition
     (page 297)

14. The sensory system that is MOST immature at birth is:
a.   sight
b.   hearing
c.   touch
d.   cognition
     (page 297)

15. Infants seem to have an innate preference for:
a. visual cliffs
b. objects with depth
c. objects with uniform colors
d. objects with varied patterns
   (page 297)

16. The visual cliff is a device used in developmental research to measure:
a. binocular vision
b. existence of depth perception
c. perception of color
d. pattern discrimination
   (page 299)

17. Infants as young as _____ can learn to discriminate their mother's voice from other female voices.
a. one hour
b. three days
c. two weeks
d. one month
   (page 300)

18. If I can use information from economists to modify what I already know about financial trends, then I am showing an ability that Piaget called:
a. assimilation
b. accommodation
c. compensation
d. conservation
   (page 300)

19. The phrase "out of sight, out of mind" fits best with Piaget's belief that young infants:
a. demonstrate egocentrism
b. show internalized speech
c. lack object permanence
d. develop action schemata
   (page 301)

20. A child who can use some symbols but who exhibits egocentrism is most likely to be in the developmental stage that Piaget termed:
a. sensorimotor
b. concrete operational
c. preoperational
d. formal operational
   (page 303)

21. Reversibility, compensation, and identity all are representative abilities of the phenomenon called:
a. assimilation
b. accommodation
c. morality
d. conservation
   (page 304)

22. The ability to think abstractly characterizes which of Piaget's stages?
a.   concrete operational
b.   formal operational
c.   sensorimotor
d.   preoperational
     (page 305)

23. Which of the following capacities is MOST likely to decline in adulthood?
a.   problem-solving skills
b.   verbal skills
c.   reasoning
d.   memory
     (page 307)

24. The "compromise" position that language and cognition (or thought) develop together is advocated by:
a.   Piaget
b.   Damon
c.   Whorf
d.   Vygotsky and Luria
     (page 309)

25. According to Vygotsky and Luria, the function of internalized speech is to:
a.   aid in problem solving
b.   aid in organized search
c.   aid in external language development
d.   express the child's fantasies
     (page 309)

26. According to Mary Ainsworth, the child that uses mother as a base from which exploration proceeds is:
a.   unattached
b.   securely attached
c.   overly attached
d.   just becoming attached
     (page 310)

27. Authoritative parents tend to be:
a.   very strict disciplinarians
b.   fairly democratic
c.   permissive
d.   low in achievement demands
     (page 315)

28. According to Erikson, the conflict over self-identity occurs during:
a.   adolescence
b.   young adulthood
c.   adulthood
d.   old age
     (page 319)

29. According to Erikson, the question most asked by young adults is:
a. Whom can I trust?
b. Can I give myself fully to another?
c. When will I be free?
d. Who am I?
    (page 319)

30. According to Erikson, the mature person is asking the question:
a. What can I offer the next generation?
b. Has my life been satisfying?
c. Can I master the necessary skills to adapt?
d. Who am I?
    (page 319)

SELF-TEST 2

1. The "death" forces in Freud's theory are called:
a. eros
b. thanatos
c. phallos
d. libido
    (page 292)

2. Concerning knowledge and development:
a. it is correct to say that children know things differently than do adults, rather than just knowing less
b. children do not actually begin accumulating knowledge until the age of about 8
c. abstract thinking can occur as early as 2 years of age
d. knowledge is formed as in packets, with many packets accumulating with age but the early ones remaining unchanged
    (page 295)

3. If third, fourth, and fifth graders all were compared on various cognitive tasks to determine changes in cognitive abilities with age, the research method would be called:
a. the sequential approach
b. longitudinal
c. cross-sectional
d. cohort analysis
    (page 296)

4. Studies with the visual cliff have shown that:
a. infants have innate preferences
b. children aged 8 already have organized search skills
c. children show internalized speech by age 5
d. infants have depth perception by the time they crawl
    (page 299)

5. According to Gibson, by the time a child is about age 10, identification of objects is made by:
a. insight
b. simple observation
c. organized search
d. trial and error
    (page 299)

6.   It has been shown that _____ can be used to teach infants to turn
their heads.
a.   operant conditioning
b.   classical conditioning
c.   modeling
d.   physical guiding
      (page 300)

7.   If I modify new information to fit into what I already know of the world,
then I am:
a.   compensating
b.   assimilating
c.   accommodating
d.   identifying
      (page 300)

8.   The development of action schemata characterizes which of Piaget's
stages of development?
a.   sensorimotor
b.   preoperational
c.   concrete operational
d.   formal operational
      (page 301)

9.   Egocentrism is characteristic of which of Piaget's stages of development?
a.   sensorimotor
b.   preoperational
c.   concrete operational
d.   formal operational
      (page 303)

10.   If the child knows that matter can be neither created nor destroyed, he
or she can master the task of:
a.   reversibility
b.   action schemata
c.   rules of permutation
d.   abstract thinking
      (page 304)

11.   Duos, two-word sentences, usually begin occurring during the _____
year of life.
a.   first
b.   second
c.   third
d.   fourth
      (page 308)

12.   Language determines thought--so says:
a.   Piaget
b.   Vygotsky and Luria
c.   Whorf
d.   Kohlberg
      (page 309)

13. The two complementary processes that work to shape the child's social development are:
a.   integration and differentiation
b.   assimilation and accommodation
c.   generalization and discrimination
d.   perception and language
     (page 309)

14. According to the most recent studies of birth order and family size:
a.   most parents who have a second child do so to keep the first from being an only child
b.   only children tend to be joiners rather than loners
c.   more emotional disorders are found in only children than other children
d.   only children have better social skills than other children
     (page 311)

15. Young children develop a wariness of strangers:
a.   shortly after birth
b.   at about two months of age
c.   between the six and twelfth month
d.   at about two years of age
     (page 311)

16. The developmental period sometimes referred to as the "terrible twos" represents a time when the child:
a.   begins to recognize itself as separate from its mother
b.   first becomes aware that the environment can be manipulated
c.   lacks inhibitory mechanisms of the brain
c.   clearly perceives differences in the environment
     (page 312)

17. During childhood, the primary focus of attachment and modeling is on:
a.   mother
b.   father
c.   peers
d.   siblings
     (page 313)

18. Empathy and a sense of morality contribute to the occurrence of _____ in children.
a.   role playing
b.   judgment
c.   self-actualization
d.   altruistic behavior
     (page 314)

19. According to Damon, in the earliest stages of morality (or fairness) the child is guided by:
a.   premoral values
b.   idiosyncratic rules
c.   heteronomous rules
d.   inner desires
     (page 314)

20. According to Piaget, which is the sequence of children's development of moral stages?
a.   autonomous, heteronomous, idiosyncratic, ideological
b.   heteronomous, ideological, idiosyncratic, autonomous
c.   ideological, idiosyncratic, autonomous, heteronomous
d.   idiosyncratic, heteronomous, autonomous, ideological
     (page 315)

21. Parents who raise their children according to which style are MOST likely to discipline their children strictly?
a.   authoritative
b.   authoritarian
c.   permissive
d.   regressive
     (page 315)

22. Research evidence suggests that parents begin sex-stereotyping their children:
a.   immediately after birth
b.   after about six months
c.   at about one year
d.   at six months for boys and one year for girls
     (page 316)

23. At what age do children tend to recognize gender differences in themselves and others?
a.   six months
b.   one year
c.   three years
d.   five years
     (page 316)

24. Which methodology does Kohlberg use in his studies of morality and moral development?
a.   case study
b.   naturalistic observation
c.   clinical interview
d.   quasi experiment
     (page 317)

25. According to Kohlberg's description of moral development, the person operating at _____ may rightly disobey society's codes in order to solve moral dilemmas.
a.   stage 1
b.   stage 2
c.   stage 3
d.   stage 6
     (page 318)

26. According to Erikson, total questioning of accepted beliefs and acute criticisms of self and society are to be expected:
a.   in late childhood
b.   in adolescence
c.   in early adulthood
d.   in mature adulthood
     (page 319)

27. The developmental theorist who views life as a series of crises is:
a. Piaget
b. Vygotsky
c. Damon
d. Erikson
   (page 319)

28. According to Erikson, if I don't know whether the world can be trusted, I am most likely to be:
a. an infant
b. an adolescent
c. a young adult
d. a mature adult
   (page 319)

29. An individual is ready to establish intimate relationships with another when:
a. the identity crisis has been resolved
b. adulthood has been reached
c. the fifth stage of morality has been entered
d. the integrity crisis has been resolved
   (page 321)

30. The major controversy in the field of adult development is:
a. do stages of development occur in fixed sequence?
b. is the identity crisis occurring earlier in adolescence?
c. does personality remain stable throughout life?
d. do cognitive capacities decline with age?

WHAT DOES IT MEAN?

OBJECTIVE

1. What methods of child rearing are most conducive to the development of psychologically healthy children?
2. How are experimental and social researchers working to combat the physical and psychological problems of aging?
3. What are the implications of the child's attachment needs for practical problems such as custody settlements after divorce and placement in day care centers?
4. What constitutes child abuse, what characterizes the abusers, and what are the consequences for the victims of abuse?

SELF-TEST

1. The most recent theories of attachment in developmental psychology show:
a. parents should hold and cuddle their children as infrequently as possible
b. affectionate parents tend to have securely attached children
c. children of affectionate parents tend to cling to them
d. children of nonaffectionate parents tend to be quite assertive and independent
   (page 325)

2.   Those personality characteristics that seem best to predict children who
may become drug abusers in adolescence are:
a.   aggressiveness and shyness
b.   intelligence and assertiveness
c.   leadership and independence
d.   dependence and shyness
      (page 326)

3.   The Hayflick limit refers to:
a.   the total number of cells in the human body
b.   the maximum life span of a species
c.   the number of cells that must be formed before an infant can survive
d.   the distance that an infant will crawl from its mother
      (page 326)

4.   Which of the following aspects of communication is suggested as
encouraging language growth in children?
a.   correct mistakes always and consistently
b.   speak in the normal discourse adults use with one another
c.   tell stories but do not read to the child
d.   discourage kiddie games in favor of sophisticated humor
      (page 327)

5.   Which of the following is recommended most as an aid in allowing people
to grow old without major illness?
a.   ten hours of sleep per night
b.   more than average exercise
c.   training in assertiveness skills
d.   megavitamin therapy
      (page 328)

6.   According to recent research on attachment needs of children, what is
the primary consideration that should be used in granting child custody after
divorce?
a.   which parent earns the most money
b.   which parent is most likely to remarry
c.   which parent loves the child the most
d.   which parent can provide the most stable relationship
      (page 329)

7.   According to psychoanalytic theory, children of divorced parents should
be placed with:
a.   the parent of the same sex
b.   the parent of the opposite sex
c.   both parents on a rotating basis
d.   a foster family with two parents
      (page 329)

8.   Of major importance to the concept of nonparental day care are research
findings from studies of monkeys and of wartime orphans that show:
a.   disattachment leads to irreversible depression
b.   disattachment leads to lack of development of language
c.   peers can take the place of parents in many respects
d.   children suffer no lasting effects of disattachment
      (page 330)

9. After their parents divorce:
a. girls seem to be affected more and for a longer time than boys are
b. boys seem to be affected more and for a longer time than girls are
c. children of both sexes are affected equally
d. children are relatively unaffected by their parents' divorce
   (page 330)

10. Farran's study on aggressive behavior in day care centers showed that:
a. children in day care were just as aggressive as were children not in
   day care
b. children in day care were less aggressive than were children not in
   day care
c. children who had come to day care as infants were the most aggressive
d. children who came to day care after age five were the most aggressive
   (page 331)

11. Instances of child abuse have not been reported in the past for all the
reasons below EXCEPT:
a. threats of retaliation from parents
b. bureaucratic red tape
c. the legal system made it difficult for teachers, doctors, and the like
   to take effective action
d. most cases of abuse occurred among the upper class
   (page 331)

12. The estimated incidence of child abuse in the United States is _____
a. 50,000 to 100,000
b. 200,000 to 250,000
c. 500,000 to 1,000,000
d. 5,000,000 to 10,000,000
   (page 331)

13. Child abusers tend to be:
a. male
b. female
c. from all strata of society
d. from the lower class
   (page 331)

14. Most child abusers:
a. are paranoid
b. were unpopular children
c. are frustrated sexually
d. were abused themselves
   (page 332)

15. Research done at the University of Colorado Medical Center uses _____
to predict parents who are likely to abuse their children.
a. biochemical tests
b. personality tests
c. tests of parent-infant eye contact
d. measures of parent-infant touching
   (page 332)

ANSWER KEY

EXERCISES

Exercise 1

1. psychoanalytic
2. instincts
3. eros
4. thanatos
5. sequential
6. oral
7. anal
8. phallic
9. latency
10. genital
11. social
12. structural

Exercise 2

1. C
2. A
c. B
4. D

4. D
5. B
6. C
8. A

Exercise 3

The temptation here is to conclude that attitudes toward sexual behavior
become more conservative as we grow older. However, the problem is that each
of these age groups were "premarital" during different eras and that attitudes
toward sexual relationships have changed drastically across these eras. Thus,
the cross-sectional differences may be "cohort" rather than developmental
differences. To determine how attitudes change over time, we also need
longitudinal data (that is, from the same people across several decades) and,
if possible, a design such as the cross-sequential panel design which
combines both cross-sectional and longitudinal data.

Exercise 4

1. vision
2. preference
3. complex
4. two-month
5. familiar
6. cliff
7. crawl
8. constancy
9. mouth
10. search
11. scanning

Exercise 5

Regarding classical conditioning, it is possible to pair a neutral tone
with the subsequent appearance of a nipple for a 3- to 4-day-old infant.
After several pairings, the infant will respond with an anticipatory sucking
response to the tone alone, and this conditioned response is somewhat
resistant to extinction.

Regarding instrumental conditioning, 3-to 4-day-old infants will learn
head-turning responses in order to obtain milk reinforcement. Thus, they can
show right or left turns in accordance with discriminative stimuli such as
buzzers or bells. They can also discriminate their mother's voice from the
voice of a stranger.

Finally, regarding imitation, in addition to being able to discriminate among different facial expressions portrayed by a live model, 1- to 2-day-old infants can mimic these expressions well enough so that observers seeing only the faces of the infant can discern an emotion (for example, happy, sad, surprised) portrayed by the model.

Exercise 6

1.	F	4.	G	7.	E
2.	I	5.	A	8.	H
3.	B	6.	C	9.	D

Exercise 7

1.	A	5.	B
2.	C	6.	A
3.	D	7.	C
4.	B	8.	D

Exercise 8

1.	crying	5.	comprehension	9.	declarative
2.	cooing	6.	holophrases	10.	transformations
3.	babbling	7.	duos	11.	rules
4.	words	8.	telegraphic	12.	1,000

Exercise 9

According to Piaget, language is one of many by-products of thought. More specifically, language is seen as a by-product of the child's ability to symbolize, which begins at the end of the sensorimotor stage.

The opposite viewpoint (the "Whorfian" hypothesis) holds that once the child has learned words and syntax, the ability to think is greatly enhanced.

The compromise position, of the Soviet psychologists Vygotsky and Luria, is that language and thought develop together. Moreover, once they have merged, it is believed that both processes become more powerful.

Exercise 10

1.	integration	5.	strange	9.	separation
2.	differentiation	6.	securely	10.	emotional
3.	attachment	7.	insecurely	11.	twos
4.	biologically	8.	father's	12.	15 months

Exercise 11

1. During the preschool and early school years, friends are seen as playmates, or as people who are frequently contacted. During this stage, friendships are based on material acts and are easily made and broken. From the middle school years through early adolescence, the friend becomes more of an associate. During this stage, friendship is based on reciprocal interest. As a result, they become more stable and are based on special qualities that friends see in one another.

2. The first step away from egocentrism is to realize that others can take their perspective and that they can take others' perspectives. This occurs during the middle school years and is called *two-way role taking*. The second stage is *third-party role taking*, which occurs by

the end of childhood. Here, the child realizes that there is an objective viewpoint that transcends individual viewpoints.

3. Role taking is believed to contribute to the child's sense of empathy (being sensitive to the needs and desires of others). Empathy, in turn, is believed to contribute to a sense of morality, which is believed to motivate prosocial, or altruistic behaviors.

Exercise 12

The correct order is C, D, A, F, E, B

Exercise 13

1. B   2. C   3. A   4. D

Exercise 14

1. authoritarian   6. girls
2. authoritative   7. boys
3. permissive   8. induction
4. instrumental   9. communication
5. girls   10. choices

Exercise 15

One study asked parents to describe their baby as they would a close friend. They were also asked to fill out a questionnaire describing their baby's physical features. Interestingly, although objective hospital records showed no difference between male and female babies, parents stereotypically described female babies differently than they did male babies, with fathers being more extreme in their differences than mothers were. In other words, even though there is little to differentiate, objectively, the male or female baby, parents find ways of doing so, and their differentiations are in keeping with traditional expectations. This implies that parents stereotype their children and do so quite early on.

From the child's perspective, there is reason to believe that even though boys and girls can play the same games, they are expected to play different games. But if a child has a severe accident that affects gender, it will, despite its biological endowment, show changes in sex roles.

Exercise 16

1. If you recall, early childhood friendships are with playmates, and later childhood friendships serve reciprocal interests. In adolescence, friendships become more intimate (that is, "chumship"), and this intimacy leads to cliquishness. The latter creates a sense of exclusivity, because friends are carefully selected.

2. According to Dunphy, the adolescent first forms isolated and unisexual cliques, which then expand to crowds (but are still unisexual). The crowds then become hierarchically organized, and this is followed by development of heterosexual cliques (wherein dating is the principal activity). In the final stage, the crowd disintegrates into loosely associated heterosexual couples.

3. Puberty brings with it sexual desires and the need to turn simple friendships into sexual relationships. Dating within the peer group helps, but it is clear that the reasons for engaging in sex in adolescence (for example, skill seeking, recreation) are less stable and enduring than are the reasons for doing so later on.

Exercise 17

1. E   2. B   3. D   4. A   5. F   6. C

Exercise 18

1. D	5. C	9. C	13. E
2. H.	6. G	10. A	14. H
3. B	7. E	11. F	15. B
4. A	8. F	12. D	16. G

Exercise 19

They all are false.

Exercise 21

1. K	5. L	9. B
2. E	6. I	10. G
3. F	7. J	11. D
4. A	8. C	12. G

Exercise 22

1. E	7. L	13. F
2. O	8. B	14. P
3. I	9. M	15. H
4. R	10. Q	16. J
5. A	11. N	17. G
6. C	12. D	18. K

MULTIPLE-CHOICE TESTS

Self-Test 1

1. d	6. a	11. c	16. b	21. d	26. b
2. c	7. b	12. d	17. b	22. b	27. b
3. b	8. b	13. a	18. b	23. d	28. a
4. d	9. b	14. a	19. c	24. d	29. b
5. a	10. c	15. d	20. c	25. a	30. b

Self-Test 2

1. b	6. a	11. b	16. a	21. b	26. b
2. a	7. c	12. c	17. c	22. a	27. d
3. c	8. a	13. a	18. d	23. c	28. a
4. d	9. b	14. a	19. d	24. c	29. a
5. c	10. a	15. c	20. d	25. d	30. c

WHAT DOES IT MEAN?

Self-Test

1.	b	2.	d	11.	d
2.	a	7.	a	12.	b
3.	b	8.	c	13.	c
4.	b	9.	b	14.	d
5.	b	10.	c	15.	c

9 Personality

OBJECTIVES

1. What are the various definitions of personality (including the text's), and what function do personality theories serve?
2. What are the major characteristics of dispositional theories, and within this major classification, what differentiates type, trait, and need theories?
3. What assumptions did Freud make about personality, and how are they expressed in Freud's personality structures, ego defense mechanisms, and stages of development?
4. What were the earlier (for example, Jung and Adler) and later (for example, ego psychology, social psychology, and transactional anlaysis) variations on Freud's theory?
5. What are the common and distinguishing features of learning and social-learning theories, and how do these theories differ from dispositional and psychodynamic theories with respect to personality assessment?
6. What distinguishes phenomenological theories from dispositional, psychodynamic, and learning theories?

SYNOPSIS

There is no universally accepted definition of personality (for example, see Table 9-1). Thus, the text adopts an eclectic definition, which is "a concept which describes and accounts for individual differences and consistencies in behavior." There are also many personality theories. In general, these theories make basic assumptions and provide working definitions. The chapter as a whole considers four classes of personality theories, namely, dispositional, psychodynamic, learning, and phenomenological theories.

As the name suggests, dispositional theories deal with tendencies or dispositions within the individual to behave in certain ways. Within this classification, there are global-type theories (for example, Sheldon's treatment of physique and temperament), less-global trait theories (for example, Allport's entities, Cattell's factors, and Eysenck's dimensions), and theories that emphasize the individual's needs or goals in relation to environmental forces (for example, Murray's need/press theory). In general, dispositional theories have been influential because they are good at describing personality and have generated a great deal of research. On the negative side, dispositional theories are weak on explanation and tend to rely too much on self-report measures.

Psychodynamic theories emphasize intrapsychic events and conflicts. In Freud's psychoanalytic theory, this translates into three assumptions, namely, psychic determinism, unconscious motivation, and the existence of sexual and aggressive instincts. The theory itself contains three components, namely, personality structures (id, ego, and superego), defense mechanisms, and psychosexual stages of development. The theory hinges on the inherent conflict between the id and the superego, which is resolved or repressed by the ego. These conflicts emerge at the phallic stage of development. Freud's methods first involved hypnosis, which he later gave up in favor of free association. Currently, psychologists use projective tests to investigate the unconscious. In general, Freud's influence on psychology and society has been immense, though his critics argue that he based his theory on a small population of patients and that many of his notions are untestable. There were also criticisms from within the movement, which resulted in a number of variations on his original theory.

Early variations on Freud's theory included Jung's criticisms that Freud overemphasized the role of sex and aggression and underestimated the scope of the unconscious. Adler argued against unconscious conflicts in favor of personal and family forces that lead each individual to develop a life-style approach overcoming inferiority in favor of superiority. Later these variations included ego psychology, which was led by Freud's daughter Anna and which emphasized the conflict-free role of the ego. This group also included Erikson, Hartmann, and Kohut. Additionally, there was a group including Horney, Fromm, and Sullivan who emphasized social-cultural influences on personality. For example, Horney argued that basic anxiety leads to neurotic needs, which in turn, promotes attitudes toward, against, and away from others. And finally, a modern variation called *transactional analysis* (led by Berne and Harris) treats the id, ego, and superego as three interpersonal states: child, adult, and parent.

In general, learning theorists reject intrapsychic events and structures in favor of the interaction between environment and behavior. Dollard and Miller attempted to rephrase Freudian notions into learning terminology, an effort that was criticized by Skinner, who believes in the functional analysis of behavior, as opposed to inferences regarding underlying constructs such as anxiety, conflict, and needs. The more modern social-learning theorists emphasize traditional learning variables but add to them the role of cognition. Rotter emphasizes the interaction between expectancy and value; Bandura emphasizes vicarious processes emanating from observation and imitation; and Mischel emphasizes the person-situation interaction. On the positive side, learning theorists use precise measuring instruments to assess personality. On the negative side, they have been criticized for their narrow perspective and their reliance on laboratory data.

Phenomenologists argue that each of the above approaches neglects the individual's unique perception of the world. This approach is based to some degree on humanistic and existential philosophy. For example, Rogers contends that we seek congruence between our direct organismic experiences and the valuation of others, and this incongruence leads to the distortion of reality. Perls argues that we as individuals need to take responsibility for our feelings. Finally, Maslow believes that we all are motivated to seek positive peak experiences but that we cannot rise to the top of the hierarchy if we cannot satisfy the more basic D-needs. In general, phenomenologists are nontraditional in their assessments of personality, and they have been criticized for their narrowness, failure to explore the causes of behavior, and vagueness in terminology.

KEY WORDS AND PHRASES

OBJECTIVE 1

personality
distinctive behavioral patterns
differences versus consistencies in behavior

OBJECTIVE 2

dispositional theories
    type theory
    trait theory
    need theory
four humors
physiognomy
physique and temperament
endomorph versus mesomorph versus ectomorph
viscerotonic versus somatotonic versus cerebrotonic
phrenology
traits as entities
    cardinal
    central
    secondary
    common versus individual traits
traits as factors
factor analysis
L-data versus Q-data versus T-data
surface versus source traits
manifestations
environmental mold traits
genetic constitutional traits
introversion
extroversion
neuroticism
psychoticism
Maudsley Personality Inventory (MPI)
need versus secondary needs
manifest versus latent needs
projective tests
objective tests
Thematic Apperception Test (TAT)

OBJECTIVE 3

Psychodynamic theories
psychic determinism
unconscious versus conscious versus preconscious
instincts (impulses)
libido
id
ego
superego
pleasure principle
reality principle

ego defense mechanisms
    repression
    denial
    reaction formation
    projection
    displacement
    rationalization
    sublimization
    sublimation
    regression
psychosexual stages
    oral stage
    anal stage
    phallic stage
    latency period
    genital stage
fixation
Oedipus complex
Electra complex
castration anxiety
penis envy
exhibitionism
hypnosis
free association

OBJECTIVE 4

analytic psychology
general psychic force
transcendent function
personal versus collective unconscious
archetypes
    hero, mother, shadow, anima, and animus
individuation
individual psychology
inferiority versus superiority
life-style
basic misconceptions
birth order
ego psychology (or analysis)
basic anxiety
neurotic needs
basic attitudes
psychosocial versus psychosexual
transactional analysis
    parent, adult, and child roles

OBJECTIVE 5

learning and social learning
measurable behavior
environmental forces
primary versus secondary needs and drives
approach-approach conflict

approach-avoidance conflict
avoidance-avoidance conflict
double approach-avoidance conflict
operant conditioning
functional analysis
expectancy versus value
locus of control
internal versus external
vicarious processes
    acquisition
    inhibition
    disinhibition
    facilitation
cognitive, behavioral, and environmental variables
reciprocal determinism
self-efficacy
person-situation interaction
behavioral sample
fear survey schedule
reinforcement survey schedule
self-monitoring
systematic observation

OBJECTIVE 6

phenomenological theories
humanism and existentialism
self-theory
self-actualization
organismic feelings
positive and negative self-regard
congruence versus incongruence
conditions of worth
distortion of reality
Gestalt therapy
responsibility for feelings
encounter and sensitivity groups
self-actualization theory
hierarchy of needs
D-needs
metaneeds (or B-values)
peak experiences
Personal Orientation Inventory (POI)

EXERCISES

EXERCISE 1: Objective 2

TITLE: PERSONALITY TYPES--AN OVERVIEW
TASK: Fill in the blanks

1. The ancient Greek physician Hippocrates assumed that the body has four
____ and used these as the basis for categorizing people into different
personality types.

2. According to Hippocrates' humor theory, _____, or a calm, apathetic temperament, is due to excess phlegm.
3. The _____, or a hot-headed temperament, is due to an excess of yellow bile.
4. The _____, or an optimistic temperament, is due to a predominance of blood.
5. And the _____, or a sad and depressed temperament, is due to too much black bile.
6. In more modern times, the nineteenth-century anthropologist, Lombroso, believed that he could judge personality from _____ features.
7. This "science" of Lombroso was called _____.
8. Recently, a more sophisticated type theory by Sheldon, related temperament to _____.

EXERCISE 2: Objective 2

TITLE: PERSONALITY TYPES--FOCUS ON SHELDON'S THEORY
TASK: Match letters to numbers

____1. The person with the soft and round physique tends to be jolly and sociable.
____2. The person with the long and skinny body tends to be restrained, fearful, introverted, and artistic.
____3. The person with the muscular body tends to be energetic and assertive.
____4. The temperament associated with the mesomorph.
____5. The temperament associated with the ectomorph.
____6. The temperament associated with the endomorph.

A. viscerotonic
B. somatatonic
C. cerebrotonic

EXERCISE 3: Objective 2

TITLE: TRAIT THEORIES--AN INTRODUCTION
TASK: Essays

1. In the general sense, what distinguishes traits from types?

2. Traits are labels--how may such labels be misused?

3. What is phrenology, and what was its fate?

EXERCISE 4: Objective 2

TITLE: FOCUS ON ALLPORT'S TRAITS AS ENTITIES
TASK: Match letters to numbers

____1. Situational traits (for example, being grouchy in the morning).
____2. The most global of traits (for example, the humanitarian).
____3. Unique traits that require the case-study approach (for example, verbal cynical aggression).

_____4. Traits that appear to some extent in everyone (for example, aggressiveness in the more general sense).

_____5. General traits that are not global (for example, being warm and outgoing).

A. cardinal traits
B. central traits
C. secondary traits
D. common traits
E. individual traits

EXERCISE 5: Objective 2

TITLE: FOCUS ON CATTELL'S TRAITS AS FACTORS
TASK: Fill in the blanks

1. Cattell based his theory on data obtained via the statistical procedure called _____.

2. In general, he obtained _____ (from life records usually supplied by other people).

3. Cattell also used _____ (from the subject's responses to question-naires).

4. Finally, he used _____ (from objective tests).

5. An example of one of these objective tests is Cattell's own _____.

6. His initial research resulted in a grouping of about 35 trait clusters characterizing overt behaviors. He called these _____ traits.

7. He considered these overt traits to be _____ or symptoms of personality--not the basic underlying personality itself.

8. Factor analysis of the surface traits produced 16 _____ traits-- or the building blocks of personality that served as the basis of the 16 PF personality test.

9. According to Cattell, these source traits stem from either _____,

10. . . . or they stem from _____ factors.

EXERCISE 6: Objective 2

TITLE: FOCUS ON EYSENCK'S TRAITS AS DIMENSIONS
TASK: Match letters to numbers

_____1. Eysenck's dimensions of personality.
_____2. His basic belief that personality traits are a function of learning.
_____3. Biological factors make some people easy or difficult to condition.
_____4. The statistical procedure he used to analyze data.
_____5. The instrument he used to obtain data for his analyses.
_____6. The combination of dimensions that leads to emotional behavior that is antisocial rather than anxiety related.
_____7. The dimension that leads to easy conditioning and, as a result, anxiety and depression.
_____8. The dimension that leads to difficult conditioning and, as a result, impulsive and unruly behavior.
_____9. The combination of dimensions that leads people to display intense emotions involving anxiety.

A. factor analysis
B. the Maudsley Personality Inventory
C. classical and instrumental conditioning
D. genetic-constitutional factors
E. introversion-extroversion, neuroticism, and psychoticism
F. introversion
G. extroversion
H. neurotic introversion
I. neurotic extroversion

EXERCISE 7: Objective 2

TITLE: MURRAY'S NEED THEORY
TASK: Fill in the blanks
1. Murray's dispositional theory concentrates on _____ or goals, rather than types or traits.
2. He postualtes 12 _____ human needs such as air, water, food, and sex.
3. He also postulated 27 secondary, or _____, needs such as achievement, dominance, autonomy, aggression, affiliation, and nurturance.
4. According to Murray, these needs combine with environmental influences called _____ to shape personality.
4. Regarding the needs, some are obvious, or _____, and can be measured by direct observation of how often, long, and intensively particular behaviors are engaged in.
6. But other needs are not so overt--instead, they are subtle or _____ (for example, expressing affection through romantic daydreams).
7. These subtle needs require indirect measurement via _____ type tests.
8. These tests are so named because the individual projects his or her personality on otherwise _____ stimuli.
9. The projective test developed by Murray is the _____.

EXERCISE 8: Objective 3

TITLE: OVERVIEW OF FREUD'S THEORY
TASK: Fill in the blanks

1. _____ theories assume that intrapsychic events and conflicts determine personality and personality development.
2. Freud's particular psychodynamic approach is called _____.
3. One assumption of Freud's theory is _____, the notion that behavior is not random but occurs because of intrapsychic causes.
4. A second assumption is that we are unaware of many ideas because they reside in the _____ portion of our minds.
5. We are aware only of those ideas in the _____ portion. . . .
6. . . . and there is also a _____ portion which consists of ideas capable of entering our awareness.
7. The third assumption is that of ongoing conflict between innate sexual and aggressive _____, or impulses and the realistic demands of society.
8. These assumptions all are incorporated into Freud's conceptualization of personality _____ (that is, id, ego, and superego),
9. . . . his ego _____ mechanisms (for example, repression),
10. . . . and his stages of _____.

EXERCISE 9: Objective 3

TITLE: FREUD'S PERSONALITY STRUCTURES--A CASE STUDY IN CONFLICT
TASK: Essay

1.   What is the main ongoing conflict between the id and superego?

2.   What is the role of the ego in resolving this conflict?

EXERCISE 10: Objective 3

TITLE: THE EGO DEFENSE MECHANISMS
TASK: Identification

1.   An unconscious hatred for your professor makes you feel uncomfortable in
     his or her presence, but you do not know why.
2.   If you hate your professor and you are aware of it, one strategy is
     to cover this up by telling the professor how wonderful today's lecture
     was.
3.   If school has gotten the best of you, one way out is to resort to
     childlike behavior--after all, when you were little, all your needs
     were taken care of.
4.   Did you hear about the worker who, after being fired by his boss, went
     home and yelled at his wife; she yelled at the kids; the kids kicked
     the family pet; and so on?
5.   For those of you who will become teachers someday, recognize that there
     will be students who, when they do poorly, will not blame themselves but,
     instead, the teacher who, after all, is boring and unreasonable and
     gives stupid tests.
6.   Some people like to stand on soap boxes and tell others how filthy and
     immoral they are for reading *Playboy* and *Playgirl* magazines. It's
     entirely possible that they are the ones with the filthy minds.
7.   Sometimes, when older people lose a mate, they go on acting as if this
     very important person were still alive--they cannot believe he or she
     is dead.
8.   I know this person who was fed up with being picked on by his boss--but
     he did not take it out on others. Instead he trained very hard and won
     the Peachtree Road Race.

EXERCISE 11: Objective 3

TITLE: STAGES OF PSYCHOSEXUAL DEVELOPMENT
TASK: Fill in the blanks

1.   The first stage of development is the _____ stage.
2.   The overindulged child faces the prospect of becoming _____ at this
     stage and developing habits such as overeating, smoking, and using
     "biting sarcasm."
3.   It is also possible for a person to _____, or return to this or other
     stages under stress.
4.   The second stage is the _____ stage, the critical feature of which is
     toilet training.
5.   Fixation at this second stage may result in the _____ pattern which is
     characterized by stinginess, obstinance, organization, and overconcern
     with cleanliness, and the like.

6. The major sexual conflicts occur in the _____ stage.
7. For the boy, the major conflict is the _____, which involves sexual feelings for his mother.
8. For the girl, the major conflict is the _____, which involves sexual feelings for her father.
9. Fearing the same-sexed parent, the boy develops _____ anxiety.
10. In comparison, the girl may develop _____ envy.
11. Freud felt that fixation at the phallic stage was responsible for aggression and sexual deviations such as _____.
12. Following the phallic stage, there is a dormant period characterized by a lack of interest in sex. This is called the _____.
13. Finally, after puberty comes the _____ stage, in which the person seeks to establish long-term sexual relationships.

EXERCISE 12: Objective 4

TITLE: EARLY VARIATIONS ON FREUD--FOCUS ON JUNG
TASK: Fill in the blanks

1. Carl Jung founded his own system of _____ psychology.
2. He argued that the _____ was a more general psychic force, not just for sex and aggression.
3. He also argued for a _____ function that harmonizes unconscious libidinal needs with real-world demands.
4. Regarding motivation, Jung proposed the _____ unconscious, consisting of what Freud called unconscious and preconscious.
5. He also proposed the _____ unconscious, which contains images and ideas shared by people from the beginning of time.
6. These images, or _____, predispose us to deal with the world in certain ways.
7. There were also archetypes representing the opposite sex in each individual. Thus, the feminine aspect of a male's personality was called the _____.
8. The masculine aspect of the female's personality was called the _____.
9. Jung used the label _____ to describe the development of personality traits.
10. For Jung, there were two types of people, _____.
11. Jung used four mental functions to describe people: _____.
12. Jung was the first to use _____ tests to measure personality.

EXERCISE 13: Objective 4

TITLE: EARLY VARIATIONS ON FREUD--FOCUS ON ADLER
TASK: Fill in the blanks

1. Adler rejected instinct theory and developed what he called _____.
2. The most important assumption of Adler's theory is that we begin life in a helpless, _____ position.
3. This helplessness creates in us a need, or a striving for _____.
4. The manner in which we strive represents our individual life _____.
5. Adler rejected the notion of unconscious conflicts and attributed maladaptive behavior to basic _____.

6. Adler used the _____ technique as his major method for assessing personality.
7. He searched through the person's early recollections for clues to his or her life style and also emphasized the _____ history.
8. Regarding the latter, Adler emphasized the importance of _____ order in shaping the life-style.

EXERCISE 14: Objective 4

TITLE: LATER CHANGES IN PSYCHOANALYSIS
TASK: Fill in the blanks

1. Interestingly, Freud's daughter Anna led a movement that became known as _____ psychology (or analysis).
2. This group, which included Erikson, Hartmann, and Kohut, suggested that the ego does not evolve entirely from the _____.
3. Indeed, the ego is seen as _____-free.
4. A second group, including Horney, Fromm, and Sullivan, emphasized _____-cultural influences.
5. For Horney, the main motivating force was _____ anxiety.
6. She identified ten _____ needs.
7. These needs constitute three attitudes, including movement toward, against, and _____ from other people.
8. Recalling the material in Chapter 8, Erikson called his stages of development _____ rather than psychosexual.
9. A more modern trend launched by psychiatrists Berne and Harris is called _____ analysis.
10. Emphasis here is on three ego states. Specifically, the parent corresponds to Freud's _____.
11. The adult corresponds to Freud's _____.
12. And the child corresponds to Freud's _____.

EXERCISE 15: Objective 5

TITLE: LERANING THEORIES
TASK: Essays

1. In general, what are the four common characteristics of learning theories?

2. How did Dollard and Miller integrate Freud's theory into a learning theory framework?

3. What was Skinner's reaction to Dollard's and Miller's efforts?

EXERCISE 16: Objective 5

TITLE: SOCIAL-LEARNING THEORIES
TASK: Fill in the blanks

1. The _____ learning theory approach emphasizes the role of cognition and imitation.
2. In Rotter's theory, behavior is dependent on a combination of what the person has come to _____ to happen . . .
3. and the _____ placed on the outcome.

4. Indeed, he has developed a locus-of-control scale to measure _____ expectancies.
5. For example, _____ work at their own pace, whereas . . .
6. _____ do better working at someone else's pace.
7. Bandura is best known for his work on _____ learning, or modeling.
8. The processes of observation and imitation are called _____ processes and include the acquisition of new responses, inhibition or disinhibition of already-learned responses, and facilitation or prompting of behavior.
9. Three important variables (cognitive, behavioral, and environmental) are seen in terms of _____ determinism.
10. However, in some situations, a person's self-_____, or learned expectation, may overcome an environmental obstacle.
11. Like Bandura, Mischel sees us as neither passive targets of _____ forces or wholly independent of these forces.
12. The important construct for Mischel is the person-situation _____.
13. For example, in Haney's, Banks's, and Zimbardo's _____ study, college students without a history of violence showed aggressive tendencies when they were put in the situation of being a guard.

EXERCISE 17: Objective 5

TITLE: LEARNING AND SOCIAL-LEARNING ASSESSMENT TOOLS
TASK: Essays

1. What distinguishes the learning approach to personality assessment from the dispositional and psychodynamic approaches?

2. What are the major types of assessment tools used by learning and social-learning theorists?

EXERCISE 18: Objective 6

TITLE: PHENOMENOLOGICAL THEORIES
TASK: Fill in the blanks

1. Phenomenologists base their theories on the individual's unique _____ of the world.
2. Many of the ideas of phenomenological theory come from humanistic and _____ philosophies (for example, Heidegger, Kierkegaard, Sartre, and Camus).
3. Rogers's self-theory uses an innate motive called self-_____.
4. For Rogers, the individual's direct experiences are called _____.
5. Rogers also sees the individual as searching for positive _____ from others in their reactions.
6. Rogers's ideal state occurs when there is _____ between organismic experiences and regard from others.
7. Incongruence leads to conditions of _____.
8. To prevent the loss of positive regard, the individual may _____ or misperceive reality (to reduce incongruity).
9. Perls is known for his writings on _____ therapy.
10. The object of this therapy is to get people to take _____ for their feelings.

11. The work of Rogers and Perls has led to the development of encounter and _____ groups.
12. Maslow, of course, is famous for his hierarchy of _____.
13. Self-actualization is impossible if we are overly concerned with our deficiency, or _____ needs.
14. For Maslow, it is the _____, or B-values that are the most important.
15. Moments of pure B-value are called _____ experiences.
16. In general, humanists are nontraditional in their assessment procedures, as evidenced by the Personal Orientation Inventory, which compares orientation with _____ versus _____.

EXERCISE 19

TITLE: KEY NAMES
TASK: Match letters to numbers.

_____1. Basic anxiety leads to neurotic needs
_____2. The person-situation interaction
_____3. Physiognomy (based on facial characteristics)
_____4. Phrenology (based on bumps in head)
_____5. Transactional analysis
_____6. Introversion, extroversion, neuroticism, and psychoticism
_____7. Personality structures, defenses, and psychosexual stages
_____8. Led ego psychology movement for the conflict-free ego
_____9. Hierarchy of needs
_____10. The four humors
_____11. Personal and collective unconscious
_____12. Experimental treatment of Freudian concepts
_____13. Internal versus external locus of control
_____14. Surface versus source of traits
_____15. Cardinal, central, and secondary traits
_____16. Congruence between self and others
_____17. The unique life-style for overcoming inferiority
_____18. Gestalt therapy--taking responsibility for feelings
_____19. Observation and vicarious processes
_____20. Functional analysis via operant conditioning
_____21. Psychogenic needs interact with the press
_____22. Relationship between physique and temperament

A.	Hippocrates	L.	A. Freud
B.	Lombroso	M.	Horney
C.	Sheldon	N.	Berne and Harris
D.	Gall and Spurzheim	O.	Dollard and Miller
E.	Allport	P.	Skinner
F.	Cattell	Q.	Rotter
G.	Eysenck	R.	Bandura
H.	Murray	S.	Mischel
I.	S. Freud	T.	Rogers
J.	Jung	U.	Perls
K.	Adler	V.	Maslow

MULTIPLE-CHOICE TESTS

SELF-TEST 1

1. Which of the following fields of study in psychology seems to encompass the broadest range of human capabilities and behaviors?
a. learning
b. personality
c. development
d. perception
   (page 334)

2. Which of the following is NOT one of the most basic assumptions of dispositional theories of personality?
a. there are a specific number of dispositions within each person
b. dispositions within a person are relatively stable in time
c. dispositions generalize across a variety of circumstances
d. knowing someone's dispositions allows you to predict his or her behavior

3. The early theorist who thought behavior could be predicted on the basis of a person's body fluids was:
a. Lombroso
b. Gall
C. Hippocrates
d. Sheldon
   (page 335)

4. If your body build were essentially "skin and bones," Sheldon would predict that you would most likely be
a. assertive and bold
b. jolly and outgoing
c. shy and scholarly
d. a little bit of each

5. Which of the following theoretical approaches to personality is most likely to result in stereotypes and prejudices?
a. dispositional
b. social-learning
c. phenomenological
d. psychodynamic
   (page 336)

6. According to Allport, only a few of us have the kind of global traits that tend to dictate our behavior in all types of situations. These traits are called:
a. cardinal
b. central
c. secondary
d. common
   (page 337)

7.   According to Cattell, some traits are overt and obvious. These traits are called _____.
a.   manifest
b.   latent
c.   surface
d.   source
     (page 339)

8.   According to Eysenck, introverts are those individuals who:
a.   are most difficult to condition and are thus likely to be impulsive and unruly
b.   are easiest to condition and thus are likely to be anxious and tense
c.   are most difficult to condition and thus are likely to be anxious and tense
d.   are easiest to condition and thus are likely to be impulsive and unruly
     (page 340)

9.   A major criticism of dispositional theories is that they:
a.   do not describe personality very well
b.   have generated little in the way of research
c.   do not explain how personality develops
d.   are written in such a way as to make prediction nearly impossible
     (page 341)

10. One of Freud's major assumptions was that human behavior does not occur randomly. This assumption is called:
a.   unconscious motivation
b.   psychic determinism
c.   pleasure principle
d.   instinct
     (page 341)

11. According to Freud, there is a constant intrapsychic conflict between our desires and our moral values. This conflict is therefore between:
a.   id and ego
b.   id and superego
c.   ego and superego
d.   id and libido
     (page 342)

12. Suppose that a bigoted individual started donating money to the groups that he or she did not like. Such an individual would be showing the defense mechanism called:
a.   reaction formation
b.   projection
c.   displacement
d.   denial
     (page 343)

13. Suppose that I took my pent-up intrapsychic energy and displaced it into something positive like teaching. If so, I would be showing which of the defense mechanisms?
a.   projection
b.   reaction formation
c.   regression
d.   sublimation
     (page 344)

14. Suppose that you have a friend who is supercompulsive and stingy. According to Freud, this friend:
a. is fixated at the oral stage
b. has regressed to the oral stage
c. is fixated at the anal stage
d. shows too much identification with mother
   (page 344)

15. According to Freud, the resolution of the Oedipal conflict is:
a. fixation at the phallic stage
b. repression of sexual desires, followed by identification with father
c. repression of sexual desires, followed by attraction to a suitable mate
d. hatred of mother
   (page 345)

16. For Jung, the transcendent function acted to:
a. allow material in the collective unconscious to move into the personal unconscious
b. modify archetypes into contemporary representations
c. bring unconscious material into consciousness
d. harmonize unconscious libidinal needs with the demands of the real world
   (page 346)

17. What Adler calls *life-style* is:
a. our unique personal unconscious
b. an expression of our neurotic needs
c. our way of achieving superiority
d. an expression of social interest
   (page 346)

18. With respect to Freud's psychoanalytic theory and the later variants by Jung, Anna Freud, Adler, Erikson, Horney, and so on:
a. all these theorists maintained Freud's notion of basic instincts of sex and aggression
b. the later theorists were more interested in aspects of healthy personality development
c. the later theorists discarded Freud's notion of unconscious processes as important to determining behavior
d. Freud emphasized the importance of social and cultural factors more than did his followers
   (page 347)

19. Basic anxiety is seen as the primary personality construct for:
a. Maslow
b. Adler
c. Erikson
d. Horney
   (page 347)

20. The theory of transactional analysis (TA) popularized in recent years by Eric Berne (for example, *Games People Play*) is considered a _____ theory of personality.
a. social-learning
b. phenomenological
c. psychodynamic
d. dispositional
   (page 348)

21. A major drawback to Freud's theory is that:
a.   it explained very little about personality
b.   it was much too descriptive
c.   it was much too behavioral
d.   it proposed concepts that were hard to measure and test
     (page 349)

22. The main difference among the various learning theories of personality
(for example, learning versus social learning) is:
a.   the type of learning process that is emphasized
b.   the assumption that behavior is measurable
c.   using the scientific method to evaluate hypotheses
d.   using heredity to explain behavior
     (page 349)

23. Suppose that you have a choice between a juicy steak and a two-pound
lobster, and you love both. According to Dollard and Miller, you have:
a.   an approach-approach conflict
b.   an approach-avoidance conflict
c.   no conflict at all
d.   an anxiety-producing situation
     (page 350)

24. The learning theorist who argues against the use of inferred concepts
such as drive is:
a.   Rotter
b.   Mischel
c.   Bandura
d.   Skinner
     (page 350)

25. According to Rotter, if you believe that events that happen to you are
beyond your control, you exhibit:
a.   an internal locus of control
b.   an external locus of control
c.   introversion
d.   extroversion
     (page 351)

26. For Bandura, the interaction of cognitive, environmental, and behavioral
variables is called:
a.   transcendent function
b.   reciprocal determinism
c.   conditions of worth
d.   vicarious process
     (page 354)

27. A major criticism of learning approaches to personality is:
a.   narrowness of approach
b.   too much emphasis on genetics
c.   insufficient data
d.   failure to consider cognitive processes
     (page 356)

28. According to Rogers, if positive regard occurs only when you do things that others approve of, you are:
a. acting out your organismic feelings
b. failing to take responsibility for your feelings and actions
c. operating under conditions of worth
d. in a dismal person-situation interaction
    (page 358)

29. According to Perls, if positive regard occurs only when you do things that others approve of, you are:
a. not taking responsibility for your feelings and actions
b. at the bottom of the hierarchy
c. not self-actualized
d. entirely external in your locus
    (page 359)

30. A major criticism of the phenomenological theories is that:
a. they are not sufficiently descriptive of behavior
b. they fail to consider conscious experience
c. they place too much emphasis on pessimistic ideas
d. they do not provide strong causal explanations
    (page 361)

SELF-TEST 2

1. In evaluating theories, such as theories of personality, adequacy of theory is judged on the basis of whether the theory:
a. is right or wrong
b. accounts for all instances of abnormal behavior
c. provides complete and testable accounts of behavior
d. is accepted by the majority of researchers in that field of study
    (page 335)

2. You are strong, brave, courageous, bold, and assertive! According to Sheldon's theory, you are most likely to be:
a. ectomorphic and somatotonic
b. mesomorphic and somatotonic
c. mesomorphic and cerebrotonic
d. endomorphic and viscerotonic
    (page 336)

3. Which of the following was essentially a trait rather than a type theory of personality?
a. phrenology
b. physiognomy
c. four humors
d. physique/temperament
    (page 337)

4. The procedure that has allowed modern trait theorists to produce efficient predictive models from the larger number of traits assigned to people is:
a. psychoanalysis
b. factor analysis
c. transcendent analysis
d. cluster analysis
    (page 339)

5.   Cattell's method of assessing the extent to which individuals manifested the various source traits was the:
a.   technique of word association
b.   TAT
c.   16 PF
d.   locus-of-control test
      (page 339)

6.   According to Murray, there are needs that we are not well aware of. These needs are referred to as:
a.   source
b.   secondary
c.   manifest
d.   latent
      (page 340)

7.   The strong suit of dispositional theory is:
a.   explanation of how the personality develops
b.   generation of the now-famous projective tests
c.   description and prediction
d.   laboratory experimentation
      (page 341)

8.   Which of the following is out of place?
a.   id
b.   pleasure principle
c.   superego
d.   libido
      (page 342)

9.   According to Freud, your conflict between obtaining something pleasurable but small now, versus obtaining something pleasurable but more substantial later on, is a conflict between:
a.   id and superego
b.   id and ego
c.   ego and superego
d.   id, ego, and superego
      (page 343)

10.   According to Freud, what was the result of the inadequate repression of id impulses?
a.   anxiety
b.   regression to an earlier stage
c.   a build-up of psychic energy
d.   occurrence of defense mechanisms
      (page 343)

11.   The individual who keeps pointing a finger at other people for engaging in immoral behavior, may actually be attributing his or her own desires to them. This is called:
a.   reaction formation
b.   displacement
c.   projection
d.   denial
      (page 344)

12. According to Freud, profound regression to the oral stage is likely to lead to:
a.   chain smoking
b.   compulsive neatness
c.   neurosis
d.   psychosis
     (page 344)

13. Which of the following is an incorrect match?
a.   Adler--superiority
b.   Jung--basic anxiety
c.   Horney--ten neurotic needs
d.   Berne--I'm OK, you're OK
     (page 346)

14. For Adler, behavior problems that arise through maladaptive life-styles were caused by:
a.   basic misconceptions about the world
b.   repressed id impulses
c.   basic anxiety
d.   intrapsychic conflicts
     (page 346)

15. The approach to personality that tends most to interpret behavior as indicative of pathology is:
a.   psychodynamic theory
b.   dispositional theory
c.   phenomenological theory
d.   learning theory
     (page 349)

16. According to Dollard and Miller, if you had a choice between volunteering for a duty that you wished to avoid or going to jail, your conflict would be:
a.   approach-avoidance
b.   existential
c.   avoidance-avoidance
d.   double avoidance-avoidance

17. Which of the following methods eliminates inferred concepts in the explanation of behavior?
a.   factor analysis
b.   psychoanalysis
c.   functional analysis
d.   reciprocal analysis
     (page 350)

18. Expectancy plays an important role in the development, maintenance, and alteration of behavior in the theory of:
a.   Skinner
b.   Rotter
c.   Bandura
d.   Dollard and Miller
     (page 351)

19. The locus-of-control scale measures:
a. source traits
b. introversion and extroversion
c. conditions of worth
d. internal versus external control
   (page 351)

20. Which of the following does not belong?
a. LOC
b. TAT
c. dream analysis
d. free association
   (page 351)

21. Vicarious processes involve:
a. intrapsychic conflicts
b. externally located stimuli
c. observation and imitation
d. self-efficacy
   (page 353)

22. A theorist who could be seen as occupying a middle ground between dispositional theorists such as Allport on the one hand and strict learning theorists such as Skinner on the other, is:
a. Freud
b. Rogers
c. Dollard
d. Mischel
   (page 355)

23. If you filled out an inventory that had you rank things that you liked in order of their liking, you would be filling out the:
a. behavioral sample
b. fear survey schedule
c. self-monitoring protocol
d. reinforcement survey schedule
   (page 356)

24. Which theorists are most likely to view unique behavior as abnormal or deviant?
a. learning
b. dispositional
c. phenomenological
d. social-learning
   (page 357)

25. The major construct in Rogers's self theory is:
a. basic anxiety
b. striving for superiority
c. tendency toward self-actualization
d. personal responsibility for behavior
   (page 358)

26. According to Rogers, distortions of reality are brought about by incongruity between:
a. organismic and self-experiences
b. conditions of worth versus lack of worth
c. B-values and D-needs
d. B-values and metaneeds
    (page 358)

27. According to Maslow, B-values lead to:
a. satisfaction of basic needs
b. positive self-regard
c. conditions of worth
d. peak experiences
    (page 359)

28. If you went to Rogers for help, he would likely assess your personality by using the:
a. MMPI
b. TAT
c. personal orientation inventory
d. internal versus external locus-of-control test
    (page 360)

29. Learning theory and phenomenological theory share a common criticism. Both are said to:
a. be too narrow
b. place too much emphasis on feelings
c. be too cognitively oriented
d. place too much concern on the development of personality
    (page 360)

30. An emphasis on experiential evidence is characteristic of which kind of theory?
a. dispositional
b. psychodynamic
c. learning
d. phenomenological
    (page 361)

WHAT DOES IT MEAN?

OBJECTIVES

1. To what extent can the various types of personality theory predict when individuals are likely to do violence to themselves or to others?
2. To what extent can tendencies to illness and disease be predicted from knowledge of an individual's personality?
3. What role do formal and informal notions of personality play in selecting candidates for jobs?
4. How is personality assessment used in the courtroom for jury selection?
5. How have personality theories contributed to the understanding of important developmental relationships, beginning with birth and extending into adulthood?
6. How has psychoanalytic theory contributed to improving and understanding competitive performance?

1. Approximately how many Americans kill themselves each year?
a. 15,000
b. 25,000
c. 50,000
d. 80,000
    (page 363)

2. MMPI data on individuals who have attempted suicide show:
a. no clear relationships
b. deviance and suicide are related
c. those who succeed at suicide tend to be paranoid
d. those who thought about suicide were less deviant than those who
    attempted suicide
    (page 363)

3. With respect to the relationship between aging and suicide:
a. the suicide rate among women is highest during adolescence
b. elderly men are more likely to commit suicide than elderly women are
c. suicide and age are directly (positively) related
d. paranoia is associated with suicide in adolescence
    (page 364)

4. With respect to the relationship between crime and personality:
a. no clear criminal personality has been identified
b. projective tests are more useful in identifying criminals than are
    objective tests
c. objective tests such as the MMPI are more useful than are projective
    tests such as the Rorschach in identifying violent from nonviolent
    criminals
d. highly abnormal responses on the TAT predict criminal behavior
    (page 364)

5. As with suicide, it is difficult to develop a criminal personality
profile because:
a. of unknown situational factors
b. criminals hide their true personality from researchers
c. criminals are usually perfectly normal
d. our society has yet to define clearly what a criminal is

6. According to hypothesized relationships between patient attitude and
psychosomatic illness, the individual who feels deprived of what is due him
or her and wants to get even is likely to develop:
a. ulcers
b. hypertension
c. asthma
d. colitis
    (page 365)

7. According to hypothesized relationships between patient attitude and
psychosomatic illness, the individual who feels frustrated and can do nothing
about it except take it out on himself or herself is likely to develop:
a. ulcers
b. eczema
c. backache
d. asthma
    (page 365)

8. According to Rosenman and others, the competitive, impatient, hard-driving individual, called Type A:
a. is likely to develop coronary heart disease
b. is likely to have a heart attack
c. works hard for a time and then relaxes totally
d. rarely has headaches
    (page 365)

9. Some recent evidence suggests that depression and repression may be linked to:
a. coronary heart disease
b. asthma
c. cancer
d. hypertension
    (page 367)

10. Job interviewers are prone to rely on _____ in selecting candidates for positions.
a. random judgments
b. stereotypes
c. psychodynamic approaches
d. their previous experience
    (page 367)

11. In selecting individuals for juries, lawyers seem to be guided most by _____ theories of personality.
a. dispositional
b. psychodynamic
c. learning
d. phenomenological
    (page 369)

12. Which type of personality theory has provided the basic rationale for hospitals allowing parents and infants to spend large amounts of time together, even when there have been complications at birth?
a. dispositional
b. psychodynamic
c. learning
d. phenomenological
    (page 367)

13. Courses on assertiveness training, stress management, social skills, and the like are based on a _____ approach to personality.
a. dispositional
b. psychodynamic
c. learning
d. phenomenological
    (page 371)

14. The practical goal of Parent Effectiveness Training is to teach parents a strategy of interacting with their children so that:
a. every parent is a winner
b. every child is a winner
c. parents and children are winners 50 percent of the time
d. neither parent nor child is a loser
    (page 371)

15. For which of the following has psychoanalytic theory prompted a method of treatment?
a. improving athletic performance
b. improving social skills
c. improving personal assertiveness
d. improving jury selection
    (page 373)

ANSWER KEY

EXERCISES

Exercise 1

1. humors
2. phlegmatic
3. choleric
4. sanguine

5. melancholic
6. facial
7. physiognomy
8. physique (or body type)

Exercise 2

1. A   2. C   3. B   4. B   5. C   6. A

Exercise 3

1. It is characteristic of type theories that they attempt to categorize the individual in simplistic ways, thus de-emphasizing individual uniqueness and interpersonal diversity. Assignment of traits to individuals recognizes the complexities of human behavior and attempts to deal with the whole individual by combining many characteristics, as in a jigsaw puzzle.

2. It is important to recognize that a label merely describes behavior. Thus, it is circular to use a trait as an explanation. For example, if a person who works hard is labeled as compulsive, it is circular then to say she works hard because she is compulsive.

3. From a historical perspective, phrenology was the first well-known trait theory. Developed by Gall and his follower Spurzheim, the belief was that 37 different traits were associated with different areas of the brain and that by examining the skull for bumps and depressions, these traits could be assessed. This approach has long since been discredited.

Exercise 4

1. C   2. A   3. E   4. D   5. B

Exercise 5

1. factor analysis
2. L-data
3. Q-data
4. T-data
6. 16PF

6. surface
7. manifestations
8. source
9. environmental-mold
10. constitutional

230

Exercise 6

1. E   5. B
2. C   6. I
3. D   7. F
4. A   8. G
5. H

Exercise 7

1. needs   6. latent
2. primary   7. projective
3. psychogenic   8. neutral
4. press   9. TAT
5. manifest

Exercise 8

1. psychodynamic   6. preconscious
2. psychoanalysis   7. instincts
3. psychic determinism   8. structure
4. unconscious   9. defense
5. conscious   10. development

Exercise 9

1. The id contains sexual and aggressive psychic energy (or libido) from
    the point of birth. If the id had its way, these impulses would be
    directly and immediately gratified (that is, the pleasure principle).
    The superego is sort of a conscience containing morals from family and
    society. Thus, it condemns the id, and there is no way of directly
    releasing psychic energy in a way satisfactory to the superego.

2. The ego operates on the reality principle--realistically, psychic
    energy must be released to maintain physical health, but in order to
    do so, both the id and the superego must be satisfied. Thus, using its
    defense mechanisms, the ego represses and/or alters the id impulses,
    and this allows for energy release in a way acceptable to the superego.
    Thus, the ego protects the organism from bodily harm, from becoming
    aware of the id impulses, and from undue condemnation by the superego.

Exercise 10

1. repression   5. rationalization
2. reaction formation 6. projection
3. regression   7. denial
4. displacement   8. sublimation

Exercise 11

1. oral   8. Electra complex
2. fixated   9. castration
3. regress   10. penis
4. anal   11. exhibitionism
5. anal-retentive   12. latency period
6. phallic   13. genital
7. Oedipal complex

Exercise 12

1. analytic
2. libido
3. transcendent
4. personal
5. collective
6. archetypes
7. anima
8. animus
9. individuation
10. introverts and extroverts
11. feeling, thinking, sensing, intuiting
12. word association

Exercise 13

1. individual
2. inferior
3. superiority
4. style
5. misconceptions
6. interview
7. family
8. birth

Exercise 14

1. ego
2. id
3. conflict
4. social
5. basic
6. neurotic
7. away
8. psychosocial
9. transactional
10. superego
11. ego
12. id

Exercise 15

1. First, learning theorists assume that the content of personality is measurable. Second, the emphasis is on environmental as opposed to genetic-biological causes. Third, learning theorists attend to experimental research in both human and nonhuman organisms. And finally, they use scientific methods rather than personality-change techniques to evaluate hypotheses.

2. Dollard and Miller turned Freud's intrapsychic events into researchable phenomena. They assumed the existence of primary and secondary (or learned) needs and the drive (or motivation) to reduce those needs. Thus, instead of having anxiety induced by conflict between personality structures (that is, id versus superego), there is conflict between opposing needs and drives (for example, approach-approach, approach-avoidance, avoidance-avoidance, and double approach-avoidance).

3. Although Skinner would approve the elimination of intrapsychic events and structures, he would still argue against the use of terms such as *anxiety*, *drive*, and *conflict* because they represent inferred constructs that are unnecessary in order to understand learning and behavior. Instead, Skinner favors a functional analysis, which explains behavior according to its antecedent conditions and environmental consequences. For example, aggressive behavior occurs not because of some innate or learned drive but because aggressive behavior has been rewarded in the past in similar situations.

Exercise 16

1. social
2. expects
3. values
4. generalized
5. internals
6. externals
7. observational
8. vicarious
9. reciprocal
10. efficacy
11. environmental
12. interaction
13. prisoner

Exercise 17

1. The dispositional and psychodynamic theorists view responses to various objective and projective tests as signs of underlying personality traits and characteristics. The learning theorists do not seek these underlying constructs, rather, they view personality and behavior as one and the same. Thus, a response to (for example) a Rorschach card is merely a sample of the individual's behavior, rather than a sign of something beneath the surface. In general, assessment focuses on how the person behaves and the circumstances that influence that behavior.

2. In general, paper and pencil measures used by learning theorists tend to be direct and straightforward (for example, the year survey schedule and the reinforcement survey schedule). There is also paper and pencil assessment of cognitive factors by the social-learning theorists (for example, the locus-of-control scale). In addition, learning and social-learning theorists ask their patients to keep tract of their own behavior (that is, self-monitoring), and they also use systematic observations of behavior by personnel specifically trained to do so. Regardless of the technique, the goal is to develop precise statements regarding behavior.

Exercise 18

1. perception
2. existential
3. actualization
4. organismic
5. regard
6. congruence
7. worth
8. distort
9. Gestalt
10. responsibility
11. sensitivity
12. needs
13. D
14. metaneeds
15. peak
16. past/present

Exercise 19

1. M
2. S
3. B
4. D
5. n
6. G
7. I
8. L
9. V
10. A
11. J
12. O
13. Q
14. F
15. E
16. T
17. K
18. U
19. R
20. P
21. H
22. C

MULTIPLE-CHOICE

Self-Test 1

1. b
2. a
3. c
4. c
5. a
6. a
7. c
8. b
9. c
10. b
11. b
12. a
13. d
14. c
15. b
16. d
17. c
18. b
19. d
20. c
21. d
22. a
23. a
24. d
25. b
26. b
27. a
28. c
29. a
30. d

Self-Test 2

1.	c	6.	d	11.	c	16.	c	21.	c	26.	a
2.	b	7.	c	12.	d	17.	c	22.	d	27.	d
3.	a	8.	c	13.	b	18.	b	23.	d	28.	c
4.	b	9.	b	14.	a	19.	d	24.	b	29.	a
5.	c	10.	a	15.	a	20.	a	25.	c	30.	d

WHAT DOES IT MEAN?

Self-Test

1.	b	4.	a	7.	b	10.	b	13.	c
2.	a	5.	a	8.	a	11.	a	14.	d
3.	b	6.	a	9.	c	12.	b	15.	a

10 Social Psychology

OBJECTIVES

1. What is the focus of social psychology, and how does the dual emphasis on social knowledge and motivation serve this focus?
2. What kinds of inferences are made from social schemata, and what are the three theories that have been proposed to explain these inferences?
3. What three factors influence attitude change, what factors affect resistance to persuasion, and why is it difficult to predict behavior from attitudes?
4. What is an attribution, and how does the process of attribution vary among internal and external factors?
5. What are the three principles related to interpersonal attraction generally, and what two theories have been used to account for enduring relationships?
6. What are the three roles of self in social behavior?
7. When are we likely to use others as a basis of self-evaluation, and whom are we likely to choose?
8. How does the mere presence of others facilitate or inhibit our behavior in social and/or group situations?
9. What is the basis for conformity in group and everyday situations, and under what conditions does conformity lead to acts that the individual would otherwise not commit?
10. How do group processes affect decision making, bargaining and negotiation, and conflict generation and resolution?

SYNOPSIS

Social psychology focuses on the behavior of people in groups and on how people are affected by social experiences. The two major parameters in social psychological research are knowledge and motivation. Knowledge is received through verbal and nonverbal transmission and is assumed to be represented in our memories as schemata. Regarding motivation, it is assumed that social needs such as approval provide incentives for us to seek positively valued outcomes and to avoid negatively valued outcomes.

Schemata are filters through which we represent social information and, therefore, from which we make inferences about persons and events. Theories of social schemata are based on the consistency principle. For example, in Heider's theory, a balance must be struck between our like or dislike for an individual and that individual's like or dislike for an object or event. In Festinger's theory, it is assumed that an imbalance (or dissonance) motivates us to rationalize and, hence, promote balance (or consonance).

The attempt to change attitudes is affected by the communicator, the communication, and situational variables. The communicator varies in credibility (expertness) and trustworthiness (prestige). The communication varies in its position relative to the recipient's position and the degree of distraction inherent in its content-relevant features. Finally, the situation also varies in its distracting factors and may or may not contain forewarnings. According to McGuire, resistance to persuasion is enhanced by acquiring knowledge of the counter arguments and practicing using them. In general, an attitude does not automatically translate into consistent behaviors. The important factors in the relationship between attitude and behaviors are attitude strength, saliency, and specificity.

Attribution is a process in which we infer causes of events and behaviors. These causes may be internal (that is, personal) or external (that is, situational). Interestingly, our attributions are biased by the desirability or undesirability of the outcome. Self-attributions tend to be personal in positive outcomes and situational in negative outcomes. Conversely, attributions regarding others tend to be situational in positive outcomes and personal in negative outcomes.

Interpersonal attraction, at least initially, is influenced by similarity (for example, of attitudes, looks), attractiveness, and proximity. Two theories have been advanced to account for more enduring, long-term relationships. One of these, social-exchange theory, views the successful relationship as involving rewards over and above the costs for both parties. Equity theory, on the other hand, views the relationship in terms of justice. That is, there is a successful relationship when the two parties share equally in the rewards and the responsibilities, or costs.

The self plays a very important role in social behavior, in three ways. First, we use self-schemata as a basis for organizing and interpreting information about others. Second, the act of thinking about ourselves (that is, self-consciousness) influences us to act in socially responsible ways. Finally, we are motivated to maintain positive self-esteem, and often in order to do so, we have to distort or discredit negative inputs.

There are many ways in which other people influence our cognitions and behaviors. Regarding cognitions, self-evaluations depend to a large extent on when and with whom we compare ourselves. We are likely to compare ourselves with others when a situation is new and/or ambiguous. That is, we need some standard for determining how we should feel about ourselves. In choosing the model for comparison, it is important to pick people who are similar to us on the dimension that is creating the need for comparison.

The mere presence of others may facilitate or inhibit our behavior in social and/or group situations. For example, the evidence suggests that the presence of others facilitates performance on simple tasks but inhibits it on complex tasks (compare the Yerkes-Dodson law). In group situations, the failure to register the individual's contribution may lead the individual to slacken, or loaf. Finally, given this loss of identity in conjunction with violations of laws and/or social norms, the resulting deindividuation may result in acts of violence (for example, the Stanford prisoner study).

Conformity is defined as a tendency to adopt the values, attitudes, and behaviors shared by other members of the group. This may be done for informational value (that is, the opinions of others may be preceived as being correct) or normative influence (that is, the belief that social approval is contingent upon holding the majority view). This is different from the small compromises we tend to make in everyday situations, which is more a matter of social etiquette. Under some conditions (for example, Milgram's shock study), it is possible to comply with others' expectations and, as a result, commit acts that are clearly immoral.

Finally, group judgments are clearly different from those made by individuals in groups. For example, in decision making, it is often the case that the group judgment is more extreme than the simple average of individual judgments. In bargaining situations (for example, prisoner's dilemma), the nature of the bargain often depends on whether the bargainers are instructed to be cooperative, competitive, or individualistic. In coalition simulations, there is a trade-off between the desire to win and what needs to be given up in order to form a majority coalition. Finally, in groups in general, if there is strong intragroup identification, there will be a tendency toward strong intergroup hostility (for example, the robber's cave study). The best way to resolve such intergroup conflict appears to be to create goals common to both groups.

KEY WORDS AND PHRASES

OBJECTIVE 1

social psychology
social knowledge
social motivation

OBJECTIVE 2

social schemata
inferences
self-fulfilling prophecy
the halo effect
positivity bias
stereotypes
consistency principle
cognitive balance theory
cognitive dissonance theory
rationalization

OBJECTIVE 3

attitude information and change
communicator, communication, and situation
credibility and trustworthiness
stated beliefs versus true beliefs
persuasiveness
discrepancy between communication and recipient
stress reduction
counterarguing
derogating the source
distraction by content-relevant features
fear arousal
coping versus noncoping
low versus moderate versus high distraction
forewarning
high versus low commitment
knowledge and practice
inoculation
attitude versus behavior
attitude strength, saliency, and specificity

OBJECTIVE 4

attributions
internal attributions
external attributions
stability of attributions
social desirability and undesirability
hedonic relevance
hedonic bias

OBJECTIVE 5

interpersonal attraction
similarity principle
attractiveness principle
proximity principle
social-exchange theory
rewards versus costs
reciprocity
equity theory
initial versus stable attraction

OBJECTIVE 6

self-schemata
false consensus bias
self-consciousness (awareness)
social responsibility
self-esteem (image)

OBJECTIVE 7

using others as a basis for self-evaluation
when to compare versus with whom to compare
need for affiliation
novel and/or ambiguous situations

OBJECTIVE 8

the presence of others
social facilitation and inhibition
Yerkes-Dodson law
simple versus complex tasks
social loafing
loss of self-identity
deindividuation
violation of law and/or social norms

OBJECTIVE 9

conformity
informational value
normative influence
social etiquette
compliance and immoral behavior

OBJECTIVE 10

group decisions
group polarization effect
risk taking
bargaining, negotiations, and coalitions
prisoner's dilemma
zero-sum games
non-zero-sum games
cooperative versus competitive versus individualistic instructions
presence versus absence of threat
intragroup identification
intergroup conflict
conflict resolution

EXERCISES

EXERCISE 1: Objective 2

TITLE: AN OVERVIEW OF SOCIAL SCHEMATA
TASK: Fill in the blanks

1. Schemata organize information about people and events and thus allow us
    to make _____ regarding what we do not know.
2. Often people modify their own behavior to conform with the expectations
    of others. This is known as _____.
3. If we assume that good-looking people do everything well, and vice versa,
    this illustrates the _____ effect.
4. In making evaluations, the tendency to give people the benefit of the
    doubt is termed the _____ bias.
5. _____ are social schemata applied to a whole class of people.
6. A prominent feature in theories of social schemata is the _____
    principle.
7. In Heider's cognitive balance theory, it is assumed that people prefer
    consistency in the pattern of their _____.
8. In Festinger's theory, cognitive dissonance will promote _____
    designed to make our decisions consonant.

EXERCISE 2: Objective 2

TITLE: FOCUS ON WEIDER'S COGNITIVE BALANCE THEORY
TASK: For each of the following examples,

        P = Peter
        O = Oscar
        X = Exercising

    How would you interpret the following four triangles.

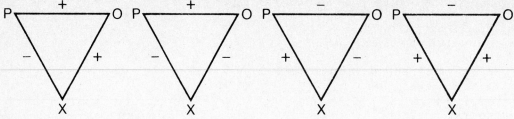

EXERCISE 3: Objective 2

TITLE: FESTINGER'S COGNITIVE DISSONANCE THEORY
TASK: Essay

Using Festinger's theory, explain how two pledges to a fraternity will react if one is given a mild initiation and the other is given a rather severe one (which one will like the fraternity better?)

EXERCISE 4: Objective 3

TITLE: ATTITUDE CHANGE--AN OVERVIEW
TASK: Fill in the blanks

1. The first important factors in attitude change are _____ variables.
2. _____ refers to the communicator's perceived expertness.
3. Communicators with high prestige are perceived as being more _____.
4. When the communicator has high prestige, people are more inclined to listen and less inclined to _____.
5. Some people report opinions similar to those of high-prestige sources simply to gain social _____. Thus, the report of belief change does not necessarily imply the true belief change.
6. People will counterargue if they perceive the communicator as trying to be _____.
7. Apart from communicator variables, a second important factor in attitude change is the _____ itself.
8. With the respect to the communication itself, the most important factor is the _____ between the position of the message and the position of the recipient.
9. Large discrepancy makes attitude change difficult and makes it easier to derogate and reject the _____.
10. Derogation becomes easier than attitude change as a means of _____ reduction.
11. Additionally, it is possible that the content-relevant features of a communication will induce _____.
12. This is particularly true with _____-arousing messages in which the recipient feels he or she cannot cope with the danger.
13. A third important factor in attitude change is the _____.
14. It is best to have conditions of _____ distraction. This allows for comprehension but prevents careful thinking.
15. Forewarn the individual prevents attitude change when the individual has high _____ to his or her position.

EXERCISE 6: Objective 3

TITLE: ATTITUDES--ADDITIONAL CONSIDERATIONS
TASK: Essays

1. According to McGuire, what are the two important factors in resisting persuasion, and how can they be effectively used?

2. What are the three factors that determine the extent to which we can or cannot predict behavior from attitudes?

EXERCISE 6: Objective 4

TITLE: ATTRIBUTION
TASK: Fill in the blanks

1. _____ serve as the basis for explaining both our own behavior and the behavior of others.
2. According to cognitive balance theory, people have a need to make the world as predictable and _____ as possible.
3. Attributions fulfill this need because they are statements of probable _____ of an event.
4. When the cause is attributed to the person, the attribution is said to be _____ or personal.
5. When the cause is attributed to an environmental factor, the attribution is said to be _____ or situational.
6. If the inferred cause is perceived to be _____, then we can expect an event or behavior to recur.
7. In general, socially _____ behaviors carry more weight in our attributions than do socially _____ behaviors.
8. More weight is also given when a person's behavior is _____ relevant to us (that is, high reward and low cost).
9. If the outcome is desirable, self-attributions will be attributed to _____ causes, whereas attributions regarding others will be attributed to _____ causes.
10. Conversely, given an undesirable outcome, self-attributions tend to involve _____ causes, whereas attributions regarding others tend to involve _____ causes.
11. The phenomenon operative in the two previous questions is termed hedonic _____.

EXERCISE 7: Objective 5

TITLE: INTERPERSONAL ATTRACTION--PRINCIPLES
TASK: Match letters to numbers

____1. There are exceptions to this rule--occasionally, opposites do attract, as when the dominant and submissive types serve each other's needs.
____2. In our society, there tends to be an implicit assumption that what is beautiful is good.
____3. We tend to like those people who share our attitudes and beliefs (that is, as in cognitive balance theory).
____4. Have you ever noticed that in a housing complex, the individuals closest to the mailboxes tend to have the most friends?

241

_____ 5. This is like the positive halo effect.
_____ 6. The basis of this principle is that we tend to interact with people quite frequently.

A. similarity principle
B. attractiveness principle
C. proximity principle

EXERCISE 8: Objective 5

TITLE: INTERPERSONAL ATTRACTION--THEORIES
TASK: Essay

The principles described in the last exercise tend to apply more to initial attraction than to enduring relationships. With respect to the latter, what are the important features of social-exchange theory and equity theory?

EXERCISE 9: Objective 6

TITLE: THE ROLE OF SELF IN SOCIAL BEHAVIOR
TASK: Fill in the blanks

1. There are three ways in which self affects social behavior. The first of these involves _____, which help us organize and retrieve information.
2. We often use information about _____ to make inferences and predictions about the behavior of others.
3. For example, we are more likely to remember information about others if we are stimulated to think about _____.
4. We often use our own opinion on a topic to judge whether or not the opinions of others (on the same topic) are _____.
5. Often, we use our own decisions to predict what others will do. This may lead to false _____ bias.
6. The second effect on social behavior concerns the degree to which we think about ourselves. This phenomenon is termed self-_____ (or self-awareness).
7. In general, a high degree of self-awareness makes us more sensitive to the consequences of our behavior. This often produces behavior that is more _____ responsible.
8. The third and final factor affecting social behavior is self-_____ or self-image.
9. In general, we are _____ to maintain a positive self-image.
10. Indeed, given negative input, we may _____ or discredit it.

EXERCISE 10: Objective 7

TITLE: USING OTHERS AS A BASIS FOR SELF-EVALUATION
TASK: Essays

1. In Schacter's experiment, why would the severe-shock subjects be more apt to choose to wait with other subjects than the mild-shock subjects would?

2. What constitutes a good model with whom to compare yourself?

EXERCISE 11:   Objective 8

TITLE: THE PRESENCE OF OTHERS
TASK: Match letters to numbers

A.   social facilitation
B.   social loafing
C.   deindividuation

_____1.   This is a form of social inhibition that occurs when the individual
          believes his or her contribution cannot be measured.
_____2.   This is more likely to occur when others are present and the task
          is simple and well learned rather than complex and not well learned.
_____3.   This follows from the Yerkes-Dodson law.
_____4.   This is a potentiation of behavior, but the outcome is undesirable
          behavior.
_____5.   The more that are present, the less will be the intensity of the
          individual cheer.
_____6.   The activity in question is likely given the loss of self-identity.
          The activity violates law and/or norms (as in the shocking of victims
          of the brutality of guards).

EXERCISE 12:   Objective 9

TITLE: CONFORMITY
TASK: Fill in the blanks

1.   _____ is defined as the tendency to adopt the values, attitudes, and
     behaviors shared by other members of the group.
2.   One basis for conforming is _____--that is, the majority view may be
     perceived as being more correct.
3.   A second basis is _____--that is, we may feel that social approval is
     contingent upon holding the majority opinion.
4.   Conformity is typically _____ when the individual feels he or she is
     the only deviant.
5.   However, conformity is reduced when there is(are) at least _____
     other deviant(s).
6.   The implication is that conformity leads to the adoption of group norms
     that _____ members find socially desirable.
7.   In everyday situations, particularly when meeting new people, we tend to
     make compromises. However, these compromises are viewed in terms of
     social _____.
8.   Nevertheless, the tendency to _____ with expectations of others can
     be strong and can lead us to commit acts we would otherwise find
     atrocious (for example, B5, Milgram's shock study).

EXERCISE 13:   Objectives 8 and 9

TITLE: SOCIAL INFLUENCE AND IMMORAL BEHAVIOR
TASK: Essay

     Looking carefully at Zimbardo's Stanford prisoner study and Milgram's
obedience study, can you make parallels to immoral behaviors that you have
witnessed or that you have read about?

EXERCISE 14: Objective 10

TITLE: DECISION MAKING, BARGAINING, AND CONFLICT
TASK: Essays

1. What is the group polarization effect, and what hypotheses have been proposed to account for it?

2. What are the implications of the prisoner's dilemma game for bargaining and negotiation?

3. How is simulation used to study bargaining and coalition?

4. What are the implications of the robber's cave study for conflict generation and conflict resolution?

EXERCISE 15

TITLE: KEY NAMES
TASK: Match letters to numbers

A. Dion, Berschield, and Walster
B. Heider
C. Festinger
D. Hovland and Janis
E. Kelman
F. McGuire
G. Snyder and Swann
H. Byrne
I. Landy and Sigall
J. Thibaut and Kelley

K. Aronson
L. Schacter
M. Zajonc
N. Bond and Titus
O. Zimbardo
P. Asch
Q. Milgram
R. Burnstein and Vinokor
S. Deutsch
T. Sherif and colleagues

_____ 1. The Stanford prisoner study
_____ 2. Information-processing approach to resisting persuasion
_____ 3. Attractiveness and the positive halo effect
_____ 4. Robber's cave study
_____ 5. Expressed versus true belief change
_____ 6. Conformity is reduced by only a single deviant
_____ 7. Social-exchange theory
_____ 8. Application of social exchange to interpersonal attraction
_____ 9. Yerkes-Dodson law and social facilitation/inhibition
_____ 10. Cognitive dissonance theory
_____ 11. Cognitive balance theory
_____ 12. Compliance in administering electric shock
_____ 13. Threat of electric shock and affiliation
_____ 14. Similarity principle and interpersonal attraction
_____ 15. Group discussion viewed as a persuasive situation
_____ 16. Attractiveness principle and interpersonal attraction
_____ 17. The three-component attitude change model
_____ 18. Review of literature relating to Zajonc's predictions
_____ 19. Effect of instructions on prisoner's dilemma
_____ 20. Attitude availability and behavioral predictions

MULTIPLE-CHOICE TESTS

SELF-TEST 1

1. The two fundamental concepts that determine much of social behavior are:
a. self-concept and self-attraction
b. social knowledge and social motivation
c. need for achievement and need for affiliation
d. approval and attraction
(page 375)

2. Need for social approval is an example of:
a. a social motive
b. social knowledge
c. a schema
d. a stereotype
(page 376)

3. If an inference based on a schema is incorrect, the behavior of another person may nonetheless match the inference. This would be an instance of:
a. a self-fulfilling prophecy
b. a social stereotype
c. a person trying to gain social approval
d. a person maintaining self-esteem
(page 377)

4. A halo effect occurs when:
a. prejudice is absent
b. there is a need for social approval
c. a person's characteristics are based on a previous global judgment
d. attractive but not unattractive persons are rated by others
(page 377)

5. Stereotypes are generally thought to be undesirable because:
a. they always convey inaccurate information about individuals
b. they are based on information (social knowledge) appropriate only to groups
c. they tend to be negative examples of social knowledge
d. they tend to contribute to prejudice and discrimination
(page 378)

6. Theories of social attitudes and interpersonal attraction are based on:
a. motivational concepts
b. the consistency principle
c. the halo effect
d. the self-concept schema
(page 379)

7. Which of the following is NOT true with respect to attitudes?
a. they are a type of schema
b. they help determine our behavior
c. they contain a strong evaluative component
d. they are unlearned
(page 379)

8. If George likes Mary, what will it take to establish cognitive imbalance?
a. Mary's liking of George
b. Mary's disliking of George
c. Mary's dislike of sex
d. Mary's liking of all of George's friends
    (page 379)

9. According to Heider's balance theory, when imbalance exists:
a. appetitive behavior will decrease
b. relationships will be terminated
c. a motivational state will be present
d. more than two people are involved in the equation
    (page 380)

10. According to Festinger, poor performance by a person who has a high
opinion of his or her own abilities is likely to result in:
a. rationalization
b. depression
c. acute anxiety
d. the self-fulfilling prophecy
    (page 380)

11. Which of the following was NOT one of the three elements that Hoveland
and Janis incorporated into their model of attitude formation and change?
a. a communicator who is motivated to convince others of his or her
    position
b. whether the communication was designed to induce an attitude change in
    the direction of the communicator's position
c. situational variables such as distraction
d. the communicator's personal characteristics (race, sex, age, and so on)
    (page 382)

12. Which of the following is a communicator variable in a persuasive
communication?
a. distraction
b. fear
c. inoculation
d. speaker's credibility
    (page 382)

13. Which of the following is a situational variable in a persuasive
communication?
a. distractions
b. fear
c. inoculation
d. speaker's credibility
    (page 383)

14. According to McGuire's research on the effects of persuasion on changing
attitudes:
a. previous arguments against a held belief increase resistance to
    persuasion
b. experience with arguments against a held belief decreases resistance to
    persuasion

246

c.   familiarity with reasons favoring one's beliefs increases resistance to persuasion
d.   it is necessary that previous arguments against the attitude be similar to the later arguments for resistance to persuasion to be increased
     (page 384)

15. With respect to the relationship between attitudes and behavior, it has been found that:
a.   attitudes toward persons and objects are excellent predictors of behavior toward that person or object
b.   attitudes toward persons and objects are not reliable predictors of behavior toward that person or object
c.   behavior tends to lead to attitude formation
d.   attitudes toward objects are correlated with behavior, but attitudes toward persons are not
     (page 385)

16. I attribute my failures to things like bad weather and bad luck and so on, I am appealing to:
a.   internal causes
b.   external causes
c.   reciprocating factors
d.   deindividuation
     (page 386)

17. An example of attribution of internal causation to yourself for good works and others for failures is:
a.   bystander apathy
b.   social facilitation
c.   hedonic bias
d.   the group polarization effect
     (page 386)

18. It seems to be generally true that we weight _____ the greatest when we judge another's personality.
a.   undesirable behaviors
b.   desirable behaviors
c.   desirable attitudes
d.   undesirable attitudes
     (page 387)

19. In regard to interpersonal attraction, it is generally true that:
a.   opposites attract
b.   similars attract
c.   there is a basic inequity
d.   no systematic relationships can be found
     (page 388)

20. According to Berscheid, Dion, and Walster, perhaps the most important determinant of success in people's lives is:
a.   the person whom they marry
b.   the environment in which they are raised
c.   their intelligence
d.   their physical attractiveness
     (page 389)

21. If I give George tickets to an important hockey play-off series, he is likely to think that he has to do something nice for me. This is an example that would be predicted by the theory of:
a. attribution
b. consensus
c. equity
d. reciprocity
   (page 391)

22. According to equity theory, long-term relationships boil down to:
a. similarity of attitudes
b. similarity of appearance
c. equalizing benefits and costs
d. chance factors
   (page 389)

23. Suppose that you liked the latest fall fashions and as a result concluded that everyone else must like them too. If so, you would be showing:
a. false consensus bias
b. social facilitation
c. social loafing
d. reciprocity
   (page 392)

24. If you remember the face of a stranger simply because that face reminds you of yours, the memory mechanism would be tied to your:
a. social schemata
b. self-schemata
c. self-consciousness
d. self-esteem
   (page 392)

25. When you are playing golf and others are watching, your dominant response may be to swing very hard. If doing so makes you perform better, the phenomenon would be called:
a. reciprocity
b. risk taking
c. normative constraint
d. social facilitation
   (page 393)

26. The equivalent to bystander apathy in a group performance situation is:
a. conformity
b. compliance
c. social loafing
d. social comparison
   (page 394)

27. In Zimbardo's simulation of a prison atmosphere, his subjects experienced "deindividuation," or a loss of:
a. self-schemata
b. self-consciousness
c. self-esteem
d. self-congruity
   (page 394)

28. The situation of one person believing that he or she is the only one disagreeing with the group's position is most likely to result in:
a. conformity
b. nonconformity
c. loss of self-esteem
d. disrespect for authority
    (page 396)

29. With respect to decisions made by groups:
a. decisions tend to be more conservative than is the average of the decisions of the individuals in the group
b. one tends to see a regression toward the mean of the individual decisions
c. the decisions tend to be more extreme than is the average individual decision
d. the decisions tend to be more risky than are individual decisions
    (page 397)

30. The results of the robber's cave experiment show us that intergroup conflict is most likely to occur when:
a. different racial and ethnic groups are mixed
b. there is strong intragroup identification
c. there is extreme overcrowding
d. group size is small
    (page 399)

SELF-TEST 2

1. It is believed that _____ is stored in our memories as schemata.
a. social motivation
b. social knowledge
c. social approval
d. social reciprocity
    (page 375)

2. The self-fulfilling prophecy has occurred when:
a. people whom we like like us in return
b. we give up our responsibility and show apathy
c. others behave the way in which we expect them to behave
d. we conform to the demands of the group
    (page 377)

3. The positivity bias refers to:
a. a tendency to evaluate others positively rather than negatively
b. a tendency to give ourselves more positive self-ratings than we give others
c. the manner in which self-schemata are formed by people in groups
d. the judgment of a group based on its behavior
    (page 378)

4. According to Heider's balance theory, if George dislikes Mary and Mary dislikes rock music, then to maintain balance:
a. George will have to dislike rock music
b. George will have to like rock music
c. Mary will have to learn to like rock music
d. Mary will have to learn to like George
    (page 379)

5. According to Festinger's cognitive dissonance theory, if you flunked an examination and previously had a high opinion of your own intelligence, you would probably attribute the failure to:
a. your overall lack of intelligence
b. internal factors
c. external factors
d. dissonance
    (page 380)

6. Which of the following theories in social psychology is based on the general consistency principle?
a. attribution theory
b. equity theory
c. social-exchange theory
d. cognitive dissonance theory
    (page 380)

7. Which of the following was NOT one of the three elements of the Hovland and Janis theory of attitude formation and change?
a. communicator variables
b. the communication itself
c. situational variables such as distraction
d. the current attitudes of the communication's target
    (page 382)

8. If you believe a communication simply because some famous actor or actress delivered it, you have been:
a. distracted
b. inoculated
c. influenced by the source
d. influenced by the message
    (page 382)

9. Who among the following would likely be LEAST swayed by a persuasive written communication?
a. someone who thought his or her reading ability was being tested
b. someone who thought the communicator was trying to influence him or her
c. someone who respected the source of the communication
d. someone who was high in self-esteem
    (page 382)

10. A person's attitude becomes more resistant to change as the:
a. message becomes more discrepant with the recipient's position
b. message becomes less discrepant with the recipient's position
c. person gets older
d. communicator moves farther away from the recipient
    (page 383)

11. As the amount of fear that a communication elicits increases, the impact of the communication:
a. increases
b. decreases
c. stays the same
d. first increases and then decreases
    (page 383)

12. If you fail to understand a portion of a lecture because you were distracted by a classmate, you have been influenced by:
a. situational factors
b. source factors
c. internal factors
d. the message itself
   (page 383)

13. Forewarning individuals that they are about to be exposed to a persuasive message:
a. always increases attitude change
b. increases attitude change when the initial commitment to a position is low
c. increases attitude change when the initial commitment to a position is high
d. never increases attitude change
   (page 385)

14. A little dose of arguing now will prevent persuasion later. This is:
a. inoculation
b. distraction
c. reciprocation
d. constraint
   (page 385)

15. One explanation for the fact that attitudes are not very reliable predictors of behavior is that:
a. the attitude may reflect too many unconscious factors
b. attitudes are too resistant to change
c. attitudinal information may not be in memory when it is time to behave
d. attitudes tend to initiate counterarguments that decrease the likelihood of consistent behavior
   (page 385)

16. The extent to which another person's behavior is rewarding or costly to us is referred to as:
a. reciprocity
b. hedonic relevance
c. attribution constraint
d. equity
   (page 387)

17. If someone whom I know gets a promotion and a raise, I am more likely to attribute that event to _____ than if I got the promotion and raise.
a. luck
b. skill
c. internal factors
d. performance
   (page 387)

18. Self-attribution theory has been shown to explain our explanations of our own behavior. Adaptive aspects of self-attribution have also been shown, particularly the notion that:
a. attributing poor performance to bad luck may reduce anxiety
b. attributing poor performance to our own lack of skill may inoculate us against future failure

c.   attributing good performance to good luck may keep us humble
d.   attributing good performance to good luck may reduce anxiety about
     performing
     (page 388)

19. You are most likely to be attracted to someone who is:
a.   rich
b.   beautiful
c.   intelligent
d.   like yourself
     (page 388)

20. "Absence makes the heart grow fonder" is inconsistent with which factor
of interpersonal attraction?
a.   similarity
b.   attractiveness
c.   consistency
d.   proximity
     (page 390)

21. Abandonment of one relationship for another in which the rewards are
higher and the costs are lower would be predicted by:
a.   balance theory
b.   social-exchange theory
c.   cognitive dissonance theory
d.   self-attribution theory
     (page 390)

22. That formulation of social-exchange theory that focuses on the costs
and benefits of group arrangements is called:
a.   self-attribution theory
b.   reciprocity of liking
c.   equity theory
d.   principle of mutual consent
     (page 391)

23. In a "just world":
a.   benefits and costs would be about equal
b.   we reciprocate
c.   we show normative constraints
d.   we are attracted to those people who are similar to us
     (page 391)

24. We might predict that a person learning to drive a car in the presence
of a group of people:
a.   would make many mistakes
b.   would learn very fast so as to escape the anxiety of the situation
c.   would learn at about the same speed as if no one was present
d.   would forget about the audience
     (page 393)

25. Milgram's study of the compliance of subjects who thought that they were
administering powerful electric shocks to others shows the great influence of
what variable:
a.   motivation to maintain self-esteem
b.   the effect of physical attractiveness on controlling behavior

c.   the effect of social pressure on conformity
d.   the ambivalence of attitudes
     (page 397)

26. In general, group decisions tend to represent:
a.   a polarized view
b.   the average of all views
c.   a view that corresponds to no single view in the group
d.   the view of one and only one very charismatic leader
     (page 397)

27. Which of the following is NOT a likely explanation for the group polarization effect?
a.   group leaders favor extreme positions
b.   high cultural value is placed on more extreme stands
c.   the extreme position with the greater number of arguments will be adopted
d.   group members lose their sense of self-awareness
     (page 398)

28. When participants in a bargaining session can both win or lose, the situation is referred to as a:
a.   zero-sum game
b.   non-zero-sum game
c.   cooperative conflict
d.   social exchange
     (page 398)

29. The best theoretical model for predicting the formation of coalitions in simulated bargaining sessions comes from which theory?
a.   balance
b.   cognitive dissonance
c.   equity
d.   attribution
     (page 399)

30. The results of the robber's cave study suggest that one effective way to end intergroup conflicts is to:
a.   punish the undesirable behavior
b.   specify competitive tasks that must be performed
c.   create a common enemy
d.   set up a mock court to settle arguments
     (page 399)

WHAT DOES IT MEAN?

OBJECTIVES

1.   How do social processes affect decisions made by juries?
2.   How do advertisers take advantage of the principles of persuasion in order to sell us their products?
3.   How does cognitive dissonance theory explain people's willingness to spend large amounts of money on physical and psychological health care?
4.   What are the social and situational variables that have been found to be important determinants of prosocial behaviors?

5. What factors have been linked with the control of aggressive and violent behavior?
6. What are important considerations in evaluating the results of opinion polls?
7. What is personal space, and what happens when personal space is invaded?
8. What are the social-psychological consequences of overcrowding?

SELF-TEST

1. Active participation in jury discussions:
a. is more probable if the jury has twelve members
b. is more probable if the jury has six members
c. occurs readily when jurors are high in prestige
d. happens most frequently if the defendant is attractive
   (page 402)

2. Physically attractive defendants receive more lenient treatment from jurors EXCEPT when:
a. the crime is related to physical appearance
b. the jurors are authoritarian
c. the jurors are high in prestige
d. the jury size is small
   (page 402)

3. Juries have a greater tendency to bring in a decision when:
a. the defendant is physically attractive
b. the jurors are prestigious
c. the jury has twelve members
d. the jury has six members
   (page 402)

4. With respect to television ads designed to persuade people to stop smoking, a major problem that has limited the effectiveness of the ads is:
a. they generate too much fear
b. getting the audience to pay attention
c. the audience's comprehension of the message
d. the opposing ads persuading people to smoke
   (page 403)

5. Fairly good success in persuading people to stop smoking has been obtained with:
a. television ads that manipulate fear
b. role playing
c. psychotherapy
d. self-punishment procedures
   (page 404)

6. Research on insomnia has shown that people given sugar pills reported feeling less restless than usual, even though they were told that the pill would make them more restless. How is this result explained?
a. the subjects did not believe the message
b. too much restlessness saps energy and induces sleep
c. the message reduced their concern about actually being restless
d. the sugar in the pills activated a calming mechanism in the brain
   (page 404)

7. Behaviors such as altruism, charity, cooperation, and rescue all are examples of:
a. prosocial behavior
b. equity models
c. the positivity bias
d. resolutions of dissonance
   (page 405)

8. Bystander apathy is believed to occur because of:
a. a tendency to attribute cause of the emergency to the victim
b. a pure and simple unwillingness to become involved
c. a decrease in perceived responsibility
d. the effects of emotional arousal brought on by the emergency
   (page 406)

9. If you were experiencing an emergency, you would be best off if:
a. you were in a crowd
b. you were alone
c. one other person was present
d. high-prestige people were present
   (page 406)

10. With respect to the most recent research reported by Berkowitz on the relation between television and aggressiveness in children:
a. aggressive behavior occurred as often in children who never watched TV as in those who watched frequently
b. young children but not older ones seemed to be more aggressive after watching aggressive characterizations
c. children quickly tired of shows that featured primarily aggressive characterizations
d. aggressive behaviors were very strongly related to watching violence on television
   (page 409)

11. Studies of prisoners who had a history of violent behavior have shown that:
a. they had little territoriality
b. they required less than normal personal space
c. they required more than normal personal space
d. their personal space requirements were inconsistent
   (page 411)

12. The typical response to invasion of personal space in our culture is:
a. flight
b. fight
c. interaction
d. insult
   (page 412)

13. According to Milgram, phenomena such as bystander apathy occur in socially crowded situations because of:
a. cognitive dissonance
b. normative constraint
c. information overload
d. deindividuation
   (page 412)

14. According to Zimbardo, vandalism is best explained by:
a. information overload
b. deindividuation
c. dissonance
d. the loss of responsibility
    (page 413)

15. According to studies done comparing urbanites with rural dwellers:
a. urbanites are more likely to use prescribed stress-reducing drugs
b. rural people are more likely to use prescribed stress-reducing drugs
c. rural people appear to have adapted better to environmental stress
d. vandalism is greater in rural communities
    (page 413)

ANSWER KEY

EXERCISES

Exercise 1

1.	inferences	5.	stereotypes
2.	self-fulfilling prophecy	6.	consistency
3.	halo	7.	attitudes
4.	positivity	8.	rationalization

Exercise 2

1. Peter likes Oscar but dislikes exercising. Thus, the fact that Oscar likes to exercise will make Peter feel uncomfortable.

2. Peter likes Oscar and dislikes exercising. However, because Oscar also dislikes exercising, there is balance.

3. Peter dislikes Oscar and likes to exercise. The fact that Oscar dislikes exercising keeps things in balance.

4. Peter dislikes Oscar and likes to exercise. Thus, the fact that Oscar likes exercising creates imbalance.

Exercise 3

According to Festinger's theory, dissonant information makes an individual feel uncomfortable, and discomfort will motivate the person to rationalize it so as to reduce the dissonance. In the above instance, the individual values the fraternity. However, he does not value the severe initiation. Thus, a good rationalization is, "to experience something truly great, one must pay the price." Stated differently, if a fraternity has only a mild initiation or no initiation at all, what can it be worth? The individual experiencing the mild initiation experiences no dissonance and has nothing to rationalize. This scenario is very much like Festinger's finding that the individual paid $1 for a boring task values the task more than the individual paid $20. After all, the individual paid $20 can say he did it for the money, whereas the individual paid only $1 will look like a fool unless, of course, he rationalizes his act.

So, who will probably like the fraternity better? It will be the fellow who had the more severe initiation.

Exercise 4

1.	communicator	6.	persuasive	11.	distraction
2.	credibility	7.	communication	12.	fear
3.	trustworthy	8.	discrepancy	13.	situation
4.	argue	9.	communicator	14.	moderate
5.	approval	10.	stress	15.	commitment

Exercise 5

1. The two factors are knowledge and practice. In experimental situations, McGuire finds that reading a counterargument provides the knowledge and that writing down the arguments provides the practice. Regarding real-world situations, he believes that if time elapses between forewarning and the persuasive message, there can be an "inoculation" effect. That is, the forewarning may bolster defenses, and this, in turn, motivates the individual to acquire knowledge and practice counterarguments.

2. The three factors are attitude strength, saliency, and specificity. That is, seemingly inconsistent behavior will occur when the individual is uncertain or ambivalent about a given belief; when the attitude is or is not available in memory at the point that behavior is required; and when the attitude is very global and vague, and the required behavior is quite specific.

Exercise 6

1.	attributions	7.	undesirable; desirable
2.	consistent	8.	hedonically
3.	cause	9.	internal; external
4.	internal	10.	external; internal
5.	external	11.	bias
6.	stable		

Exercise 7

1. A   2. B   3. A   4. C   5. B   6. C

Exercise 8

According to social-exchange theory, a relationship is maintained if the rewards for each individual are greater than the costs. For example, we might abandon a potentially rewarding long distance relationship because it is too costly, whereas we might maintain a less rewarding local relationship because it is relatively uncostly. It should be noted that factors such as attractiveness and reciprocity influence the perceived degree of reward.

According to equity theory, rewards and costs are equally divided among the group (or pair) members. For example, people who are equally attractive or share the same attitudes make equal contributions to a relationship. Also, equity theory explains the attraction of opposites by assuming that the initial attractions are often not followed (for example, we might not pursue a more beautiful person for fear that such a relationship would be inequitable to us).

Exercise 9

1. schemata
2. ourselves
3. ourselves
4. favorable
5. consensus
6. consciousness
7. socially
8. esteem
9. motivated
10. distort

Exercise 10

1. In general, we need others for a basis of comparison when we need to evaluate ourselves but have no internalized norms for making the evaluation. This need is most likely to arise in new and/or ambiguous situations. The severe-shock condition is clearly the more ambiguous situation, and the subjects do not know how worried or upset they actually are. Thus, other subjects in the same situation provide the standard for comparison.

2. As implied above, the most useful model is the one who is in the "same boat." Thus, a beginner should not make comparisons with experts. In general, the model should be as similar as possible on the relevant dimensions of the comparison. For example, a severe-shock subject in Schacter's study would be foolish to use a subject who has (presumably) already completed the severe-shock condition, because this subject no longer (presumably) experiences ambiguity and fear.

Exercise 11

1. B   2. A   3. A   4. C   5. B   6. C

Exercise 12

1. conformity
2. informational
3. normative
4. greatest
5. one
6. few
7. etiquette
8. comply

Exercise 13

The prisoner study illustrates how a loss of self-identity can lead to violent antisocial behavior. Specifically, the "guards," by virtue of their uniforms, lose individual identity and commit acts that they probably would not commit in normal social situations. A good parallel is the behavior of crowds at sporting events. Because the crowd is so large, the individual is unidentified. Thus, often, there is uncontrolled antisocial behavior that ordinarily does not occur (for example, hurling objects on the field, abusive language, and perhaps even violence in the stands).

The Milgram study illustrates what happens when an individual loses his or her sense of responsibility. In the study, experimental subjects committed acts (under instructions from the experimenter) that the control subjects claimed they would never commit. Similar claims occurred at the Nazi war trials after the Second World War, when many individuals claimed they were just "taking orders." Thus, the moral of the Milgram story is that giving up one's responsibility is very dangerous.

1. The group polarization effect is defined as a group decision that is more extreme than the average of individual judgments. In general, the direction of the extreme judgment (that is, risk versus conservatism) goes in the direction that the group is leaning toward initially. Explanations of this effect include the possibility that the group leader(s) holds the extreme position and, more plausibly, that either higher cultural value is placed on extreme, as opposed to average, positions or that group discussion is persuasive situation in which the group takes the majority view, be it risk or conservatism. These three explanations are not mutually exclusive.

2. In the prisoner's dilemma, two prisoners commit a crime, and both can confess, neither can confess, or one can rat on the other. In other words, one can win at the other's expense (that is, zero-sum), or both can win or lose (that is, non-zero-sum). Interestingly, when subjects are given cooperative instructions, they will tend to cooperate. But they will cooperate less if instructed to be individualistic, and even less if instructed to be competitive.

3. Simulation produces interesting results in voting situations in which a clear majority is required but is not obtained by any of more than two candidates. The trade-off in this situation is between the number needed by the coalition to form the majority and the amount of patronage the higher vote getter would have to have given up in order to form the coalition.

4. In the robber's cave study, a simulated summer camp situation was used to create and resolve conflict. It was created by initially creating identification with two groups. This led to hostility between the groups. The two groups could be brought together with respect to a common enemy, but this still represented hostility. Ultimately, the resolution of conflict depended on finding goals common to both groups.

Exercise 15

1.	O	6.	P	11.	B	16.	I
2.	F	7.	J	12.	Q	17.	D
3.	A	8.	K	13.	L	18.	N
4.	T	9.	M	14.	H	19.	S
5.	E	10.	C	15.	R	20.	G

MULTIPLE-CHOICE

Self-Test 1

1.	b	6.	b	11.	d	16.	b	21.	d	26.	c
2.	a	7.	d	12.	d	17.	c	22.	c	27.	b
3.	a	8.	b	13.	a	18.	a	23.	a	28.	a
4.	c	9.	c	14.	a	19.	b	24.	b	29.	c
5.	d	10.	a	15.	b	20.	d	25.	d	30.	b

Self-Test 2

1.	b	6.	d	11.	d	16.	b	21.	b	26. a
2.	c	7.	d	12.	a	17.	a	22.	c	27. d
3.	a	8.	c	13.	b	18.	a	23.	a	28. b
4.	b	9.	b	14.	a	19.	d	24.	a	29. c
5.	c	10.	a	15.	c	20.	d	25.	c	30. c

WHAT DOES IT MEAN?

Self-Test

1.	c	4.	b	7.	a	10.	d	13.	c
2.	a	5.	b	8.	c	11.	c	14.	b
3.	d	6.	c	9.	c	12.	a	15.	b

11 Psychopathology

OBJECTIVES

1. What is the definition, and what are the six viewpoints of psychopathology?
2. What are the two functions of diagnostic classification, and how are these treated in the five axes of DSM-III?
3. What are the seven organic mental disorders, and what distinguishes them from functional disorders?
4. What are the three anxiety disorders, and how do they promote primary and secondary gains?
5. What characterizes the somatoform disorders, and what are the four types?
6. Considering both causes and treatment, what are the major differences between substance-use disorders involving alcohol, as opposed to other drugs such as heroin?
7. What are the four classes of psychosexual disorders?
8. What are the three types of affective disorders, and what are the proposed genetic, biochemical, and psychological causes?
9. What are the four types of schizophrenic disorders, and what are the proposed genetic, biochemical, and psychological causes?
10. What are the five Axis II (personality) disorders, and what distinguishes them from the Axis I anxiety and schizophrenic disorders?

SYNOPSIS

The definition of psychopathology incorporates both behavior that deviates from social norms and maladaptive behavior that is detrimental to the individual and society. The early history of psychopathology shows a variety of crude beliefs regarding the causes of pathological behavior (for example, spirits, gods and goddesses, the devil). In more modern times, six viewpoints have guided our thinking with respect to both cause and treatment. These include the biological, psychodynamic, behavioral, phenomenological, ethical, and cognitive viewpoints.

Diagnostic categories are important in that they allow us to enumerate the various types of disorders and allow professionals to communicate more readily with one another. The current classification scheme (DSM-III) has a total of five axes, and these axes consider current symptoms (Axis I), personality disorders (Axis II), medical disorders (Axis III), level of stress (Axis IV), and adaptive functioning (Axis V). This chapter discusses seven of the Axis I disorders (organic mental, anxiety, somatoform, substance-use, psychosexual, affective, and schizophrenic disorders) and the personality disorders of Axis II.

Organic mental disorders are characterized as problems (sometimes inborn) in the nervous system, damage through injury, damage caused by toxic substances, or general deterioration as a result of aging. Included among these disorders are delirium, dementia, amnestic syndrome, organic delusional syndrome, intoxication syndrome, and atypical or mixed-brain syndrome.

The anxiety disorders are presumed to be functional in origin. Collectively, they involve escape/avoidance strategies that reduce anxiety (that is, primary gain) and promote sympathy (that is, secondary gains). But paradoxically, these gains are temporary and serve to perpetuate the underlying conflicts. The three anxiety disorders are phobias, anxiety states, and obsessive-compulsive disorders.

There are four somatoform disorders (somatization disorder, hypochondriasis, conversion disorder, and psychogenic pain disorder). These disorders are also considered to be functional. They are the expression of psychological problems through physical symptoms for which there are no demonstrable causes.

The principal substance-use disorder pertains to alcohol. Although there is some evidence for genetic predisposition, it is generally concluded that immature, impulsive, and dependent personalities turn to alcohol during periods of stress. Although conditioning treatments have been tried, the most common treatment prescribes abstinence in conjunction with a change in life-style. Heroin addiction is a second major category. Unlike alcoholics, heroin addicts tend to be antisocial personalities who have no desire to behave in socially appropriate ways. At this time, the major treatments are substituting drugs such as methadone and naloxone for the heroin.

The psychosexual disorders characterize individuals who are confused about their sexual identity (gender-identity disorders), individuals who use bizarre acts and/or unusual practices to achieve sexual satisfaction (paraphilias), the failure to follow the normal sexual response cycle of appetite, excitement, orgasm, and resolution (psychosexual dysfunctions), and homosexuals who feel uncomfortable with this role (ego-dystonic homosexuality).

The affective disorders include dysthynic disorder (formerly called neurotic depression) and the two major disorders (bipolar disorder and major depression). There are genetic, biochemical, and psychological theories regarding the causes of affective disorders.

The schizophrenic disorders are characterized by cognitive and emotional problems and a marked distortion of reality. In general, the disorders may be rapid in onset (that is, reactive) or slow and progressive (that is, process). The specific disorders include disorganized, paranoid, catatonic, and chronic-undifferentiated schizophrenia. As with affective disorders, the proposed causes are genetic, biochemical, and psychological.

The Axis II (personality) disorders often occur in combination with Axis I problems. In general, there are long-standing dominant personality traits that lead to maladaptive behavior. Personality disorders do not usually include a stress component. The five major disorders in this catagory are passive-aggressive, paranoid, antisocial, dependent, and compulsive personalities.

KEY WORDS AND PHRASES

OBJECTIVE 1

psychopathology
deviation from the norm
maladaptive behavior
functional causes
organic causes
prehistoric viewpoint
ancient Greek viewpoint
viewpoint in Dark Ages
viewpoint in sixteenth century
biological viewpoint
psychodynamic viewpoint
behavioral viewpoint
phenomenological (humanistic) viewpoint
ethical viewpoint
cognitive viewpoint

OBJECTIVE 2

diagnosis
types of disorders
communication among professionals
DSM-III
Axis I (current symptoms)
Axis II (personality disorders)
Axis III (medical disorders)
Axis IV (current level of stress)
Axis V (adaptive functioning)

OBJECTIVE 3

organic mental disorders in Axis I
delirium
dementia
amnestic syndrome
organic delusional syndrome
organic personality syndrome
intoxication syndrome
atypical or mixed-brain syndrome
hallucinosis
organic hallucinosis

OBJECTIVE 4

anxiety disorders
neurotic paradox
primary gain
secondary gain
phobias
acrophobia
claustrophobia

agoraphobia
zoophobia
xenophobia
anxiety states
anxiety attacks (panic disorder)
obsessive-compulsive disorder

OBJECTIVE 5

somatoform disorders
somatization disorder
hypochondriasis
conversion disorder
psychogenic pain disorder
hysteria
glove anesthesia
malingering

OBJECTIVE 6

substance-use disorders
alcohol
stimulant versus depressant
physical versus psychological addiction
prealcoholic, prodromal, crucial, and chronic phases
withdrawal
delirium tremens
genetic predisposition
aversive conditioning
electric shock
antabuse
covert sensitization
abstinence
Alcoholics Anonymous
prescription medications
Valium and Librium
barbiturates
cocaine
amphetamines
heroin
morphine
methadone
naloxone
contagion effect
tolerance
cold turkey

OBJECTIVE 7

psychosexual disorders
gender-identity disorders
paraphilias
psychosexual dysfunctions
ego-dystonic (unwanted) homosexuality

fetishism
voyeurism
exhibitionism
zoophilia
pedophilia

OBJECTIVE 8

affective (mood) disorders
dysthymic disorders
major affective disorders
anxiety and guilt
bipolar disorder
major depression
cyclothymic disorder
delusions
hallucinations
suicide
hereditary causes
concordance rates
biochemical causes
tricyclic antidepressants
reserpine
psychological causes
personal loss
Freud's theory
Rogers's theory
behavioral theory
learned-helplessness theory

OBJECTIVE 9

schizophrenic disorders
reactive schizophrenia
process schizophrenia
disorganized schizophrenia
paranoid schizophrenia
catatonic schizophrenia
chronic-undifferentiated schizophrenia
genetic, biochemical, and psychological causes
diasthesis-stress theory
dopamine
marital skew
marital schism
double bind
schizophrenogenic parent

OBJECTIVE 10

personality disorders
long-standing dominant traits
passive-aggressive personality
passive obstructionism
paranoid personality

antisocial personality (sociopath)
dependent personality
compulsive personality

EXERCISES

EXERCISE 1: Objective 1

TITLE: DEFINITION AND EARLY VIEWPOINTS
TASK: Fill in the blanks

1. There are two components to the definition of psychopathology. The first is the failure to behave in socially appropriate ways, or _____ from the norm.
2. The second component includes _____ behavior that is detrimental to both the individual and society.
3. Psychopathological behavior may reflect _____ causes (for example, genetic abnormality, biochemical imbalance, or brain damage).
4. Psychopathological behavior may also reflect _____ deficiencies (for example, lack of knowledge, competence, or motivation).
5. In _____ times, it was assumed that "crazy" people were possessed by demons or evil spirits.
6. In ancient _____, abnormal behavior was attributed to the acts of gods and goddesses.
7. It was the Greek physician Hippocrates who took the _____ viewpoint and introduced the notion of mental illness.
8. During the Dark Ages and under the Church's influence, abnormal behavior was attributed to the _____.
9. The common treatments during this era included torture, _____, and burning at the stake.
10. During the sixteenth century and under the influence of the medical profession, abnormal behavior was attributed to _____ damage--thus the treatment became confinement to hospitals and insane asylums.

EXERCISE 2: Objective 1

TITLE: MODERN VIEWPOINTS
TASK: Match letters to numbers

A. biological viewpoint
B. psychodynamic viewpoint
C. behavioral viewpoint
D. phenomenological viewpoint
E. ethical viewpoint
F. cognitive viewpoint

_____1. Psychopathology is viewed as maladaptive learning. Thus the treatment is unlearning, and/or relearning.
_____2. Psychopathology is viewed as failure to take responsibility for one's behavior. Thus, treatment is designed to promote acceptance of this responsibility.
_____3. Psychopathology is viewed as an organic disorder. Thus, the treatment is physical (for example, medication, rest).

_____4. Psychopathology is viewed as faulty thinking. Thus, treatment is designed to teach new ways of interpreting life's experiences.

_____5. Psychopathology is viewed as the lack of meaning and/or distortion of life's experiences. Thus, treatment focuses on the development of awareness and openness.

_____6. Psychopathology is viewed as unconscious conflicts. Thus, treatment is designed to give insight into these conflicts.

EXERCISE 3: Objective 2

TITLE: DIAGNOSIS OF PSYCHOPATHOLOGY
TASK: Fill in the blanks

1. Categories of psychopathology are useful in enumerating the various types of disorder. In the biological and dynamic viewpoints, this process is called _____.

2. One of the main advantages of diagnosis is that it permits _____ among professionals.

3. The most common classification system uses behavioral or emotional characteristics, which, because of the influence of the medical/dynamic viewpoint, are often called _____.

4. The most recent formal classification scheme is termed _____.

5. In this scheme, the person's _____ set of current symptoms is on Axis I.

6. Long-standing problems that need to be considered separately, or _____ disorders, are considered on Axis II.

7. _____ disorders are considered on Axis III.

8. The severity of _____ in a person's life is rated on Axis IV.

9. Finally, the individual's highest level of _____ functioning is considered on Axis V.

EXERCISE 4: Objective 3

TITLE: ORGANIC MENTAL DISORDERS
TASK: Match letters to numbers

A. dementia1
B. delirium
C. amnestic syndrome
D. organic delusional syndrome
E. organic personality syndrome
F. intoxication syndrome
G. mixed-brain syndrome

_____1. Loss of intellectual abilities such as reasoning, judgment, and abstract thinking. May be irreversible (as in senility) or remain steady with periods of improvement.

_____2. Confused or clouded state of consciousness in which one is unaware of what is happening in the environment. Includes inability to sustain attention, misperception of stimuli, and disordered thought processes.

_____3. Maladaptive behavior caused by toxic substances. Leads to socially inappropriate behavior. Withdrawal occurs with cutting down on such substances.

_____4. Dramatic personality changes (for example, temper tantrums, fits of crying). Includes poor social judgment (for example, sexual misbehavior). Frequently caused by actual sturctural damage.

_____5. Catch-all term for disorders with presumed organic basis but with no clearly defined pattern.

_____6. Experiencing delusions (that is, false beliefs), but with no confusion or memory loss. May be some intellectual impairment and some bizarre behavior. May be combined with hallucinosis that may or may not be organic in origin.

_____7. Disruption or impairment of memory. May be inability to learn new material (short-term memory deficit) or an inability to remember past events (long-term memory deficit).

EXERCISE 5: Objective 4

TITLE: ANXIETY DISORDERS
TASK: Fill in the blanks

1. Because they appear to depend upon experience, the anxiety disorders are presumed to be _____ rather than organic.

2. Because anxiety is conceptualized as aversive in nature, these disorders are characterized by _____ strategies that, when blocked, lead to anxiety attacks.

3. Because the removal of anxiety becomes an overriding concern, these disorders are also characterized by _____ behavior.

4. The need being served by the behavior that removes the anxiety seems insatiable which leaves the person unable to _____.

5. Because escape and avoidance strategies lead to only temporary solutions, the problems become self-perpetuating. This is termed the neurotic _____.

6. The immediate reduction of anxiety is called _____ gain.

7. Additional positive consequences of the anxiety-removing behavior (such as sympathy from friends) is called _____ gain.

8. Included among these disorders are _____ which are intense and irrational fears of objects and situations.

9. Anxiety _____ include irrational feelings of anxiety that cannot be attributed to specific causes.

10. Sometimes an individual will experience feelings akin to those of terror or impending doom; these are called anxiety _____, or panic disorder.

11. Another anxiety disorder that includes repetitive thoughts of behaviors is called _____ disorder.

12. Obsession refers to repetitive _____.

13. Compulsion refers to repetitive _____.

14. Obsessions and compulsions are considered pathological when they prevent the individual from behaving in a(n) _____ manner.

15. Sometimes, obsessive thoughts or compulsive bahaviors can be best explained by realizing that they may bear a(n) _____ relationship to the anxiety-provoking thought (for example, an expression of guilt or fear of punishment).

EXERCISE 6: Objective 4

TITLE: A CASE STUDY IN ANXIETY STATES
TASK: Essay

Mary is an attractive nineteen-year-old woman who regards intimate sexual behavior as an activity that should be reserved for marital relationships. Her boyfriend, John, cares for Mary but does not understand why she clings so tightly to what he considers to be an outdated morality. After many arguments on the topic, John has told Mary that they either will engage in sexual activities or the relationship is over. Last Friday, John arrived at Mary's house at 8 p.m. fully expecting that Mary was going to accede to his wishes. However, Mary's mother answered the door and told John that Mary was extremely sick and was unable to go out that evening. Mary did indeed feel ill but was at a loss to explain her extreme tension, increased heartbeat, faintness, sweating, and so forth. John forgot his previous intentions for the evening and went away feeling concerned for Mary's health.

The question is, what is happening to Mary? (Hint: think in terms of conflict, neurotic paradox, primary gains, and secondary gains).

EXERCISE 7: Objective 5

TITLE: SOMATOFORM DISORDERS
TASK: Match letters to numbers

a. somatization disorder
B. hypochondriasis
C. conversion disorder
D. psychogenic pain disorder

_____1. Involves a pattern of vague but recurring complaints and is typically established before age thirty.

_____2. A general overconcern with one's health that is typically found after age thirty.

_____3. A report of pain where there is no physical basis for it.

_____4. Reducing anxiety by inactivating (that is, paralysis) a part of the body.

_____5. Often referred to as the *medical student syndrome*.

_____6. Formerly called *hysteria*, it provided much of the impetus for Freud's psychoanalytic theory.

_____7. The faker, or "malingerer," often has a clear secondary gain such as workman's compensation.

_____8. Patients are likely to be women who continuously seek medical attention, frequently changing doctors.

EXERCISE 7: Objective 5

TITLE: ALCOHOL ABUSE
TASK: Fill in the blanks

1. In a(n) _____ addiction, the individual is addicted to a drug with a few addictive properties of its own (for example, marijuana).

269

2. In a(n) _____ addiction, the substance (for example, heroin) has highly addictive properties.
3. In the case of the alcoholic, excessive drinking interferes with socially _____ behavior.
4. Contrary to popular belief, alcohol is a(n) _____, not a stimulant
5. The first stage in alcoholism, called _____, is when the social drinker turns to alcohol to relieve tension.
6. In the _____ phase of alcoholism, the person drinks in the morning and experiences blackouts.
7. In the _____ phase of alcoholism, the individual loses control over drinking and often loses his or her family and job.
8. Finally, in the _____ phase, there are long binges and evidence of thought impairment.
9. In extreme cases of withdrawal from alcohol, the individual experiences terrifying visual hallucinations--this is called _____.
10. Although there is some evidence of genetic predisposition, the majority belief is that alcoholics are under severe _____.
11. Also, alcoholics tend to be impulsive, immature individuals who cannot tolerate _____.
12. One commonly used treatment for alcoholism is _____ conditioning, in which drinking is paired with either electric shock or drugs such as antabuse, which cause extreme nausea.
13. A more cognitive approach to treatment is _____ sensitization, which involves imagining repulsive events along with alcohol use.
14. The majority of workers believe that _____ is the only reliable approach to dealing with alcoholism.
15. Thus, in programs such as _____, the emphasis is on learning new ways to spend their time in place of drinking.

EXERCISE 9: Objective 6

TITLE: DRUG ADDICITON
TASK: Fill in the blanks

1. The most widely abused drugs other than alcohol are the _____ medications (for example, antianxiety drugs such as Valium and Librium, sleeping medications such as barbiturates, pain relievers such as cocaine, and diet drugs such as amphetamines).
2. Heroin has both physical and psychological consequences, not the least of which is that addicts introduce newcomers to the drug--an effect called _____.
3. Heroin produces _____ rather than just tension reduction.
4. Also, more heroin is needed to maintain a given level of high. In other words, there is a rapid increase in _____ which often leads to an overdose.
5. However, tolerance disappears if the addict goes _____.
6. As opposed to alcoholics, who frequently are immature, impulsive, and dependent, heroin addicts tend to be _____.
7. It may be difficult to treat heroin addicts because they are frequently not motivated to act in socially _____ ways.
8. One treatment for heroin is preventing withdrawal symptoms by using the drug _____.

9. What is interesting about the use of methadone is that many years ago, heroin was touted as a cure for _____ addiction.
10. Other drugs, such as _____, serve as heroin antagonists and prevent the high from occurring.

EXERCISE 10:   Objective 7

TITLE: OVERVIEW OF PSYCHOSEXUAL DISORDERS
TASK: Match letters to numbers

A.   gender-identity disorders
B.   paraphilias
C.   sexual dysfunctions
D.   ego-dystonic homosexuality

____1.   Inability to experience the normal cycle of appetite, excitement, orgasm, and resolution.
____2.   A clear and compelling discomfort with one's biological sex.
____3.   Homosexuals who consider their life-style inappropriate.
____4.   Bizarre acts and/or unusual practices are needed to become sexually excited.
____5.   The transsexual.
____6.   The homosexual who wants to be heterosexual.
____7.   The "peeping Tom."
____8.   Impotence and frigidity.

EXERCISE 11:   Objective 7

TITLE: FOCUS ON THE PARAPHILIAS
TASK: Identify each of the following disorders

1.   Sexual attachemnt to animals (formerly called beastiality).
2.   The "peeping Tom."
3.   Sexual attraction to children.
4.   The need to use unusual objects or situations in order to achieve sexual satisfaction.
5.   The need to expose one's sexual parts to others.

EXERCISE 12:   Objective 8

TITLE: OVERVIEW OF THE AFFECTIVE DISORDERS
TASK: Fill in the blanks

1.   Affective disorders involve depression and/or elevation in _____.
2.   This disorder used to be called neurotic depression but DSM-III is called _____ disorder.
3.   In dysthymic disorder there is excessive depression accompanied by anxiety and guilt. However, contact is maintained with _____.
4.   A more major affective disorder is cycling between depression and mania and is called _____ disorder.
5.   Here, there is evidence of loss of contact with reality. For example, there are gross misbeliefs, or _____.

6. There are also reports of visions and of hearing voices, or _____.
7. When the two moods are not excessively severe, the disorder is termed _____.
8. The _____ condition in which there is only depression is termed major depression (it used to be called psychotic depression).
9. Contrary to commonly held beliefs, the depressed individual lacks the _____ to commit suicide.
10. However, suicide is a possibility when the individual swings out of depression, or on major _____.
11. In general, suicide ranks _____ among causes of death in the United States.
12. Interestingly, _____ are more likely to attempt to commit suicide . . .
13. . . . and _____ are more likely to succeed.

EXERCISE 13: Objective 8

TITLE: GENETIC AND BIOCHEMICAL CAUSES OF AFFECTIVE DISORDERS
TASK: Essay

    What evidence is there for genetic and biochemical contributions to affective disorders?

EXERCISE 14: Objective 8

TITLE: PROPOSED PSYCHOLOGICAL CAUSES OF DEPRESSION
TASK: Identify each of the following

1. Depression that occurs because of the death of a loved one, a serious financial setback, or even the achievement of an important goal.
2. Depression that is caused by the inability to express outwardly hostility and anger, even when it is appropriate to do so.
3. Depression that results from the lack of self-actualization. That is, there is too great a discrepancy between the real self and the ideal self.
4. Depression that results because the individual spends more time avoiding punishment than obtaining positive reinforcement.
5. Depression that results because the individual believes that he or she has no control over anxiety-provoking situations and therefore gives up.

EXERCISE 15: Objective 9

TITLE: OVERVIEW OF SCHIZOPHRENIC DISORDERS
TASK: Essays

1. What are the major characteristics of schizophrenic disorders?

2. What differentiates reactive from process schizophrenia?

EXERCISE 16: Objective 9

TITLE: TYPES OF SCHIZOPHRENIA
TASK: Identify the following

1. This type of schizophrenia may be reactive or process, and the reactive

form has the best prognosis of all types of schizophrenia. The major characteristic is immobility for hours at a time. While immobile, the individual may show "waxy flexibility."

2. This type of schizophrenic tends to experience delusions of persecution. Being so singled out, the individual feels special and thus develops delusions of grandeur.

3. This type of schizophrenia, formerly called hebephrenia, is characterized by inappropriate affect. There are usually no delusions, but the individual is likely to be withdrawn socially.

4. There is also a "wastebasket" category for schizophrenia in which there are characteristics belonging to more than one subtype.

EXERCISE 17: Objective 9

TITLE: CAUSES OF SCHIZOPHRENIA
TASK: Fill in the blanks

1. As with behavioral genetic studies of manic-depression, Kallman has collected data on _____ rates for schizophrenia for identical twins.

2. However, the general consensus is that Kallman's data exaggerate the _____ component in schizophrenia.

3. The criticisms of Kallman's data are that too many of the pairs are _____ and that the rates are higher when the severity of affliction is high.

4. These criticisms have led to the _____ theory, which includes both genetic and environmental components.

5. The genetic component is termed a _____ .

6. Given this, stress acts as the _____ .

7. From a biochemical viewpoint, it is argued that _____ are altered so that they act like hallucinogenic drugs.

8. The major transmitter implicated in the biochemical viewpoint is _____ .

9. It is unclear whether the biochemical changes reflect the _____ or the _____ of schizophrenia.

10. Environmental factors in schizophrenia include marital _____ , in which serious pathology in one parent is accepted and/or supported by the other parent.

11. In marital _____ , there is open warfare between the parents.

12. There is also the possibility of contradictory demands placed on the child, a situation known as the _____ .

13. The term used to describe the kind of parent who supposedly induces schizophrenia in his or her offspring is _____ .

EXERCISE 18: Objective 10

TITLE: OVERVIEW OF PERSONALITY DISORDERS
TASK: Essay

What defines personality disorders and differentiates them from anxiety and schizophrenic disorders?

EXERCISE 19: Objective 10

TITLE: THE VARIOUS DISORDERS
TASK: Identify each of the following

1.   These individuals lack self-confidence and allow others to dominate
     their lives. They rarely make their own decisions, and they may
     tolerate extensive physical abuse.
2.   These individuals manipulate others by procrastinating, acting helpless,
     being stubborn (that is, passive obstructionism), acting helpless, and
     so forth. They are satisfied with themselves and would persist in their
     behaviors if others left them alone.
3.   These are individuals who are perfectionists who become preoccupied with
     details, often at the expense of major issues. They are rigid and
     stubborn, yet indecisive and fearful of making mistakes.
4.   These are hedonistic individuals who lack moral behavior. They are
     bright and manipulative and often physically attractive. They are also
     called *sociopaths*.
5.   These individuals are afraid that others are out to do them harm. They
     are often preoccupied with moral issues and believe thay are 100 percent
     correct. They may or may not have accompanying severe Axis I
     disturbance.

EXERCISE 20

TITLE: IMPORTANT NAMES
TASK: Match letters to numbers

A.   Freud
B.   Szasz
C.   Glazer
D.   Kraepelin
E.   Vaillant
F.   Kallman
G.   Rogers
H.   Seligman
I.   Lidz
J.   Bateson

_____1.   Learned helplessness and depression
_____2.   The "myth of mental illness"--also the ethical viewpoint
_____3.   Reality therapy--also the ethical viewpoint
_____4.   The genetic basis of alcoholism
_____5.   The dynamic viewpoint--and its account of depression
_____6.   The phenomenological viewpoint--and its account of depression
_____7.   Proponent of the double-bind theory in schizophrenia
_____8.   The precursor to modern-day classifications such as DSM-III
_____9.   Concordance rates for manic-depression and schizophrenia
____10.   A proponent of the theory of marital skew in schizophrenia

MULTIPLE-CHOICE TESTS

SELF-TEST 1

1. Which of the following psychopathologies afflicts the most Americans?
a. catatonic schizophrenia
b. profound depression
c. alcohol abuse
d. process schizophrenia
    (page 416)

2. Which of the following does NOT comprise part of the definition of psychopathology?
a. maladaptive consequences of behavior for the individual
b. maladaptive consequences of behavior for society
c. socially inappropriate behavior
d. behavior that results in individual failure
    (page 415)

3. Probably the most important implication of the therapist's viewpoint of psychopathology is:
a. the cost of treatment
b. the determination of whether a psychopathology exists
c. the kind of drug that is prescribed
d. whether the family is brought into therapy
    (page 417)

4. According to the _____ view, psychopathological behavior is a function of underlying intrapsychic conflicts.
a. medical
b. dynamic
c. phenomenological
d. cognitive behavioral
    (page 418)

5. The viewpoint of psychopathology that, by definition, argues against the insanity defense in a court of law is the _____ viewpoint.
a. ethical
b. phenomenological
c. dynamic
d. biological
    (page 420)

6. Communication among professionals is one of the main goals of:
a. theories of psychopathology
b. research on psychopathology
c. psychodiagnosis
d. psychotherapy
    (page 420)

7. The DSM-III is:
a. a system of psychodiagnosis
b. a form of schizophrenia
c. a new drug used in the treatment of depression
d. a method of monitoring blood-alcohol levels
    (page 421)

8. On the DSM-III, the amount of current stress that an individual is suffering would be reflected on:
a. Axis I
b. Axis II
c. Axis III
d. Axis IV
    (page 421)

9. Which of the following would NOT be considered a diagnostic category on Axis I of the DSM-III?
a. personality disorder
b. organic-mental disorder
c. somatoform disorder
d. affective disorder
    (page 421)

10. Whether or not the patient is in contact with reality would be the key distinction that would differentiate between:
a. organic and functional disorders
b. psychosis and neurosis
c. personality disorder and anxiety disorder
d. prealcoholic and alcoholic syndrome
    (page 423)

11. _____ is an organic disorder that involves dramatic personality changes in the form of temper outbursts, explosive behavior, fits of crying and so on.
a. Organic personality syndrome
b. Intoxication syndrome
c. Organic delusional syndrome
d. Antisocial behavior
    (page 425)

12. Which of the following is characteristic of anxiety disorders?
a. irrational thoughts about other family members
b. feelings that one's body is rotting
c. overly rigid behavior that the person feels compelled to complete
d. relaxation during events that normally produce anxiety
    (page 425)

13. If the neurotic person is given a break because we feel sorry for him or her, the phenomenon would be called:
a. anxiety reduction
b. primary gain
c. secondary gain
d. self-fulfilling prophecy
    (page 426)

14. A housewife who considers killing her husband to prevent him from seeing other women suddenly develops such a fear that she will cut herself with a knife that she can't even prepare food. This would be an anxiety disorder called:
a. the amnestic syndrome
b. obsessive-compulsive disorder
c. phobia
d. cognitive-behavioral activation
    (page 426)

15. Which of the following is NOT considered a somatoform disorder?
a. hypochondriasis
b. conversion disorder
c. psychogenic pain disorder
d. amnestic syndrome
   (page 427)

16. In wartime, soldiers have sometimes developed paralyses and consequently have been taken out of combat. Interestingly, there were no physical bases for these paralyses. This syndrome is called:
a. psychogenic pain disorder
b. somatization disorder
c. conversion disorder
d. hypochondriasis
   (page 428)

17. Which of the somatoform disorders listed below would likely be identified with a patient who had insisted on having many needless surgeries performed?
a. somatization disorder
b. conversion disorder
c. hypochondriasis
d. psychogenic pain disorder
   (page 429)

18. Which of the following symptoms would you expect with increased levels of alcohol intoxication?
a. increased sexual activity
b. inability to make fine discriminations
c. increased perception of discomfort
d. facilitation of motor behavior
   (page 429)

19. The first sign of alcoholism is:
a. the prodromal phase of addiction
b. impairment of rational thinking
c. a social drinker who relieves daily tensions with a drink
d. a social drinker who experiences his or her first blackout
   (page 429)

20. Probably the most controversial approach to the treatment of alcoholism is:
a. controlled drinking
b. aversive conditioning
c. Alcoholics Anonymous (AA)
d. antabuse therapy
   (page 433)

21. Impotence and frigidity are:
a. psychosexual dysfunctions
b. gender-identity crises
c. symptoms of homosexuality
d. paraphilias
   (page 434)

22. A person who was able to manage day-to-day life despite his or her feelings of depression, weakness, exhaustion, and anxiety would likely be diagnosed as having:
a. bipolar disorder
b. major depression
c. dependent personality disorder
d. dysthymic disorder
    (page 435)

23. Dysthymic disorder is to major depression as cyclothymic disorder is to _____.
a. paranoid schizophrenia
b. bipolar disorder
c. intoxication syndrome
d. phobia
    (page 435)

24. If concordance rates were higher among identical twins than fraternal twins, the tendency would be to attribute the cause of a disorder to:
a. environmental factors
b. genetic factors
c. bipolar factors
d. random factors
    (page 437)

25. According to the learned-helplessness account of depression:
a. you feel that you have no control over your life
b. you don't live up to your expectations
c. you can't get any satisfaction
d. you have experienced personal loss
    (page 439)

26. Schizophrenia is characterized by:
a. emotional disturbance in the form of extreme anxiety
b. extreme shifts of mood in the form of mania and depression
c. motivational problems that lead to harmful acts against society
d. thought disturbances as characterized by delusions and hallucinations
    (page 439)

27. According to the stress-diathesis hypothesis, schizophrenia is:
a. all genetic
b. all environmental
c. a genetic predisposition that needs an environmental trigger
d. a biochemical problem
    (page 442)

28. If a parent were to ask her child to clean up his room and then criticize him for being too compulsive, this would represent:
a. passive agression
b. skewed behavior
c. a double bind
d. antisocial behavior
    (page 443)

29. Which class of disorders seems LEAST related to stress?
a. personality disorders
b. anxiety disorders
c. intoxication syndrome
d. dystheymic disorder
(page 445)

30. A person diagnosed as _____ personality disorder would probably be singled out as the "cold fish" of a group of people.
a. dependent
b. antisocial
c. passive-aggressive
d. compulsive
(page 446)

SELF-TEST 2

1. Survey data concerning the incidence of psychiatric disorders among Americans shows that most disorders are found in what age range?
a. 5 to 15 years of age
b. 15 to 24 years of age
c. 25 to 44 years of age
d. 45 to 65 years of age
(page 416)

2. The notion of "mental illness" was first introduced by:
a. Freud
b. Hippocrates
c. Galen
d. Spurzheim
(page 417)

3. Conceptualizing abnormal behavior as a symptom of underlying physical or physiological problems is characteristic of the _____ viewpoint of psychopathology.
a. biological
b. ethical
c. cognitive
d. psychodynamic
(page 417)

4. According to which viewpoint of psychopathology are the same principles used to account for normal as well as abnormal behavior?
a. biological
b. psychodynamic
c. phenomenological
d. behavioral
(page 419)

5. According to the ethical viewpoint of psychopathology:
a. psychotics should be removed from society
b. psychosis is due to environmental factors
c. psychosis is due to existential anxiety
d. psychotics should be held responsible for their behavior
(page 420)

6. On the DSM-III, current symptomotology would be indicated on:
a. Axis I
b. Axis II
c. Axis III
d. Axis IV
    (page 421)

7. If a disorder is due to psychological rather than physical causes, we say that it is:
a. functional
b. organic
c. reactive
d. process
    (page 421)

8. Which of the following would NOT be considered an organic mental disorder?
a. amnestic syndrome
b. mixed-brain syndrome
c. delirium
d. cyclothymic disorder
    (page 424)

9. It is said that the avoidance behavior of the anxious individual may temporarily reduce anxiety, but at the expense of greater anxiety in the future. This is referred to as:
a. the dystonic effect
b. the neurotic paradox
c. the amnestic syndrome
d. secondary gain
    (page 425)

10. A person who ran away screaming upon the approach of a harmless little dog would likely be diagnosed as suffering from:
a. dementia
b. phobia
c. dependent personality disorder
d. the neurotic paradox
    (page 426)

11. When psychological problems are expressed by way of actual physical symptoms, the Axis I diagnostic category would be:
a. organic mental disorder
b. anxiety disorder
c. somatoform disorder
d. affective disorder
    (page 427)

12. The *medical student syndrome* is representative of the Axis I diagnosis:
a. conversion disorder
b. somatization disorder
c. hypochondriasis
d. psychogenic pain disorder
    (page 428)

13. "Glove" anesthesia occurs when a person loses feeling in the hand in the area that corresponds to the skin covered by a glove. This would be considered:
a.   a psychogenic disorder
b.   a conversion disorder
c.   an organic brain disorder
d.   hypochondriasis
     (page 428)

14. The criterion for physiological addiction is:
a.   physiological withdrawal symptoms
b.   blackout
c.   direction of all of one's behavior toward obtaining the drug
d.   deterioration of the thought processes
     (page 429)

15. If an individual can control starting to drink but not stopping once he or she has started, he or she would be in the _____ stage of alcoholism.
a.   prealcoholic
b.   prodromal
c.   crucial
d.   chronic
     (page 430)

16. In his research on the causes of alcoholism, Vaillant came to the startling conclusion that:
a.   there are more than 100 million alcoholics in the United states
b.   alcoholism is the result of underlying biochemical abnormalities
c.   the alcoholic personality is the result of alcoholism, not the cause
d.   alcoholics can be taught to drink in a mature way, without returning to the alcoholic pattern of drinking
     (page 432)

17. Methadone controls heroin addiction by:
a.   curing the addictive habit
b.   blocking the heroin "high"
c.   allowing the addict to concentrate on the causes of the addiction
d.   causing the withdrawal syndrome to occur if heroin is taken
     (page 433)

18. The paraphilias include all EXCEPT:
a.   voyeurism
b.   exhibitionism
c.   frigidity
d.   fetishism
     (page 434)

19. According to the American Psychiatric Association, homosexuality:
a.   is no longer listed as psychopathological
b.   continues to be listed as always psychopathological
c.   is psychopathological only when it is unwanted by the individual
d.   is psychopathological if it disrupts the family
     (page 434)

20. Disturbances in mood are characteristic of individuals who would be diagnosed as having:
a.   an affective disorder
b.   a psychosexual dysfunction
c.   psychogenic pain disorder
d.   personality disorder
     (page 435)

21. The risk of suicide in a depressed patient is often greatest when:
a.   the depression is most intense
b.   the cause of the depression reappears
c.   the person is unable to sleep properly
d.   the depression lifts
     (page 436)

22. If concordance rates between identical and fraternal twins were about equal, there would be strong evidence for _____ causes of psychopathology.
a.   organic
b.   genetic
c.   biochemical
d.   environmental
     (page 437)

23. According to the dynamic viewpoint of psychopathology, the cause of depression is:
a.   anger turned inward
b.   childhood rejection
c.   genetic and biochemical
d.   discrepancy between the real and the ideal self
     (page 437)

24. Schizophrenic disorders are characterized by all of the following EXCEPT:
a.   thought disturbance
b.   delusional behavior
c.   anxiety
d.   emotional blunting
     (page 439)

25. "Waxy flexibility" and "hostility by immobility" characterize:
a.   bipolar disorder
b.   catatonic schizophrenia
c.   dysthymic disorder
d.   dependent personality
     (page 440)

26. Excess amounts of the brain neurotransmitter _____ may be a likely part of a biochemical mechanism for schizophrenia.
a.   dopamine
b.   norepinephrine
c.   serotonin
d.   acetylcholine
     (page 442)

27. Current research efforts aimed at identifying brain structures that may be linked to schizophrenia have concentrated on the examination of the:
a.   thalamus
b.   hypothalamus
c.   hippocampus
d.   midbrain
     (page 443)

28. When open warfare exists between parents:
a.   there is a double bind for the children
b.   a schism is said to exist
c.   there is skew
d.   the neurotic paradox will occur
     (page 443)

29. A dependent individual who was afraid of directly expressing anger at another would probably be diagnosed as:
a.   dependent personality disorder
b.   mixed-brain syndrome
c.   passive-aggressive personality disorder
d.   hypochondriac
     (page 445)

30. Assessment of individuals in jails would probably turn up a large number who fit the diagnosis of:
a.   paranoid schizophrenic
b.   antisocial personality
c.   organic mental disorder
d.   posttraumatic stress syndrome
     (page 446)

WHAT DOES IT MEAN?

OBJECTIVES

1.   How does the definition of psychopathology as applied to individuals relate to culture and society?
2.   How reliable and valid is psychodiagnosis, and what are the implications of psychodiagnosis for the therapist and client?
3.   Why should psychodiagnosis be left in the hands of professionals?
4.   What considerations must be addressed when mental patients are moved from hospitals back into communities?
5.   What is the insanity defense, and why is its use surrounded by controversy?

SELF-TEST

1.   With respect to psychodiagnosis and abnormal behavior:
a.   there is a natural standard that determines what behavior is abnormal
b.   diagnostic criteria may change as a society's values change
c.   diagnostic criteria remain unchanged year after year by their very nature
d.   most societies seem to have the same criteria for calling behavior abnormal
     (page 448)

2. One of Szasz's main criticisms of the concept of psychopathology is that:
a. sick people should not be held responsible for their actions
b. psychopathology is partly defined by a fallible society
c. mental illness is an adaptive behavior in modern times
d. it makes the medical student's syndrome too probable
   (page 448)

3. According to Laing:
a. legislators are insane
b. homosexuality is psychopathological
c. more emphasis should be placed on cognitive functioning in diagnosis
d. diagnostic labels keep us from communicating with disturbed people
   (page 448)

4. Research that assessed the reliability and validity of psychodiagnosis showed that:
a. there were an insufficient number of diagnostic categories
b. schizophrenia was diagnosed 90 percent of the time
c. interclinician reliability was suprisingly low
d. the reliability of diagnosis improved in regard to subcategories
   (page 449)

5. A psychodiagnosis can lead to a self-fulfilling prophecy because it:
a. contains expectancies
b. says too much about feelings and not enough about behavior
c. is much too cognitive
d. is much too unreliable

6. Which of the following fits in best with the medical student's syndrome?
a. a little learning is a dangerous thing
b. to be or not to be
c. you can't teach old dogs new tricks
d. a stitch in time saves nine
   (page 451)

7. When releasing mental patients from hospitals into the community:
a. most states provide adequately for the reentry of these individuals into society
b. many of the patients never receive further care after release
c. about 10 percent will reenter the hospital within two years
d. most patients will be capable of resuming their lives in an effective manner
   (page 452)

8. It is estimated that about _____ percent of all released mental patients reenter the hospital within a year of release.
a. 10
b. 25
c. 50
d. 75
   (page 452)

9. The insanity defense:
a. is a psychiatric rather than a legal term
b. requires that the defendant acted on impulse regardless of whether he or she knew that the act was wrong
c. results in fairly straight-forward presentation of the issue by prosecution and defense experts
d. aims at absolving the defendant from responsibility for the crime
(page 453)

10. The American Psychiatric Association has suggested that regarding the insanity defense:
a. antisocial personalities be held accountable for their actions
b. persons found innocent by reason of insanity should not be sent to mental institutions
c. psychiatrists rather than judges are best capable of determining who is likely to be dangerous
d. the insanity defense should be abolished altogether
(page 453)

ANSWER KEY

EXERCISES

Exercise 1

1. deviation
2. maladaptive
3. organic
4. functional
5. prehistoric
6. Greece
7. medical
8. devil
9. exorcism
10. brain

Exercise 2

1. C   2. E   3. A   4. F   5. D   6. B

Exercise 3

1. diagnosis
2. communication
3. symptoms
4. DSM-III
5. primary
6. personality
7. medical (or physical)
8. stress
9. adaptive

Exercise 4

1. A   2. B   3. F   4. E   5. G   6. D   7. C

Exercise 5

1. functional
2. escape and avoidance
3. rigid
4. relax
5. paradox
6. primary
7. secondary
8. phobias
9. states
10. attacks
11. obsessive-compulsive
12. thoughts
13. behaviors
14. appropriately
15. symbolic

Exercise 6

Obviously, Mary has a realistic conflict--whether to remain true to her beliefs or to accede to her boyfriend's wishes. She cannot do both. As long as she avoids making a decision, she keeps herself in a constant state of anxiety that may sometimes escalate into a full-blown anxiety attack such as the one she experienced on Friday night. Mary's symptoms give her an excuse to stay away from John and avoid the issue, which reduces her anxiety. This is a primary gain. When John leaves, she feels better. The sympathy that she receives from John is a secondary gain. The paradoxical aspect is that the solution is only temporary and will shortly result in a resumption of high anxiety.

POSTSCRIPT: Anxiety states do not have to be this sensational. If you are constantly having conflicts over whether to study or whether to party and you constantly choose the latter, this is not pathological. But if your way out of the conflict is consistently to make up reasons that you cannot take the exam on time, this is different. You will only prolong the agony!

Exercise 7

1. A   5. B
2. B   6. C
3. D   7. D
4. C   8. A

Exercise 8

1. psychological   6. prodromal   11. failure
2. physiological   7. crucial   12. aversive
3. appropriate   8. chronic   13. covert
4. depressant   9. delirium tremens 14. abstinence
5. prealcoholic   10. stress   15. Alcoholics Anonymous

Exercise 9

1. prescription   6. antisocial
2. contagion   7. appropriate
3. euphoria   8. methadone
4. tolerance   9. morphine
5. cold turkey   10. naloxone

Exercise 10

1. C   5. A
2. A   6. D
3. D   7. B
4. B   8. C

Exercise 11

1. mood
2. voyeurism
3. pedophilia
4. fetishism
5. exhibitionism

Exercise 12

1.	mood	6.	hallucinations	10.	holidays
2.	dysthymic	7.	cyclothymic	11.	tenth
3.	reality	8.	unipolar	12.	women
4.	bipolar	9.	energy	13.	men
5.	delusions				

Exercise 13

The evidence for genetic contributions is correlational and applies mainly to bipolar disorder. Kallman found that the concordance rate for manic-depression (as it was then called) is about 25 percent for siblings and parents of an afflicted individual (that is, if the individual is diagnosed as manic-depressive, a sibling or parent has a one in four chance of also being so diagnosed). This compares with a concordance rate of only 0.5 percent in the general population. In comparison, the concordance rate for fraternal twins is comparable to that for siblings and parents (that is, 26.5 percent) but is much higher (that is, 95.7 percent) for identical twins. Because identical twins share identical genes, one possible conclusion is that the difference between 95.7 percent and 26.5 percent is due to genetic causes. However, it should be noted that in Kallman's studies, there were no controls for environmental contributions (that is, it is quite possible that identical twins also share a more similar environment than do fraternal twins).

The evidence for biochemical contribution is very indirect. It has been hypothesized that lower levels of the neurotransmitters norepinephrine and setotonin contribute to mood changes. Given this, it is known that the tricyclic antidepressants, which alleviate depression, also raise the level of these neurotransmitters, whereas reserpine, a drug that tends to induce depression, lowers the level of these neurotransmitters.

Exercise 14

1. personal loss
2. Freud's theory
3. Rogers's theory
4. behavioral (learning) theory
5. learned-helplessness theory

Exercise 15

1. Schizophrenia refers to a group of psychotic disorders in which there are disturbances in thought processes and emotions and a marked distortion of reality. There are a number of potential symptoms, including withdrawal from interpersonal relationships, blunted and/or inappropriate emotional responses, depersonalization, and a preoccupation with inner fantasies (for example, hallucinations and delusions). This general lack of attention to the external environment can lead to low IQ scores.

2. In reactive schizophrenia, the onset of symptoms is sudden, and the prognosis is good. In comparison, in process schizophrenia, there is a slow and gradual development of withdrawal and thought deterioration over many years, and the prognosis is poor.

Exercise 16

1. catatonic
2. paranoid
3. disorganized
4. chronic-undifferentiated

Exercise 17

1. concordance
2. genetic
3. female
4. diasthesis-stress
5. predisposition
6. trigger
7. neurotransmitters
8. dopamine
9. cause and effect
10. skew
11. schism
12. double bind
13. schizophrenogenic

Exercise 18

Personality disorders are defined by their clearly maladaptive long-standing patterns of behavior. Such individuals are capable of criminal acts (including violence), and they do not see themselves as having a problem. Thus, they are unlikely to seek help and to experience anxiety with respect to their behaviors. Also, unlike the anxiety and schizophrenic disorders, personality disorder is not defined by reactions to stress, conflict, and the like.

Exercise 19

1. dependent personality
2. passive-aggressive personality
3. compulsive personality disorders
4. antisocial personality
5. paranoid personality

Exercise 20

1. H   6. G
2. B   7. J
3. C   8. D
4. E   9. F
5. A   10. I

MULTIPLE-CHOICE

Self-Test 1

1.	c	6.	c	11.	a	16.	c	21.	a	26.	d
2.	d	7.	a	12.	c	17.	d	22.	d	27.	c
3.	b	8.	d	13.	c	18.	b	23.	b	28.	c
4.	b	9.	a	14.	b	19.	c	24.	b	29.	a
5.	a	10.	b	15.	d	20.	a	25.	a	30.	d

Self-Test 2

1.	c	6.	a	11.	c	16.	c	21.	d	26.	a
2.	b	7.	a	12.	c	17.	b	22.	d	27.	c
3.	a	8.	d	13.	b	18.	c	23.	a	28.	b
4.	d	9.	b	14.	a	19.	c	24.	c	29.	c
5.	d	10.	b	15.	c	20.	a	25.	b	30.	b

WHAT DOES IT MEAN?

Self-Test

1.	b	3.	d	5.	a	7.	b	9.	d
2.	b	4.	c	6.	a	8.	c	10.	a

12 Psychotherapy

OBJECTIVES

1. What is the definition of psychotherapy, and what characterizes the mental health professionals and paraprofessionals who administer therapeutic services?
2. What are the four classes of drugs used in chemotherapy, and why have they limited the relative roles of hospitalization and convulsive therapy and virtually eliminated the role of psychosurgery?
3. What are the goals and methods of Freudian psychoanalysis, and what changes have occurred in the revised versions?
4. Which learning principles are used in the behavior therapies, and what cognitive techniques have been added to create the cognitive-behavioral therapies?
5. How do the phenomenologists view abnormal behavior, and how are these views incorporated in client-centered and Gestalt therapy and in encounter groups?
6. What was the impetus for the community mental health movement, how does its emphasis differ from those of the various psychotherapies, and what three important services are provided?
7. What are the negative and positive conclusions regarding the future of psychotherapy?

SYNOPSIS

Psychotherapy is defined as a corrective experience that helps a person behave in more socially appropriate, adequate, and adaptive ways. At the professional level, therapeutic services are provided by degreed mental health professionals, including clinical psychologists, psychiatrists, psychoanalysts, psychiatric social workers, school psychologists, counseling psychologists, and psychiatric nurses. Often, these professionals enlist the aid of paraprofessionals from the community.

The various modes of treatment include medically oriented therapies, psychodynamic therapies, behavioral and/or cognitive therapies, phenomenological therapies, and community mental health services.

The most promising of the medical therapies is drug therapy, or chemotherapy, which uses sedatives, tranquilizers, antidepressants, and antipsychotics. Thanks to these drugs, there is much less need for traditional hospital care and virtually no need (if there ever was one) for psychosurgery. Moreover, the use of electroconvulsive therapy is now limited mainly to certain depressed patients.

Psychoanalysis is the original psychodynamic therapy. Created by Freud, it is designed to help a client gain insight into unresolved, unconscious, and infantile conflicts. The therapist must overcome the client's unconscious resistance, interpret what the major conflicts are, and then help the client work through them. In this endeavor, Freud tried and quickly abandoned hypnosis in favor of free association. Other important techniques include interpretation of symptomatic acts, dream analysis, and use of transference. The newer or revised versions of psychoanalysis rely less on infantile conflicts and more on self-directed problem-solving strategies. There is also more of an emphasis on group therapies (for example, family therapy and psychodrama), which answers a major criticism against classical psycho-analysis--that it is inefficient.

The emphasis in behavioral therapy is on learning history. The procedures used are variants of classical conditioning (for example, systematic desensitization and aversion therapy), operant conditioning (for example, positive reinforcement and punishment), and modeling. The cognitive-behavioral therapies rely not only on behavioral principles but also on changing irrational beliefs, imagination of both stimuli and responses (for example, covert sensitization), and methods for coping with stress.

The phenomenological viewpoint emphasizes the individual's unique perception of himself or herself and others. From this perspective, Rogers's client-centered therapy uses a more passive atmosphere of acceptance in which to encourage the client to experience his or her immediate feelings. Perls's Gestalt therapy is more active, and its purpose is to induce the client to overcome barriers to self-awareness, which prevent him or her from taking responsibility for his or her feelings. Often, Gestalt therapy is used in groups. For example, in the encounter group, the emphasis is not on specific problem areas but on sensitization to feelings.

Although all forms of psychotherapy are designed to help people after problems have occurred, the purpose of the community mental health movement is to prevent problems, or at least to deal with them as quickly as possible. The movement was initiated by legislation proposed by President John F. Kennedy and enacted in the administration of President Lyndon B. Johnson. Primary services are designed to prevent problems from occurring; secondary services are designed to minimize the impact of problems once they have developed; and tertiary services are designed to minimize the long-term effects of emotional problems.

In their concluding comments, the authors caution against assuming that "diagnosis-treatment-rehabilitation-cure" is a sequence that works smoothly and often. However, they also point to positive changes in therapeutic services, particularly as they relate to the diagnosis, training of therapists, and administration of services.

KEY WORDS AND PHRASES

OBJECTIVE 1

psychotherapy
clinical psychologist
psychiatrist
psychoanalyst
psychiatric social worker
school psychologist
counseling psychologist
psychiatric nurse
paraprofessional

OBJECTIVE 2

medical orientation
drug therapy (chemotherapy)
sedatives (for example, alcohol, barbiturates)
tranquilizers (for example, Valium)
antidepressants (for example, Iproniazid, lithium)
antipsychotics (for example, reserpine, chlorpromazine)
hospitalization
criteria for admission
social-learning therapy
milieu therapy
medication and custodial care
psychosurgery
prefrontal lobotomy
side effects of lobotomy
convulsive therapy
insulin and metrazol
ECT
side effects of convulsions

OBJECTIVE 3

psychodynamic therapies
insight
psychoanalysis
resistance
free association
symptomatic acts
manifest content
latent content
transference
interpretation
working through
analytical orientation
self-directed problem solving
family therapy
psychodrama
protagonist

OBJECTIVE 4

behavioral therapies
cognitive-behavioral therapies
systematic desensitization
reciprocal inhibition
hierarchy of anxiety-provoking stimuli
relaxation training
positive reinforcement
shaping
token economy
punishment
aversion therapy
time out from reinforcement

biofeedback
modeling
social-skills training
assertiveness training
rational emotive therapy
irrational beliefs
"straight thinking"
coping
covert sensitization
stress-inoculation training
preparation, acquisition, rehearsal, and application

OBJECTIVE 5

phenomenological approach
unique perception of self and others
client-centered therapy
self-knowledge
denial of feelings
nondirective therapy
self-concept
empathic understanding
unconditional positive regard
congruence
immediate feelings
Gestalt therapy
barriers to self-awareness
responsibility
encounter groups
self-description
eyeball to eyeball
blind walk
trusting exercises
hot seat
positive and negative bombardment

OBJECTIVE 6

community mental health
primary services
secondary services
tertiary services

OBJECTIVE 7

oversimplification
positive changes

EXERCISES

EXERCISE 1: Objective 1

TITLE: MENTAL HEALTH PROFESSIONALS (AND PARAPROFESSIONALS)
TASK: Match letters to numbers

A. clinical psychologist   E. school psychologist
B. psychiatrist   F. counseling psychologist
C. psychoanalyst   G. psychiatric nurse
D. psychiatric social worker   H. paraprofessional

_____ 1. The graduate work is either in psychology or education; the degree is either an M.A., Ph.D., or Ed.D.; and the specialization is in either counseling or educational testing.

_____ 2. The graduate work usually involves residency training after the M.D. degree, and the specialization is in psychotherapy, management of medication, or electroconvulsive therapy.

_____ 3. After a short orientation in a service facility, the nondegreed individual specializes in communicating with people from his or her own community.

_____ 4. After graduate training in either an academic or professional psychology program, the Ph.D. or Psy.D. specializes in research, therapy, and diagnostic testing.

_____ 5. The degree can have an M.D., Ph.D., or Psy.D. but is usually the M.D. who seeks additional specialized training.

_____ 6. The degree is R.N., and the specialization is in counseling, therapy, and care of hospitalized mental patients.

_____ 7. The degree is M.S.W., and the specialization is in individual and family therapy and counseling, and community orientation.

_____ 8. The graduate work is in psychology or education; the degree is an M.A., Ph.D., or Ed.D.; and the specialization is in counseling, therapy, vocational counseling, and rehabilitation.

EXERCISE 2: Objective 2

TITLE: DRUG THERAPY (CHEMOTHERAPY)
TASK: Fill in the blanks

1. _____ reduce anxiety and tension by inducing muscle relaxation, sleep, and inhibition of the cognitive centers.
2. The most common sedative is _____.
3. Other sedatives include the _____ bromides and chloral hydrate.
4. _____ also reduce anxiety, but without the sleep-inducing side effects of the sedatives.
5. The most popular tranquilizer currently is _____.
6. Mood elevators, or _____, are used for depressed patients.
7. The original antidepressant drug was _____.
8. These drugs seem to work by _____ the amount of norepinephrine and serotonin in the brain.
9. The element _____ has been used in recent years, particularly to counteract mood swings, as seen in bipolar disorder.

10. The original antipsychotic drug was _____ .
11. Unfortunatley, as a side effect, this drug can induce severe _____ .
12. The phenothiazines, particularly _____ have replaced reserpine.
13. The side effects of this drug include _____ stiffness and dryness of the mouth.
14. The long-term effects include _____ , which is a disfiguring and irreversible disturbance of motion control.
15. Antipsychotics are believed to work by _____ dopamine activity.

EXERCISE 3: Objective 2

TITLE: HOSPITALIZATION
TASK: Essays

1. What are the various reasons that people are hospitalized?

2. What are the statistics regarding first-time admissions, average size of the hospital population, average stay, and readmission rate?

3. What are social-learning and milieu therapy, and how do they compare in effectiveness with medication and traditional custodial care?

EXERCISE 4: Objective 2

TITLE: PSYCHOSURGERY AND ELECTROCONVULSIVE THERAPY
TASK: Fill in the blanks

1. In the prefontal _____ , pathways in the prefrontal region of the brain are severed.
2. The purpose of lobotomies is to calm _____ behavior.
3. The basis for performing lobotomies was early research of calming effects in _____ .
4. During the 1940s and 1950s, lobotomies were performed on hospitalized _____ , depressives, and some neurotics.
5. The side effects of lobotomy include seizures, catatoniclike stupor, and even _____ .
6. Fortunately, psychosurgery is now a nearly extinct procedure, made so by the advent of _____ drugs.
7. Regarding convulsive therapy, there was early evidence in the 1930s that _____ overdose reduced psychotic symptoms.
8. Also, it was noted that _____ rarely appears among schizophrenics.
9. The early convulsive procedures used the drugs insulin and _____ .
10. The current procedure involves electroconvulsive shock and is abbreviated _____ .
11. A common by-product of ECT is retrograde _____ .
12. ECT is used somewhat effectively in alleviating _____ .
13. But ECT is not effective with other problems; it is not known why it works with depressives; and there is no evidence of alleviation of _____ depressions.

EXERCISE 5: Objective 3

TITLE: PSYCHOANALYSIS
TASK: Match letters to numbers

A.   free association
B.   resistance
C.   symptomatic acts
D.   manifest content
E.   latent content
F.   transference
G.   working through

_____1. If one believes in psychic determinism, then slips of the tongue,
         errors in writing, lateness for appointments, and the like can be
         interpreted to have unconscious meaning.
_____2. The hidden meaning of a dream that needs to be interpreted.
_____3. Freud abandoned hypnosis in favor of a technique in which the client
         is instructed to say whatever comes to mind.
_____4. Once the therapist has interpreted the client's unconscious conflicts,
         he or she tries to help the client understand and resolve them.
_____5. The content of a dream that is obvious and conscious.
_____6. The client often forms a relationship with the therapist that is
         similar to relationships that the client had with his or her parents
         (and others) in childhood.
_____7. Given the unconscious nature of conflicts, the client has a tendency
         to block or to be unaware of anxiety-provoking thoughts, feelings,
         wishes, or impulses.

EXERCISE 6: Objective 3

TITLE: REVISED VERSIONS OF PSYCHOANALYSIS
TASK: Essays

1.   What are two main differences between classical psychoanalysis and the
     revised versions?

2.   What are the four main advantages of group therapy?

3.   What are the four goals of family therapy?

4.   What are the two important roles in psychodrama, and what are the
     potential advantages of this form of group therapy?

EXERCISE 7: Objective 4

TITLE: BEHAVIORAL THERAPIES: HISTORICAL BACKGROUND
TASK: Essays

1.   What is the basic behavioral objection to psychoanalysis, and to what
     position instead do behaviorists ascribe?

2.   What are the essential features of the early studies in the conditioning
     and "deconditioning" of fear?

3. What historical procedure (that is still used today) was developed to treat enuresis (bed-wetting)?

EXERCISE 8: Objective 4

TITLE: OVERVIEW OF THE BEHAVIORAL THERAPIES
TASK: Match letters to numbers

A. systematic desensitization
B. positive reinforcement
C. shaping
D. token economy
E. punishment
F. aversion therapy
G. time out
H. biofeedback
I. modeling
J. social-skills training
K. assertiveness training

_____1. Application of an unpleasant stimulus contingent upon inappropriate behaviors.
_____2. Application of external rewards for appropriate behaviors.
_____3. Learning by observing how others around us do things.
_____4. The use of reciprocal inhibition (that is, counteracting anxiety-provoking stimuli with relaxation).
_____5. An extension of classical conditioning in which the client is taught to associate an inappropriate response (for example, excessive drinking) with an unpleasant stimulus (for example, nausea).
_____6. Focuses on teaching a broad range of socially appropriate behaviors. Can include modeling, role playing, groups, or whatever.
_____7. Use of positive reinforcement for components of a complex behavioral sequence. Involves differential reinforcement of behaviors that more successively approximate the desired response.
_____8. Use of electronic devices to monitor and control physiological responses. Often combined wiht other techniques of stress reduction.
_____9. Focuses on teaching people how and when to express their feelings and stand up for their rights. Can include modeling, role playing, groups, or whatever.
_____10. Use of positive reinforcement. The patient is allowed to exchange credits for appropriate behavior for desired goods or privileges.
_____11. A form of punishment that involves removing or delaying positive reinforcement.

EXERCISE 9: Objective 4

TITLE: FOCUS ON SYSTEMATIC DESENSITIZATION
TASK: Fill in the blanks

1. The pairing of opposing responses such as relaxation and anxiety is called _____ inhibition.
2. Reciprocal inhibition serves as the basis for Wolpe's technique called systematic _____.

3. The first step in systematic desensitization is to establish a
_____ of fear-provoking stimuli (from mild to intense).
4. In the second step of systematic desensitization, _____ training
begins as the client is taught to control specific muscle groups and
to breathe deeply and slowly.
5. In the third step of systematic desensitization, the subject tries to
relax as he or she _____ fearful stimuli on the hierarchy.

EXERCISE 10: Objective 4

TITLE: A CASE STUDY IN OPERANT CONDITIONING
TASK: Essay

Little Johnny is a head banger. Often, he gets up and begins banging
his head against the wall and continues to do so until his parents stop him.
How would you explain and treat this behavior from the operant perspective?

EXERCISE 11: Objective 4

TITLE: THE COGNITIVE-BEHAVIORAL THERAPIES
TASK: Fill in the blanks

1. _____ therapy focuses on mistaken or distorted beliefs that people
have about themselves or others.
2. For example, a person who thinks he or she has to please everyone would
be given training in _____ thinking.
3. When cognitive procedures are used in conjunction with desentization
procedures, the client imagines anxiety-provoking situations but also
that he or she is _____ with the anxiety or stress.
4. Also, clients may be asked to record their self-_____, and these
are later subjected to modification.
5. Covert _____ is a cognitive therapy created to resolve both
inconveniences and ethical problems associated with administering
unpleasant stimuli.
6. Here the client _____ both inappropriate behaviors and aversive
stimuli associated with the inappropriate behaviors.
7. Yet another cognitive therapy is stress-_____ training.
8. The first stage in this training is _____, in which the therapist
helps the client understand the nature of stress and explores self-
statements made under stress.
9. The next stage involves _____ and _____, in which the client learns
and practices more adaptive self-statements.
10. Finally, in the _____ stage, the client practices using these
coping strategies while under mild and controlled stress in the
therapist's office.

EXERCISE 12: Objective 5

TITLE: THE PHENOMENOLOGICAL THERAPIES
TASK: Essays

1. How does the phenomenological (or humanistic) view of behavior differ
from the psychoanalytical and behavioral viewpoints?

2. What is the role of the phenomenological therapist relative to that of the psychoanalyst or behavioral therapist?

EXERCISE 13: Objective 5

TITLE: CLIENT-CENTERED AND GESTALT THERAPIES
TASK: Fill in the blanks

1. In client-centered therapy (formerly called nondirective therapy), the main concept is the _____ concept.
2. The self-concept is defined as a relatively consistent and enduring framework of self-regarding _____.
3. The disturbed person has experiences or feelings that are _____ with these self-attitudes.
4. The purpose of client-centered therapy is to promote an atmosphere of acceptance in which the client can face _____ feelings.
5. The goal is to create an _____ frame of reference in which the client no longer relies on others for evaluation.
6. The client-centered therapist shows _____ understanding, or an attempt to understand the client's immediate feelings.
7. The client-centered therapist also shows _____ positive regard, which is an acceptance of the client as being worthwhile, irrespective of the contingencies.
8. Finally, the client-centered therapist shows _____, which means that what the therapist perceives is consistent with what the therapist says.
9. In comparison with the client-centered therapist, the Gestalt therapist is seen more _____ (active/passive).
10. The Gestalt therapist tries to deal with _____ the person is feeling and _____ the person is behaving.
11. More specifically, the therapist tries to help the client overcome barriers to self-_____.
12. Often this is done in _____ rather than individual therapy sessions.
13. Gestalt therapists rely on both verbal and nonverbal behaviors and often use _____ playing, the purpose being to help their clients get in touch with and communicate their feelings.
13. The goal is for the client to accept _____ for his or her feelings or behaviors.

EXERCISE 14: Objective 5

TITLE: ENCOUNTER GROUPS
TASK: Match letters to numbers

A. self-description
B. eyeball to eyeball
C. the blind walk
D. trusting exercises
E. hot seat
F. positive and negative bombardment

____1. Being lifted and passed around in a circle formed by group members.
____2. After each participant writes down three adjectives about himself or herself, a given set of adjectives is randomly selected, and the group discusses the kind of person being described.

299

_____ 3. Similar to the hot seat--but the focus is on good or bad feedback.
_____ 4. Two people stare at each other for a minute or two and communicate as much as possible. They discuss their feelings afterwards.
_____ 5. While at the center of attention, the rest of the group gives the individual honest feedback about how he or she affects them.
_____ 6. All participants are paired off, and one from each pair leads the other around until the follower is sensitized to the environment.

EXERCISE 15: Objective 6

TITLE: OVERVIEW OF COMMUNITY MENTAL HEALTH
TASK: Essays

1. How does the community mental health movement differ in emphasis from psychotherapy, and what are its two major concerns?

2. Which two important historical factors led to the restructuring of the nation's mental care policy?

EXERCISE 16: Objective 6

TITLE: PRIMARY, SECONDARY, AND TERTIARY SERVICES
TASK: Match letters to numbers

A. primary services
B. secondary services
C. tertiary services

_____ 1. Concern for long-term effects of emotional problems.
_____ 2. Concern for immediate impact of problems once they have developed.
_____ 3. Concern for preventing problems from ocurring.
_____ 4. Crisis intervention (for example, suicide prevention) centers that use both storefront clinics and paraprofessionals.
_____ 5. Rehabilitation.
_____ 6. Institution of changes in punishment techniques used in prisons.
_____ 7. In the schools, the emphasis has shifted from memorizing facts to solving problems.
_____ 8. Counseling intended to get people back into the community. This may involve job training, help in learning how to get a job, and development of social skills.
_____ 9. In a crisis, people are likely to receive therapy that is more directive and confrontive than are most forms of traditional therapy.

EXERCISE 17: Objective 6

TITLE: SUICIDE
TASK: True/False

_____ 1. In general, older people represent a greater suicide risk than younger people do.
_____ 2. The exception is for black males, where the greatest risk is from age 20 to 24.
_____ 3. Men are three times more likely than women are to attempt suicide.
_____ 4. Women are three times more likely than men are to succeed at suicide.
_____ 5. The more specific the suicide plan is, the greater the risk will be.

_____ 6. Pills pose a greater suicide danger than guns do.

_____ 7. People with little social support (for example, friends, relatives, clergy) pose a greater risk than others do.

_____ 8. Divorced people have a suicide rate that is three to four times lower than the national average.

EXERCISE 18: Objective 7

TITLE: CONCLUDING COMMENTS
TASK: Essays

1. Why is the diagnosis-treatment-rehabilitation-cure sequence an over-simplified description of mental health care?

2. What are the five promising trends in mental health?

EXERCISE 19

TITLE: KEY NAMES
TASK: Match letters to numbers

A. Hippocrates   J. Skinner
B. Rush   K. Bandura
C. Paul and Lentz   L. Ellis
D. Moniz   M. Dush, Hirt, and Schroeder
E. Freud   N. Rogers
F. Watson and Raynor   O. Perls
G. Mary Cover Jones   P. Lieberman
H. Mowrer   Q. John F. Kennedy
I. Wolpe   R. Lyndon B. Johnson

_____ 1. Systematic desensitization
_____ 2. Conditioning Little Albert's fear of rats
_____ 3. Decondition Peter's fear of rabits
_____ 4. Ancient Greek remedies such as bleeding and purging
_____ 5. Proposal to Congress to establish mental health centers
_____ 6. Conversion of the proposal into law
_____ 7. The father of American psychiatry
_____ 8. Popularization of lobotomies in the 1940s
_____ 9. Negative results in 16 of 170 students in encounter groups
_____ 10. Classical psychoanalysis
_____ 11. Operant procedures
_____ 12. Gestalt therapy
_____ 13. Client-centered therapy
_____ 14. Comparison of social-learning and millieu therapies with traditional custodial care
_____ 15. Research showing success with self-statement modification
_____ 16. Rational-emotive therapy
_____ 17. Classic treatment of enuresis (bed-wetting)
_____ 18. Modeling

MULTIPLE-CHOICE TESTS

SELF-TEST 1

1. One of the first questions that a therapist asks himself or herself when a new client seeks help is:
a. why is this person here?
b. how much should I charge this person?
c. what method of treatment should I employ?
d. how long should I keep this person in therapy?
    (page 455)

2. In chemotherapy, _____ are used because they reduce anxiety without inducing sleep.
a. sedatives
b. tranquilizers
c. antidepressants
d. antipsychotics
    (page 458)

3. _____ is an effective chemical agent in the treatment of bipolar disorder.
a. norepinephrine
b. reserpine
c. lithium
d. Valium
    (page 458)

4. A medicated mental patient who began exhibiting severe motion impairments most likely had been taking which kind of drug?
a. sedative
b. tranquilizer
c. antidepressant
d. antipsychotic
    (page 458)

5. The main purpose of hospitalization is to:
a. prepare patients for ECT of psychosurgery
b. administer long-term psychoanalysis
c. maintain those patients incapable of functioning in the community
d. bring the community closer to the medical profession
    (page 458)

6. Based upon Paul's and Lentz's research, the best form of therapy to return chronically hospitalized mental patients successfully to the community is:
a. social-learning therapy
b. milieu therapy
c. medication
d. electric shock
    (page 460)

7. The need for psychosurgery and ECT has been greatly reduced, thanks to:
a. an increase in the number of hospitals
b. milieu therapy
c. paraprofessionals
d. chemotherapy
    (page 460)

8. The psychosurgical procedure known as the lobotomy was developed to:
a. reduce aggressive behavior
b. cure schizophrenia
c. relieve depression
d. treat epilepsy
    (page 460)

10. The initial aim of psychoanalysis is to:
a. produce transference
b. overcome unconscious resistance to remembering repressed wishes and the like
c. encourage the clients to accept themselves as they really are
d. develop a strong ego
    (page 461)

11. You were supposed to meet your analyst for a 3 p.m. appointment and you forgot. This would be viewed as:
a. latent content
b. denial
c. a symptomatic act
d. incongruence
    (page 462)

12. In psychoanalysis, the therapist uses the technique of free association in order to:
a. induce transference
b. overcome resistance
c. promote congruence
d. reduce discrepancy between self and experience
    (page 462)

13. When the therapy patient begins viewing the analyst as if he were his or her father, the process called _____ has occurred.
a. resistance
b. congruence
c. interpretation
d. transference
    (page 463)

14. Which of the group therapies is geared toward improving communication, decision making, and conflict resolution?
a. encounter
b. family
c. assertiveness
d. rehabilitation
    (page 465)

15. The behaviorist who was influential in the development of cognitive behavior therapy is:
a. Skinner
b. Watson
c. Bandura
d. Mowrer
    (page 466)

16. In _____, the object is to inhibit fear reciprocally by pairing a fearful stimulus with relaxation.
a.   covert sensitization
b.   systematic desensitization
c.   stress inoculation
d.   RET
     (page 466)

17. Biofeedback would be a useful technique to employ in training clients to relax as part of:
a.   punishment training
b.   aversion therapy
c.   overt sensitization
d.   systematic desensitization
     (page 467)

18. A behavioral approach that has been used successfully in institutions and that has reduced the frequency of passive, dependent behavior among the patients is:
a.   the token economy
b.   systematic desensitization
c.   RET
d.   aversion therapy
     (page 468)

19. Aversion therapy is usually based on the principles of:
a.   operant conditioning
b.   classical conditioning
c.   modeling
d.   cognition
     (page 469)

20. In order to be truly effective, punishment procedures must:
a.   eliminate the problem behavior on the first application
b.   employ electric shock as the punishing stimulus
c.   be combined with positive reinforcement of appropriate behavior
d.   be combined with deprivation of the consequences of the punished
     behavior
     (page 469)

21. Which of the following cognitive therapies has as its goal the changing of irrational beliefs?
a.   RET
b.   stress inoculation
c.   systematic desensitization
d.   covert sensitization
     (page 471)

22. A child molester might be told to imagine a child and then imagine that his or her insides were falling out. This would be done in:
a.   systematic desensitization
b.   RET
c.   stress inoculation
d.   covert sensitization
     (page 472)

23. Which of the following is NOT one of the stages of stress inoculation training?
a. preparation
b. rehearsal
c. relaxation
d. application
    (page 473)

24. When the client-centered therapist understands the immediate feelings of her client, she is showing:
a. transference
b. empathic understanding
c. unconditional positive regard
d. congruence
    (page 475)

25. Which of the following best illustrates unconditional positive regard?
a. So, you think that I am your father!
b. I think that I know how you are feeling.
c. I care for you, regardless of your nasty actions.
d. I don't think that you are being completely honest.
    (page 475)

26. Barriers to self-awareness are what prevent you from taking responsibility for your feelings, according to:
a. Wolpe
b. Perls
c. Freud
d. Bandura
    (page 478)

27. The goal in primary service is:
a. prevention
b. rehabilitation
c. maintenance
d. crisis intervention
    (page 478)

28. Suicide intervention counseling is an example of:
a. primary services
b. secondary services
c. tertiary services
d. mixed services
    (page 479)

30. Which of the following is NOT a contemporary trend in psychotherapy?
a. crisis intervention
b. short-term psychotherapy
c. little or no hospitalization
d. narrowing of therapy approaches to a few that are known to be effective
    (page 481)

SELF-TEST 2

1. Which of the following mental health professionals is most likely to
have a degree in medicine?
a. clinical psychologist
b. psychiatrist
c. clinical social worker
d. paraprofessional
    (page 456)

2. Alcohol, barbiturates, and bromides are members of the class of drugs
called:
a. sedatives
b. tranquilizers
c. antipsychotics
d. antidepressants
    (page 458)

3. Which two neurotransmitters in the brain are increased by the action of
antidepressant medications?
a. dopamine and epinephrine
b. acetylcholine and endorphin
c. serotonin and neoepinephrine
d. acetylcholine and serotonin
    (page 458)

4. The disorder called tardive dyskinesia:
a. occurs as part of bipolar depression
b. causes delusions and hallucinations
c. is treated through the use of reserpine
d. occurs as a side effect of antipsychotic medication
    (page 458)

5. When someone is hospitalized with mental and emotional problems, the
average length of confinement is about:
a. four days
b. two weeks
c. six months
d. two years
    (page 459)

6. Research has shown that the brain chemical _____ is found to be at an
increased level after electroconvulsive therapy (ECT).
a. norepinephrine
b. dopamine
c. lithium
d. beta-endorphin
    (page 461)

7. Which of the following would be considered an insight therapy?
a. behavior modification
b. covert sensitization
c. psychoanalysis
d. systematic desensitization
    (page 461)

8.   Quite early in his career, Freud gave up on the use of _____ as a way of overcoming resistance.
a.   surgery
b.   dream analysis
c.   free association
d.   hypnosis
      (page 461)

9.   The use of dream analysis in psychoanalysis:
a.   depends most on the dream's manifest content
b.   requires some knowledge of the client's pattern of associations
c.   is fairly straightforward and generalizable
d.   is well accepted by most psychologists
      (page 462)

10.   Most clients who are in psychoanalytic therapy:
a.   are from the middle or upper class
b.   are children
c.   exhibit thought disorders
d.   are women
      (page 464)

11.   Which of the following is NOT one of the reasons that group psychotherapy may be more effective than individual psychotherapy is?
a.   finding that others have similar problems
b.   experiencing helping someone else through their problems
c.   elimination of the transference stage
d.   having a sounding board for new behaviors and feelings
      (page 464)

12.   A form of group psychotherapy in which members of the group assume roles in order to help a "protagonist" work through interpersonal problems is:
a.   RET
b.   encounter training
c.   milieu therapy
d.   psychodrama
      (page 465)

13.   Watson's experiment with Little Albert:
a.   suggested ways in which phobias could be learned
b.   showed how bed-wetting could be eliminated
c.   revealed the limits on learning in infants
d.   produced a massive counterreaction to behaviorism
      (page 466)

14.   Mowrer's treatment of bed-wetting in children:
a.   was based on principles of operant conditioning
b.   was based on principles of classical conditioning
c.   required shocks to be delivered when urine was released
d.   turned out to cause neurosis in adulthood
      (page 466)

15. In behavior therapy, such as systematic desensitization:
a. the main goal is fostering insight into the phobia
b. remote causes of problems are sought
c. the behavior therapist has little need to talk with the client
d. unconscious processes are ignored
   (page 467)

16. The non-cognitive-behavioral therapist is most likely to use which method below in treatment?
a. shaping
b. covert sensitization
c. RET
d. modeling
   (page 468)

17. Putting snakes in a wine glass to discourage drinking alcohol would be a crude form of:
a. RET
b. aversion therapy
c. systematic desensitization
d. encounter therapy
   (page 469)

18. Biofeedback techniques have been applied to many disorders, each of which has an underlying relationship to:
a. disease
b. age
c. stress
d. repression
   (page 470)

19. Social-skills and assertiveness training techniques bear a close resemblance to:
a. encounter therapy
b. RET
c. family therapy
d. psychodrama
   (page 471)

20. _____ is like punishment by imagination.
a. systematic desensitization
b. punishment training
c. aversion therapy
d. overt sensitization
   (page 472)

21. Which of the following is NOT a goal of client-centered therapy?
a. help people show how they really feel
b. promote acceptance of self
c. produce peak experiences
d. overcome denial of true feelings
   (page 474)

22. Psychoanalysis is to client-centered therapy as:
a. empathy is to congruence
b. resistance is to interpretation
c. conditioned is to unconditional positive regard
d. past is to present
   (page 474)

23. Congruence means that the therapist:
a. works through the conflict with the client
b. is honest and genuine with the client
c. loves the client
d. understands the client
   (page 474)

24. In which form of psychotherapy is the therapist least intrusive?
a. client-centered
b. psychoanalytic
c. Gestalt
d. behavioral
   (page 474)

25. Sensitizing oneself and others to one another's feelings is a primary goal of:
a. psychodrama
b. client-centered therapy
c. encounter groups
d. psychoanalysis
   (page 476)

26. Positive and negative bombardment is most likely to occur in:
a. RET
b. family therapy
c. encounter groups
d. Gestalt therapy
   (page 476)

27. Which of the following does NOT fit?
a. trusting exercises
b. blind walk
c. social-skills training
d. eyeball to eyeball
   (page 476)

28. Social and political activism occurs frequently among mental health professionals who are engaged in the delivery of:
a. primary services
b. secondary services
c. tertiary services
d. crisis intervention
   (page 479)

29. If there were an emergency, which class of community-based services would likely be involved first?
a. primary
b. secondary
c. tertiary
d. quaternary
   (page 479)

30. Which of the following is NOT true concerning contemporary trends in psychotherapy?
a.   therapists are becoming more and more specialized
b.   therapists are moving away from traditional forms of psychotherapy
c.   behavior modification techniques show promise for altering problem behaviors
d.   an increased reliance on psychosurgery
      (page 481)

WHAT DOES IT MEAN?

OBJECTIVES

1.   What factors make it difficult to assess accurately the effectiveness of psychotherapy?
2.   What are the traits that characterize successful therapists?
3.   What kinds of problems motivate people to seek therapy, and what is likely to happen in therapy?
4.   How does the confidential relationship between therapist and client affect the process of therapy?
5.   What short-term solutions have been used in modern times to broaden the reach of therapists in a community?

SELF-TEST

1.   According to Wysneck's study of psychotherapy effectiveness:
a.   psychoanalytic therapy was much more effective than nonpsychoanalytic therapy was
b.   nonpsychoanalytic therapy was much more effective
c.   patients who received no therapy improved more than patients who did
d.   behavior modification was the most effective treatment
      (page 483)

2.   Which of the following was NOT a major problem with Eysenck's research on psychotherapy effectiveness?
a.   the data were not collected in a standard manner
b.   cure was not operationally defined
c.   differences between those who did and did not seek psychotherapy were not controlled
d.   too few of the subjects were diagnosed as suffering from depression, and not enough were suffering from adjustment disorders
      (page 483)

3.   Perhaps the most optimistic conclusion that we can draw from Eysenck's study on the effectiveness of psychotherapy is that:
a.   people frequently solve their own personal problems
b.   people rarely need psychotherapy
c.   most therapists provide effective therapy
d.   few people are hurt by being in therapy
      (page 483)

4.   The "demand for improvement" effect occurs when after finishing therapy, the client:
a.   feels worse than when he or she started
b.   feels pressure to be cured
c.   feels cheated because more did not happen
d.   is pressured to return for follow-up treatments
     (page 483)

5.   Many training programs in clinical psychology are apt to select students on the basis of _____ criteria.
a.   intellectual
b.   socioeconomic
c.   personality
d.   empathic skills
     (page 484)

6.   The probability of an ideal relationship between therapist and client increases with the therapist's
a.   intelligence
b.   experience
c.   attractiveness
d.   patience
     (page 484)

7.   Which of the following characteristics of a therapist was NOT seen to be important for positive change in therapy?
a.   accurate empathy
b.   nonpossessive warmth
c.   self-actualization
d.   genuineness
     (page 484)

8.   In general, the successful therapist:
a.   is always experienced
b.   is always warm
c.   remains aloof from his or her clients
d.   sometimes does not succeed with all types of problems
     (page 484)

9.   The most common reported problems for which people seek help is:
a.   marital difficulties
b.   problems with parents
c.   problems on the job
d.   depression
     (page 486)

10. When in need of psychological help, most people turn first to a:
a.   psychologist
b.   clergyman
c.   psychiatrist
d.   friend
     (page 486)

11. Shuman's study of what people do and do not tell their therapists
revealed that:
a.   most people had committed crimes that they were afraid to reveal
b.   the most censored topic was sexual thoughts and acts
c.   many people were afraid that their therapist would tell others of their
     innermost thoughts and feelings
d.   90 percent of clients did not hide any information from their therapist
     (page 487)

12. In which of the following situations would a communication between
client and therapist NOT be considered to be bound under the principles of
confidentiality?
a.   a woman admitted that she sometimes drove drunk with her children in
     the car
b.   a man revealed that he was tempted by thoughts of incest
c.   a man revealed that he planned to murder his wife in order to collect
     insurance money
d.   a boy admitted that he was using marijuana and amphetamines
     (page 487)

13. Which of the following has NOT been a contemporary response to the
shortage of therapists?
a.   use of paraprofessionals
b.   use of computers for personality testing
c.   greater use of group therapy
d.   greater reliance on insight oriented psychotherapies such as
     psychoanalysis
     (page 488)

14. The movement toward community mental health has been sparked by the
a.   failure of psychotherapy to cure people
b.   dissatisfaction with drugs
c.   shortage of therapists
d.   development of a milieu therapy
     (page 488)

15. Which of the following is NOT a contemporary application of computers to
the field of psychotherapy?
a.   use of robot computers for behaviorally oriented psychotherapies such
     as systematic desensitization
b.   administration of personality tests
c.   collection of interview data
d.   training of specific skills such as problem solving
     (page 488)

ANSWER KEY

EXERCISES

Exercise 1

1.	E	5.	C
2.	B	6.	G
3.	H	7.	D
4.	A	8.	F

Exercise 2

1. sedatives
2. alcohol
3. barbiturates
4. tranquilizers
5. Valium
6. antidepressants
7. Iproniazid
8. increasing
9. lithium
10. reserpine
11. depression
12. chlorpromazine
13. muscle
14. tardive dyskinesia
15. reducing

Exercise 3

1. Persons may be hospitalized because they cannot handle the pressures of everyday life, because they are unresponsive to outpatient psychotherapy and/or medication, because they are a danger to themselves or others, or because they do not respond favorably to traditional psychotherapy in the office setting.

2. There are about 250,000 new admissions each year, and the average size of the mental hospital population is about 750,000 at any given time. This latter figure at least equals that for all physical illness combined. Also, the average stay of a mental patient is about two weeks, although 20 percent of those admitted stay a year or more. Finally 50 percent of all admitted return at a later point.

3. Social-learning therapy is based on learning principles, and milieu therapy involves the self-government of wards. In a six-year study comparing these two forms of therapy with traditional medication and custodial care, 90 percent of those treated with social-learning therapy remained in the community after release. This compares with 70 percent for milieu therapy and only 50 percent for traditional custodial care.

Exercise 4

1. lobotomy
2. aggressive
3. animals
4. schizophrenics
5. death
6. antipsychotic
7. insulin
8. epilepsy
9. metrazol
10. ECT
11. amnesia
12. depression
13. future

Exercise 5

1. C   2. E   3. A   4. G   5. D   6. F   7. B

Exercise 6

1. First, from a theoretical standpoint, in which classical psychoanalysis focuses on unconscious infantile conflicts, the more modern ego-analysis focuses on the establishment of adaptive ego functions that promote self-directed problem solving. Second, from a structural standpoint, classical psychoanalysis is inefficient because of the one-to-one therapist-client relationship. The revised versions have been adapted for the group situation.

2. First, the individual often learns that his or her problems are not unique, that others have the same problems. Second, the individual receives

feedback from several different points of view. Third, group members may fulfill one another's needs. And finally, the individual can try out new behaviors in a safe and accepting atmosphere.

3. The family therapist views an individual's problem in the context of a family network that maintains a certain balance and certain rules. Given this, the therapist's goals are to improve communication within the family, encourage autonomy and empathy among members, help develop new ways of making decisions, and help resolve conflicts.

4. In psychodrama, the protagonist is the main actor (who usually describes a given problem in interpersonal relationships), and the therapist and other group members either play roles relating to the protagonist's personality or simply observe the drama. The belief is that this situation is less threatening because it is make-believe and because key people in the protagonist's life are not usually present. Thus, the protagonist is freer to express feelings and try out alternative solutions to problems. Often, the audience may become as emotionally involved as the protagonist is.

Exercise 7

1. The basic belief of behaviorists such as Skinner is that psychoanalysis emphasizes private events (that is, unconscious conflicts) that are difficult to measure and that rely on subjective inference. The behavioral position is that therapy should focus on directly observable behavior.

2. In an early study, Watson and Raynor (1920) reported that they classically conditioned baby Albert to fear a white rat. According to the report, after several pairings of the white rat--the CS--with loud noise-- the UCS--Albert developed a fear of the white rat, as well as fear of stimuli resembling the white rat. In a subsequent report by Mary Cover Jones (1924), Peter, who had a natural fear of rabbits, was "deconditioned." The method used taught Peter to relax as the situation was made progressively more fearful (that is, bringing the rabbit closer and closer). This procedure is much like Wolpe's systematic desensitization procedure.

3. O. H. Mowrer (1938) used a classical conditioning procedure to counteract bed-wetting. The procedure used an electronic sensing device that woke the child just as the flow of urine began. The child would then get up and complete his urination in the toilet. Mowrer's belief was that this procedure promoted an association between the stimulus of a full bladder and the response of waking and inhibiting urination.

Exercise 8

1.	W	5.	F	9.	K
2.	B	6.	J	10.	D
3.	I	7.	C	11.	G
4.	A	8.	H		

Exercise 9

1. reciprocal
2. desensitization
3. hierarchy
4. relaxation
5. images

Exercise 10

According to the operant viewpoint, something must be reinforcing Johnny's head banging. The best guess here is that under normal conditions, Johnny receives little or no attention from his parents. However, when he hurts himself, they come running and shower him with perhaps too much affection and attention. Thus, it may be that attention is maintaining the head banging. Given these assumptions, the recommended treatment is to ignore (that is, extinguish) head banging and, in addition, pay attention to Johnny when he is not banging his head. If you recall from Chapter 4, this is an omission procedure in which the absence of head banging is being socially reinforced, as are appropriate behaviors that are incompatible with head banging.

Exercise 11

1. rational-emotive
2. straight
3. coping
4. statements
5. sensitization
6. imagines
7. inoculation
8. preparation
9. acquisition; rehearsal
10. application

Exercise 12

1. In comparison with the psychoanalytic viewpoint, which emphasizes unconscious conflicts, and the behavioral viewpoint, which emphasizes learning history, the phenomenological viewpoint attributes behavior to the individual's unique perception of the world. The individual is most knowledgeable with respect to his or her own problems.

2. To use the language of the text, the phenomenological therapist is seen not as an "all-knowing judge" or a "behavior modifier" but instead as an "attentive helper." The therapist's main task is to create conditions that allow the client to become aware of important perceptions, feelings, and conflicts. Given this awareness, it is assumed that progression toward positive changes will occur naturally.

Exercise 13

1. self
2. attitudes
3. inconsistent
4. denied
5. internal
6. empathic
7. unconditional
8. congruence
9. active
10. what; how
11. awareness
12. group
13. role
14. responsibility

Exercise 14

1. D   2. A   3. F   4. B   5. E   6. C

Exercise 15

1. Whereas psychotherapy is designed to help people deal with problems after they have developed and caused considerable hardship, the purpose of community mental health is to prevent problems before they occur, or at least to deal with them as early as possible. The two major concerns in community mental

health are the need for more efficient and comprehensive mental health services and the need to consider the community as a whole, as opposed to the individuals within it.

2.   In 1963, President John F. Kennedy proposed to Congress the establishment of community mental health centers. Legislation was passed under President Lyndon B. Johnson's administration which required mental health centers to provide short-term hospitalization, outpatient care, 24-hour emergency services, day care, night care, and consultation with community agencies.

Exercise 16

1.	C	4.	B	7.	A
2.	B	5.	C	8.	C
3.	A	6.	A	9.	B

Exercise 17

1.	T	5.	T
2.	T	6.	F
3.	F	7.	T
4.	F	8.	F

Exercise 18

1.   There is often disagreement with respect to diagnoses, and it is rarely the case that psychologists are aware of causes, let alone cures. Furthermore, psychotherapy is not uniformly effective. Results vary with the type of therapy and the skills of the therapist. In general, all therapies appear to be effective with some problems, and no therapy appears to be effective with all problems.

2.   According the authors, the five positive trends include less emphasis on diagnostic labels, training that permits therapists to be skilled in a wide variety of techniques, the use of behavior modification for specific disorders, movement away from traditional psychotherapeutic approaches, and movement toward the community mental health approach.

Exercise 19

1.	I	7.	B	13.	N
2.	F	8.	D	14.	C
3.	G	9.	P	15.	M
4.	A	10.	E	16.	L
5.	Q	11.	J	17.	H
6.	R	12.	O	18.	K

MULTIPLE-CHOICE

Self-Test 1

1.	a	6.	a	11.	c	16.	b	21.	a	26.	b
2.	b	7.	d	12.	b	17.	d	22.	d	27.	a
3.	c	8.	a	13.	d	18.	a	23.	c	28.	b
4.	d	9.	d	14.	b	19.	b	24.	b	29.	c
5.	c	10.	b	15.	c	20.	c	25.	c	30.	d

Self-Test 2

1. b	6. d	11. c	16. a	21. c	26. c
2. a	7. c	12. d	17. b	22. d	27. c
3. c	8. d	13. a	18. c	23. b	28. a
4. d	9. b	14. b	19. d	24. a	29. b
5. b	10. a	15. a	20. d	25. c	30. d

WHAT DOES IT MEAN?

Self-Test

1. c	4. b	7. c	10. b	13. d
2. c	5. a	8. d	11. b	14. c
3. a	6. b	9. a	12. c	15. a

Appendix A
Elementary Statistics

OBJECTIVES

1. What is the function of descriptive statistics?
2. What are the three measures of central tendency?
3. Why is it important to know about variability, and how is variability measured?
4. What are major characteristics of the normal frequency distribution, and what do z-scores represent?
5. What is the relationship between correlation and regression?
6. What are the procedures followed in inferential statistics, and how do they differ from those used in descriptive statistics?
7. How does analysis of variance relate to the t-test, and how does factor analysis relate to the correlation coefficient?

SYNOPSIS

Psychologists use statistics both to anlayze data gathered from their research and to produce and refine psychological tests. Basically, descriptive statistics are used to organize and describe sample data, whereas inferential statistics are used to estimate population characteristics and test hypotheses regarding behavior in these populations.

In descriptive statistics, the mean (average), median (middlemost score), and mode (most frequent score--a crude measure) are measures of central tendency, whereas the range (a very crude measure), standard deviation, and variance are measures of variability. The normal distribution has a number of important characteristics (for example, symmetry), and z-scores allow us to characterize the area under the normal curve in standard (deviation) units. Correlation coefficients allow us to describe the relationship between two sets of events (positive or negative covariation), and regression represents a use of correlation in which we can predict specific values of a set of events (that is, the regression line). When more than one variable is correlated with the criterion variable, multiple regression analyses are used.

With inferential statistics, we test the (null) hypothesis that the results of a given piece of research are due to chance. In the simplest case (that is, an experimental versus a control group), we use the t-test to compare the two means. If the difference between means is not likely due to chance, we call it statistically significant and reject the null hypothesis. Depending on the nature of the research, the investigator may wish to guard against either a Type I error (rejecting the null hypothesis when it is true) or a Type II error (accepting the null hypothesis when it is false).

More complicated experimental designs require more complicated statistics. Analysis of variance, for example, is an extension of the logic behind the t-test and is used when there are more than two groups (and/or more than one variable under study). Factor analysis extends the logic behind correlation to more than only two sets of events. For example, there may be a number of factors that underlie personality, and so factor analysis is a good technique for identifying these factors.

KEY WORDS AND PHRASES

OBJECTIVE 1

descriptive statistics

OBJECTIVE 2

arithmetic mean
median
mode

OBJECTIVE 3

variability
individual differences
range
standard deviation
variance

OBJECTIVE 4

normal distribution
z-scores
probability

OBJECTIVE 5

correlation coefficient
positive covariation
negative covariation
Pearson produce-moment correlation coefficient
scatter plot
regression
linear regression
regression line
prediction
multiple regression

OBJECTIVE 6

random sampling
hypothesis testing
population
mean difference
null hypothesis
t-test
Type I error
Type II error

OBJECTIVE 7

analysis of variance
F-test
factor analysis

MULTIPLE-CHOICE TEST

1.   Statistics used to describe and summarize the results of research is called _____ statistics.
a.   descriptive
b.   summary
c.   hypothesis
d.   inferential
      (page 490)

2.   Statistics used to infer conclusions about the meaning of experimental results are called _____ statistics.
a.   descriptive
b.   correlational
c.   normal
d.   inferential
      (page 490)

3.   When you add up all the scores and divide by the number of cases in your sample, you are calculating the:
a.   mean
b.   median
c.   mode
d.   range
      (page 490)

4.   The middlemost score and most frequently occurring score are, respectively:
a.   mean and mode
b.   mean and median
c.   mode and mean
d.   median and mode
      (pages 490, 491)

5.   If the scores in a distribution were skewed, the most appropriate measure of central tendency to describe them would be the:
a.   mean
b.   median
c.   mode
d.   standard deviation
      (page 490)

6.   What is the median of the following set of scores: 2, 6, 6, 7, 10, 16, 19, 25?
a.   6
b.   10
c.   8.5
d.   11.4
      (page 490)

7.   A measure of variability that is calculated by subtracting the lowest score from the highest score is the:
a.   variance
b.   range
c.   standard deviation
d.   mode
     (page 492)

8.   The standard deviation reflects the extent to which scores are spread out around their:
a.   mean
b.   median
c.   mode
d.   all three
     (page 492)

9.   Which of the following is NOT a measure of variability?
a.   range
b.   frequency
c.   variance
d.   standard deviation
     (page 493)

10. The square root of the variance of a set of scores is called the:
a.   range
b.   correlation coefficient
c.   difference score
d.   standard deviation
     (page 493)

11. If a set of scores were normally distributed, then:
a.   each half of the distribution should mirror the other
b.   the frequency of scores should be low at one end and high at the other
c.   the mean, mode, and median should have identical values
d.   the most frequent scores should be at the beginning and at the end
     (page 493)

12. Which of the following expresses in units of standard deviations the degree of distance from center:
a.   t-test
b.   F-test
c.   regression line
d.   z-score
     (page 494)

13. A descriptive statistic that allows a researcher to make comparisons among scores that represent different qualities is the:
a.   t-test
b.   median
c.   Z-score
d.   mean
     (page 494)

14. If the mean score on an English exam were 75 and the standard deviation were 8, then a z-score of 2.5 would be an exam score of:
a. 65
b. 85
c. 95
d. 100
   (page 494)

15. If sexiness and IQ were negatively correlated, then:
a. sexy people should be smart
b. unsexy people should be dumb
c. unsexy people should be smart
d. the correlation coefficient would be zero
   (page 495)

16. If scores on two separate tests change in the same direction, then the two are:
a. positively correlated
b. negatively correlated
c. bicorrelated
d. uncorrelated
   (page 495)

17. If there is absolutely no relationship between two variables, then the Pearson product moment correlation coefficient should have a value:
a. between -1 and +1
b. between -1 and zero
c. between zero and +1
d. approximately zero
   (page 497)

18. If the scores of people on the same test were compared from one administration to another, then the correlation coefficient would be a measure of:
a. validity
b. reliability
c. predictability
d. efficiency
   (page 497)

19. In linear regression we try to:
a. compare two group means
b. find factors that underline a given psychological phenomenon
c. find the best fitting line for a given scatter plot
d. see if our samples are random relative to the population
   (page 497)

20. If we use linear regression to make a prediction, our accuracy will be determined by the:
a. degree of correlation between two variables
b. direction of correlation between the two variables
c. absolute means of the two variables
d. factor loadings of the two variables
   (page 497)

21. When all potential participants have an equal chance of participating in any of the groups in an experiment, we say that the sampling is:
a. random
b. haphazard
c. contrived
d. controlled
   (page 499)

22. We use random sampling to make sure that our sample is _____ the population.
a. correlated with
b. random with respect to
c. representative of
d. not influenced by
   (page 499)

23. A difference is said to be statistically significant if it is:
a. scientifically important
b. consistent with the null hypothesis
c. very unlikely to have occurred by chance
d. very large
   (page 500)

24. According to the null hypothesis, in an experiment:
a. the results are not due to the independent variable
b. the results are due to the independent variable
c. there is a correlation but no cause
d. the data lack variability
   (page 500)

25. In a t-test, the measure calculated is a ratio of the difference between the means and:
a. the estimated means
b. the null hypothesis
c. the regression line
d. an estimate of the variability
   (page 501)

26. A Type I error is made when:
a. a false null hypothesis is rejected
b. a false null hypothesis is not rejected
c. a true null hypothesis is rejected
d. a true null hypothesis is accepted
   (page 501)

27. If you were going to test the null hypothesis regarding the difference between just two groups, you would use:
a. a correlation coefficient
b. a t-test
c. an analysis of variance
d. a factor analysis
   (page 501)

28. An analysis of variance (F-test) is used instead of a t-test when:
a. the groups are very large
b. the variability is very large
c. more than two groups are compared
d. the variance needs to be analyzed
    (page 502)

29. The results of a factor analysis will show:
a. clusters
b. means
c. variabilities
d. variances
    (page 502)

30. The statistical procedure called factor analysis has been used extensively in:
a. learning and motivation
b. memory and cognition
c. biopsychology and development
d. intelligence and personality assessment
    (page 502)

ANSWER KEY

1. a	6. c	11. a	16. a	21. a	26. c
2. d	7. b	12. d	17. d	22. c	27. b
3. a	8. a	13. c	18. b	23. c	28. c
4. d	9. b	14. c	19. c	24. a	29. a
5. b	10. d	15. c	20. a	25. d	30. d

Appendix B
Neurons: The Building Blocks
of the Nervous System

OBJECTIVES

1. What are the structural components of the nerve cell?
2. What are the structural components of the synaptic region?
3. What physical and chemical properties of ions interact to produce the resting membrane potential?
4. What are the ionic changes that occur during the action potential?
5. How is the "message" of the action potential transmitted to the post-synaptic neuron?
6. With respect to the common neurotransmitters, what commonalities and differences do the basic processes of synthesis, storage, release, reception, and termination of action share?
7. How can drugs alter the normal effects of neurotransmitters?

SYNOPSIS

Structrually, the nerve cell contains a nucleus and many smaller organelles that keep the neuron alive and functioning. The dendrites receive information from the sensory receptors or other neurons, and the axon carries that information to the organs, muscles, and other neurons.

Within the neuron, there are electrical properties that are based on the distribution of chemicals inside relative to outside the semipermeable cell membrane. At rest, the cell membrane is polarized so that the inside is 70 millivolts more negative than the outside is. In general, at rest, more sodium and chloride ions are outside than inside, whereas more potassium and protein ions (the latter being too big to cross the membrane) are inside than outside.

The action potential is said to be all or none. That is, an initial depolarization brought about by a small influx of sodium ions either will or will not reach the threshold (that is, depolarize by about 10 millivolts). If the threshold is reached, the inside will rise from -70 millivolts to +40 millivolts. The action potential begins at the axon hillock and moves sequentially to the terminal button. During this interval the axon is in an absolute refractory state (that is, no other action potentials can occur). Subsequently, both sodium and potassium are pumped out of the axon, resulting in a state of hyperpolarization. The normal resting membrane potential is recovered when the postassium reenters the axon in the usual amounts.

The action potential at the presynaptic terminal initiates the release of neurotransmitter substances from the terminal button across the synaptic space to make contact with receptors on the postsynaptic neuron. These transmitters are manufactured within the presynaptic neuron, and after either exciting or inhibiting the postsynaptic neuron, they are either broken down by enzymes or taken back up, resynthesized, and restored in the synaptic vesicles for later use.

We have learned a great deal in recent years about three of these neurotransmitters. Acetylcholine (ACh) is present in all of the neuromuscular junctions of the body, where its effect is excitatory. However, it can have inhibitory effects elsewhere. ACh seems to inhibit behavior, whereas norepinephrine (NE) excites behavior. Thus, there is evidence that ACh and NE function antagonistically to each other. Dopamine (DA), precursor of NE, has attracted attention recently, having been implicated in schizophrenia, Parkinson's disease, and the loss of muscle control in senility.

In general, the drugs that we take have four effects, each involving some aspect of synaptic structure or function. More specifically, drugs may mimic a transmitter, prevent its breakdown and reuptake, prevent its main action (for example, by blocking release or preventing contact with post-synaptic endorphins), and, finally, affect the neuromodulators (for example, the endorphins), which affect the neurotransmitters.

KEY WORDS AND PHRASES

OBJECTIVE 1

neuron
nucleus
dendrite
axon
organelles
mitochondria
ribosomes
hillock
myelin
nodes of Ranvier
telodendria

OBJECTIVE 2

boutons (terminals)
cleft (space)
presynaptic neuron
postsynaptic membrane
vesicles
presynaptic membrane
postsynaptic neuron

OBJECTIVE 3

resting membrane potential
polarization
sodium ions
potassium ions
chloride ions
proteins
semipermeable membrane
diffusion
electrical charge
inside/outside

OBJECTIVE 4

action potential
depolarization
hyperpolarization
absolute refractory period
all-or-none principle
saltatory conduction

OBJECTIVE 5

synaptic transmission
neurotransmitter
excitation
EPSP
inhibition
IPSP
spatial summation
temporal summation

OBJECTIVE 6

synthesis
precursor
enzymes
transport
storage
release
receptor molecules
degradation
reuptake
ACh
NE
DA

OBJECTIVE 7

neuromodulators
mimic
blockade

MULTIPLE-CHOICE TEST

1. The _____ controls all aspects of cell activity.
a. synapse
b. nucleus
c. axon
d. mitochondria
    (page 504)

2. The production of energy in the nerve cell occurs in the:
a. mitochondria
b. telodendria
c. node of Ranvier
d. organelle
   (page 504)

3. The part of the neuron at which the action potential begins is called the:
a. node of Ranvier
b. axon hillock
c. telodendria
d. terminal button
   (page 504)

4. Unlike other types of cells in the body, neurons:
a. do not produce their own energy
b. do not require nutrients
c. do not have a semipermeable membrane
d. do not reproduce
   (page 504)

5. The small branches at the ends of axons that contact other cells are called:
a. dendroglia
b. nodes of Ranvier
c. myelin
d. telodendria
   (page 505)

6. The space that divides the presynaptic terminal from the postsynaptic neuron is the:
a. synapse
b. synaptic cleft
c. node of Ranvier
d. telodendria
   (page 505)

7. If one were to look microscopically at the area of the synapse, large numbers of _____ would be seen.
a. ribosomes
b. mitochondria
c. nuclei
d. axon hillocks
   (page 505)

8. The value of the resting membrane potential on most nerve cells is approximately:
a. -10 microvolts
b. -20 millivolts
c. -70 millivolts
d. -230 millivolts
   (page 506)

9. When the cell membrane is at rest, it is said to be:
a. polarized
b. unpolarized
c. inhibited
d. depolarized
    (page 506)

10. The notion that the cell membrane is semipermeable means that:
a. all ions can pass through
b. no ions can pass through
c. some ions can pass through
d. no ions can leak out
    (page 506)

11. The principle of _____ says that substances in solution move from regions of high concentration to regions of low concentration.
a. diffusion
b. attraction
c. potential charge
d. permeability
    (page 506)

12. According to the attraction principle of charged particles, one would expect Na+ to _____ K+.
a. repel
b. attract
c. combine with
d. have no effect on
    (page 506)

13. When a nerve cell was at its resting membrane potential, which ion would be MOST concentrated outside the membrane?
a. proteins
b. potassium
c. sodium
d. chloride
    (page 506)

14. Which event triggers the release of transmitter molecules from the presynaptic terminal?
a. the EPSP
b. the IPSP
c. the resting membrane potential
d. the action potential
    (page 507)

15. Which ionic event occurs during the depolarization phase of the action potential?
a. influx of sodium into the axon
b. efflux of potassium from the axon
c. influx of potassium into the axon
d. efflux of sodium from the axon
    (page 507)

16. The fall in voltage during the latter phase of the action potential is brought about by the:
a. influx of sodium into the axon
b. efflux of potassium from the axon
c. influx of potassium into the axon
d. efflux of sodium from the axon
   (page 507)

17. According to the all-or-none principle:
a. a neurotransmitter either excites or inhibits the postsynaptic membrane
b. an action potential maintains all its characteristics during axonal conduction
c. protein molecules either cross or fail to cross the cell membrane
d. the dendrite either receives or does not receive a message
   (page 507)

18. During the action potential:
a. there is a polarity change of about 110 millivolts
b. another action potential can be produced at any time
c. potassium enters the axon from outside, hyperpolarizing the membrane
d. proteins are released from the axon hillock
   (page 508)

19. The rate of conduction of action potentials in large-diameter, myelinated axons is approximately:
a. at the speed of light
b. 1 foot per second
c. 130 meters per second
d. 1,000 miles per hour
   (page 508)

20. Where there are myelinated fibers with nodes of Ranvier, the impulse will jump from node to node. This is called _____ conduction.
a. ribosomic
b. dopaminergic
c. axonal
d. saltatory
   (page 508)

21. At excitatory synapses, the postsynaptic membrane is _____ by the neurotransmitter.
a. mimicked
b. blocked
c. depolarized
d. hyperpolarized
   (page 509)

22. When action potentials from several different neurons lead to convergence of transmission at several places on a single neuron, _____ has occurred.
a. absolute refraction
b. degradation
c. temporal summation
d. spatial summation
   (page 509)

23. The actual process of production of neurotransmitters within the synaptic terminals is called:
a. reuptake
b. absorption
c. synthesis
d. neuromodulation
   (page 510)

24. Dopamine is said to be a _____ of norepinephrine.
a. precursor
b. mimic
c. blocker
d. receptor
   (page 510)

25. In order for synthesis to occur, _____ are needed to catalyze reactions.
a. blockers
b. enzymes
c. precursors
d. mimics
   (page 510)

26. The relationship between ACh and NE is said to be:
a. excitatory
b. inhibitory
c. antagonistic
d. enziomatic
   (page 511)

27. Which neurotransmitter has been implicated in schizophrenia and Parkinsonism?
a. acetylcholine
b. doapmine
c. norepinephrine
d. beta-endorphin
   (page 511)

28. Norepinephrine and dopamine appear to be two transmitters that are concentrated in the _____ and important to the regulation of eating.
a. thalamus
b. hypothalamus
c. medulla
d. cerebellum
   (page 512)

29. Drugs that interfere directly with a neurotransmitter are called:
a. enzymes
b. blocking agents
c. mimics
d. neuromodulators
   (page 512)

30. A dietary substance that potentially could affect mood disorders, schizophrenia, and Parkinson's disease is:
a. tyrosine
b. tryptophan
c. choline
d. vitamin D
   (page 513)

ANSWER KEY

1.	b	6.	b	11.	c	16.	b	21.	c	26.	c
2.	a	7.	b	12.	a	17.	b	22.	d	27.	b
3.	b	8.	c	13.	c	18.	a	23.	c	28.	b
4.	d	9.	a	14.	d	19.	c	24.	a	29.	b
5.	d	10.	c	15.	a	20.	d	25.	b	30.	a

Appendix C
Psychological Tests
and Assessment Techniques

OBJECTIVES

1. What factors must psychologists consider when constructing tests?
2. What differentiates the rational (theoretical) and empirical approaches to test construction, and how are tests and test items evaluated?
3. What differentiates reliability and validity, and how is each determined?
4. What is item-response theory, and how does its application in testing eliminate some of the external problems?
5. What four things do tests test, and what are the two types of decisions to which test results contribute?
6. What are the various objective and projective tests, and how do these two types of tests differ?
7. What is the difference berween a sign and a behavioral sample, and what implication does this difference have for psychological testing?
8. What are the relative advantages and disadvantages of projective tests and self-report measures?

SYNOPSIS

In the rational approach to test construction, the psychologist depends on theory and common sense in constructing items. In comparison, empirical test items need bear no resemblance to what's being measured. For example, the MMPI contains a number of scales that historically have elicited different but predictable responses from different patient populations. Another empirical approach entails using a statistical procedure such as factor analysis to determine commonality among already-constructed tests (for example, Cattell's 16 PF).

Standardization is the key ingredient in test and test-item evaluation. In standardization, the test is administered to large samples of subjects. In so doing, fine details of the test procedure can be worked out, and norms can be established (for example, as in intelligence tests).

It is important that tests be both reliable and valid. Reliability means repeatability--that is, the ability to yield consistent results. This can be established through alternative forms, split-half, or test-retest methods. Reliability is a prerequisite for validity, but the two are far from isomorphic. A test is valid if it measures what it is supposed to measure (for example, a personality test should measure personality and not intelligence). There is concurrent validity (how a test correlates with other tests), predictive validity (can it predict some behavioral outcome?), and construct validity (do the results conform to the requirements of a theory?).

Attempts at standardization and at maximizing the reliability and validity of tests have sometimes contributed to biases in tests and test interpretations. One method of ensuring that an individual's test score is an unbiased estimate of his or her ability is the threshold determination measure used in computerized adaptive testing, an application of item-response theory.

In general, tests have been used to measure (1) intelligence, (2) personality, (3) ability, and (4) attitudes, interests, preferences, and values. This information has been used primarily for mental health decisions and prognostications.

Objective (for example, MMPI, 16PF) tests require answers of a yes or no type. They are easy to score but depend greatly on the subject's honesty. On the other hand, projective tests (for example, Rorschach and TAT) do not suffer from the subject's potential dishonesty as they present ambiguous stimuli (for example, inkblots). However, as a result, there is a problem in scoring, which is, by definition, subjective.

Finally, there is some dispute regarding what test results actually represent. Some psychologists view these results as indicative of signs, or things inside the subject (for example, trait theorists). On the other hand, behaviorists treat these results as just another sample of behavior.

KEY WORDS AND PHRASES

OBJECTIVE 1

test construction

OBJECTIVE 2

rational (theoretical) approach
empirical approach
face validity
reference groups
factor analysis
standardization
norms

OBJECTIVE 3

reliability
validity
reliability coefficients
concurrent validity
test-retest
alternative forms
split-half
predictive validity
construct validity

OBJECTIVE 4

computerized adaptive testing
item-response theory

OBJECTIVE 5

mental health decisions
prediction decisions

OBJECTIVE 6

objective tests
projective tests
MMPI
16 PF
Rorschach Inkblot Test
TAT

OBJECTIVE 7

sign
behavioral sample

OBJECT 8

self-report
subjective judgment
objective scoring
subject honesty

MULTIPLE-CHOICE TEST

1.   In the _____ approach to test construction, test items are based on
theoretical principles.
a.   rational
b.   empirical
c.   psychoanalytic
d.   standard
     (page 515)

2.   An overt, or common-sense, relationship between test items and what is
being tested constitutes _____ validity.
a.   face
b.   predictive
c.   concurrent
d.   construct
     (page 515)

3.   In the _____ approach to test construction, test items are based on
the ability to distinguish among classifications (for example, depressive or
nondepressive).
a.   rational
b.   theoretical
c.   empirical
d.   statistical
     (page 515)

4. A psychologist who constructed a test to measure a characteristic by including questions that differentiated known reference groups from others would be using the _____ approach.
a. rational
b. theoretical
c. empirical
d. statistical
   (page 515)

5. The MMPI represents a personality test that was constructed using the _____ approach to test construction.
a. empirical
b. projective
c. rational
d. factor analytic
   (page 516)

6. You would use the Strong Vocational Inventory if you wanted to know:
a. your intelligence level
b. what to pursue for a career
c. what kind of mental health decision to make
d. about discovering source traits
   (page 516)

7. Factor analysis was used by Cattell to develop the:
a. TAT
b. MMPI
c. Strong Vocational Inventory
d. 16PF
   (page 516)

8. The purpose of _____ is to refine the testing procedure and to establish norms.
a. reliability coefficients
b. validity checks
c. standardization
d. factor analysis
   (page 516)

9. The norms for a psychological test would be expressed as:
a. means and standard deviations
b. an F-ratio
c. the results of a factor analysis
d. the conditions necessary for optimum performance
   (page 517)

10. If test results are repeatable, we say that they are:
a. reliable
b. valid
c. efficient
d. constructive
   (page 517)

11. Which does not belong?
a. split-half
b. test-retest
c. concurrent
d. alternative forms
   (page 518)

12. If a test measures what it is supposed to measure, we say that it is:
a. reliable
b. valid
c. operational
d. significant
   (page 518)

13. Which does not fit?
a. concurrent
b. predictive
c. construct
d. split-half
   (page 518)

14. If an IQ rest correlates positively with school performance, it gains in
_____ validity.
a. face
b. predictive
c. concurrent
d. construct
   (page 518)

15. If a newly constructed test yields results similar to those from
already-constructed tests, the new test will gain in _____ validity.
a. face
b. predictive
c. concurrent
d. construct
   (page 518)

16. If test results agree with the results of theoretical speculations, the
test will gain in _____ validity.
a. face
b. predictive
c. concurrent
d. construct
   (page 518)

17. Test norms are established by:
a. estimating the average score from a theoretical model
b. computing the average score and variability of a reference group
c. keeping a running average of scores of all test takers through the years
d. computing the validity scales on each test
   (page 518)

18.   The advantage of item-response theory as applied to psychological tests is that:
a.   the need for projective tests is eliminated
b.   tests can be taken over the telephone
c.   interpretation of the score does not depend on the scores of other persons
d.   the subjects' anxiety is reduced significantly
     (page 519)

19.   A procedure that establishes a borderline level of ability for a person by showing which questions he or she can answer correctly and which he or she cannot is called:
a.   factor analysis
b.   computerized adaptive testing
c.   standardization
d.   normalization
     (page 519)

20.   The most important and frequent use of psychological tests is:
a.   to diagnose mental disorders
b.   to establish criteria for retardation programs
c.   to screen candidates for the military
d.   to predict vocational abilities
     (page 519)

21.   For many psychologists, the first step in diagnosing mental disorders and establishing a plan of therapy is:
a.   interview with family members
b.   establishing the potential for suicide or violent behavior
c.   assessment of personality
d.   observation in a real-life setting
     (page 519)

22.   In a _____ test, ambiguous stimuli are presented, thus nullifying the problem of subject dishonesty.
a.   projective
b.   objective
c.   theoretical
d.   rational
     (page 520)

23.   The only one of the following that proves troublesome for the MMPI test is:
a.   scoring
b.   the lack of an empirical basis
c.   subject dishonesty
d.   it's too subjective to understand
     (page 520)

24.   The answer format on the MMPI is:
a.   multiple-choice
b.   true-false
c.   five-point scale from agree to disagree
d.   open-ended
     (page 520)

25. The personality assessment scale that consists of many multiple-choice items that are separated into a number of clusters by way of factor analysis is:
a.   the MMPI
b.   the TAT
c.   the Rorschach
d.   the 16PF
     (page 521)

26. Rorschach is to MMPI as:
a.   objective is to projective
b.   projective is to objective
c.   empirical is to rational
d.   rational is to empirical
     (page 522)

27. In the _____, you are faced with a true-life picture, but one that does not have any obvious implications.
a.   Rorschach
b.   TAT
c.   MMPI
d.   16PF
     (page 522)

28. To behaviorists such as Skinner, test results represent:
a.   inferred constructs
b.   functional analysis
c.   a sample of behavior
d.   underlying signs
     (page 524)

29. To trait theorists such as Cattell, test results represent:
a.   manifest needs
b.   a sample of behavior
c.   latent needs
d.   underlying signs
     (page 524)

30. Subjective judgment is to objective scoring as:
a.   projective is to self-report
b.   projective is to empirical
c.   projective is to rational
d.   empirical is to honesty
     (page 525)

ANSWER KEY

1.	a	6.	b	11.	c	16.	d	21.	c	26.	b
2.	a	7.	d	12.	b	17.	b	22.	a	27.	b
3.	c	8.	c	13.	d	18.	c	23.	c	28.	c
4.	c	9.	a	14.	b	19.	b	24.	b	29.	d
5.	a	10.	a	15.	c	20.	a	25.	d	30.	a

Appendix D
Altered States
of Consciousness

OBJECTIVES

1. What is consciousness, and how do we differentiate normal from altered states?
2. What are the differences between REM and non-REM sleep, in terms of both brain-wave data and dreaming?
3. What three conclusions about why we sleep seem the most likely?
4. What are the psychological (for example, perceptual, memorial) effects and physiological correlates of dreaming?
5. What are the direct effects of hypnosis, and what are the posthypnotic effects?
6. What are the psychological effects of alcohol intoxication, and why is such intoxication dangerous?
7. What are the effects of marijuana intoxication?
8. What distinguishes drug use from drug abuse, and how do these distinctions apply to the various drugs discussed in the text?
9. What are the different types of meditation, and what are the psychological and physiological effects?
10. How has biofeedback contributed to our understanding of altered states of consciousness, and why should the consumer be careful when purchasing biofeedback equipment?

SYNOPSIS

Consciousness describes the extent to which we are aware of and attend to the overall information flow in our environment. Normal and altered states of consciousness are defined according to deviations from our day-to-day pattern of experience. Sleep, hypnosis, drug intoxication, meditative states all have been categorized as altered states of consciousness.

In a given night's sleep, we pass through four stages, based on differences in EEG patterns. During sleep, periods of rapid eye movements (REM) alternate with non-REM periods. Dreaming is reported about 80 percent of the time during REM periods. During dreams, our psychological perceptions are altered, our performance is minimal, and our cognitive processes are somewhat unusual, if not distorted. We may also have intense emotional experiences, heightened memory, and variable identity. Despite all this, time sense in a dream is the same as in the waking state.

Three theories about why we sleep are considered. First, empirical evidence shows that without sleep, physical health and well-being cannot be maintained. Second, sleep serves a restorative function for various bodily systems. Third, sleep is a time when special biological events occur (for example, release of growth hormone).

Hypnosis involves suggestibility, to be sure, and there are vast individual differences in susceptibility. Under hypnosis, perception may be restructured, awareness may be focused on internal or external processes, and identity may be radically altered. Nevertheless, the subject is not the "zombie" that the media make him or her out to be. Posthypnotic suggestions may also be made. Some researchers (for example, Barber) believe that there is nothing done in hypnosis that cannot be done in a normal (albiet a highly motivated) waking state. Hypnosis can be a useful psychological tool in the hands of the responsible professional, but a dangerous tool in the hands of a charlatan.

At high levels, alcohol clearly alters our perception and self-awareness. Unfortunately, in doing so, it may give us more confidence in our abilities than is justified. As with alcohol, marijuana alters our perceptions and relaxes us. However, unlike alcohol users, marijuana users tend to quiet down and are seemingly not nearly as retarded on motor tasks (at least in the case of experienced users).

Drugs can be used appropriately as long as they do not impair the user's functioning and the user does not pose a threat to others. However, drugs frequently are abused. More people are victims of alcohol abuse than any other single drug, with tranquilizers such as Valium and Librium running second. Aside from overusing a given drug, there is also the very dangerous possibility of using two drugs that potentiate each other's effects. For example, alcohol increases the effects of barbiturates.

The focus of psychologists on meditation is a recent undertaking. There are two classes of meditation, namely, concentrative, which restricts attention to one object over a long period, and opening-up, or paying full attention to everything continuously. In a process similar to opening-up meditation (called self-remembering), one tries to dissociate oneself from the surrounding events. In general, meditation is practiced by those in Zen, Yoga, and transcendental meditation.

Biofeedback equipment has been particularly helpful in the objective study of the physiological correlates of meditation. It has been shown, for example, that one can actually throw one's heart into fibrillation. Biofeedback equipment can also be of help when subjects need to learn how to relax their muscles. However, in the commercialization of biofeedback, there have been many exaggerations of its benefits and uses.

KEY WORDS AND PHRASES

OBJECTIVE 1

consciousness
ordinary state of consciousness
altered state of consciousness

OBEJCTIVE 2

sleep
dreams
EEG
EOG
brain waves
alpha

delta
sleep stages 1 through 4
REM

OBJECTIVE 3

sleep deprivation
restoration theory
slow-wave sleep
insomnia

OBJECTIVE 4

hypnogogic
hypnopompic
psychological effects of dreaming
        perception
        performance
        cognition
        emotion
        memory
        identity
        time sense

OBJECTIVE 5

hypnosis
hypersuggestibility
simulator control groups
hypoesthesia
hidden observer
regression
posthypnotic effects
automatic writing

OBJECTIVE 6

alcohol
intoxication
blood concentration
false competence
lowered inhibition

OBJECTIVE 7

marijuana
potential effect
pure drug effect

OBJECTIVE 8

drug abuse
potentiation
tolerance
addiction

tolerance
Valium
Librium
amphetamines

OBJECTIVE 9

meditation
concentrative
opening-up
self-remembering
Zen
Yoga
transcendental meditation

OBJECTIVE 10

biofeedback
fibrillation
relaxation

MULTIPLE-CHOICE TEST

1. A person who is awake but not engaged in eyes-open mental activity would
show the EEG waveform called:
a.   alpha
b.   beta
c.   delta
d.   theta
      (page 527)

2.   Dreaming (REM sleep) is MOST likely to occur:
a.   during the first 30 minutes of sleep
b.   towards the end of the sleep period
c.   in stage 4 of sleep
d.   in the middle of the sleep period
      (page 528)

3.   In normal sleep periods, the length of the cycles between successive
dreaming episodes is about:
a.   30 minutes
b.   60 minutes
c.   90 minutes
d.   120 minutes
      (page 528)

4.   The age at which the MOST REM sleep occurs is:
a.   3 to 5 months
b.   2 to 3 years
c.   20 to 25 years
d.   65 to 70 years
      (page 528)

5. Which of the following is NOT a consequence of prolonged sleep deprivation?
a. severe deterioration in psychological functioning
b. physical impairment
c. build up of chemical by-products that are usually purged during sleep
d. increase in nervous and behavioral activity
   (page 528)

6. Following extreme exercise, such as running a long distance race, during the next two nights:
a. REM sleep time increases
b. slow-wave sleep time increases
c. total sleep time decreases
d. dreams occur at the beginning rather than at the end of the sleep period
   (page 529)

7. Which endocrine hormone tends to be released primarily during sleep?
a. growth hormone
b. thyroxin
c. ACTH
d. testosterone
   (page 529)

8. The process of going from wakefulness to sleep is called:
a. EOG
b. hypnogogic
c. hypnopomic
d. transcendental
   (page 529)

9. With respect to motor output during sleep:
a. sleep walking occurs during dream sleep
b. the dreaming person is almost paralyzed
c. only hand and feet movements occur during dreaming
d. talking occurs equally often during dreaming and nondream sleep
   (page 531)

10. Which of the following treatments has been found to be effective in relieving insomnia?
a. resting frequently during the day so that the body is not bone-tired at night
b. satying in bed until sleep comes, no matter how long it takes
c. getting up at the same time each morning, regardless of when you went to bed
d. napping once in the morning and once in the afternoon
   (page 531)

11. Surprisingly, during a dream:
a. our perception is clear
b. our motor output is high
c. our time sense is unaltered
d. cognitions outweigh emotions
   (page 532)

12. When Wilse Webb asked students to create stories about rapidly presented artificial images and then compared these stories with dreams:
a. the artificial dreams resulted in real dreams of similar content
b. the artificial dreams were totally unlike real dreams
c. the artificial dreams seemed more like delusions than dreams
d. the artificial dreams had similar content with real dreams
   (page 533)

13. Perhaps the greatest controversy concerning the nature of hypnosis is:
a. does hypnosis represent an altered state of consciousness?
b. can hypnotized subjects really deaden pain?
c. is suggestibility heightened during hypnosis?
d. can all people be hypnotized?
   (page 533)

14. During hypnosis, awareness can be split in half via the technique called:
a. heightened motivation
b. hypothesis
c. regression
d. hidden observer
   (page 536)

15. If analgesia is the aim in hypnosis, the procedure to use is:
a. hypoesthesia
b. simulation control
c. the hidden observer
d. regression
   (page 536)

16. If heightened self-awareness (identity) is the goal in hypnosis, then the procedure to use is:
a. hypoesthesia
b. simulation control
c. the hidden observer
d. regression
   (page 536)

17. With respect to changes in memory during hypnosis:
a. subjects cannot be made to forget events that have actually occurred
b. there is not much evidence that suggests that memory is improved
c. memories are improved by as much as 50 percent
d. memory improves only when posthypnotic suggestion is used
   (page 536)

18. According to T. X. Barber, with regard to hypnosis:
a. the hidden observer successfully dissociates the personality
b. pain is successfully dulled
c. regression is produced
d. nothing happens that could not happen in any highly motivated subject
   (page 537)

19. One of the major dangers of hypnosis is:
a. it is so easy to learn that incompetent persons may use it
b. some people regress to an earlier age and never recover
c. subjects injure themselves in attempting to accomplish impossible feats
d. it never really accomplishes therapeutic goals
(page 538)

20. A quantitative definition of an alcohol-induced state of consciousness is a:
a. 0.01 percent blood alcohol level
b. 0.10 percent blood alcohol level
c. 1.0 percent blood alcohol level
d. 10.0 percent blood alcohol level
(page 539)

21. Which of the following is a typical effect of alcohol intoxication?
a. decrease in auditory sensitivity
b. increase in mechanical competence
c. increase in fantasies of power
d. decreased feelings of confidence and ability
(page 539)

22. Most of the common experiences of marijuana intoxication have been shown to be due to its _____ effects.
a. pure drug
b. potential
c. psychedelic
d. summation
(page 539)

23. The recent report from the National Academy of Sciences on the long-term effects of marijuana on health concluded that:
a. regular marijuana use reduces sexual potency in men and women
b. heavy marijuana use causes chromosomal damage
c. regular marijuana use impairs the body's immune system
d. heavy marijuana use may lead to respiratory tract cancer
(page 541)

24. The primary addictive problem with cocaine is:
a. psychological
b. physical
c. physiological
d. cellular
(page 542)

25. Concerning drug abuse:
a. it occurs whenever a psychoactive drug is taken
b. if the ability to function has not been significantly impaired, it has not been abused
c. it applies only to certain classes of drugs
d. it could not occur with over-the-counter medications such as aspirin
(page 543)

26. When one drug enhances the effect of another drug taken simultaneously, the effect is called:
a. summation
b. tolerance
c. potentiation
d. addiction
   (page 543)

27. Concentrative meditation is:
a. restrictive
b. nonrestrictive
c. self-defeating
d. expansive
   (page 546)

28. Self-remembering is akin to:
a. concentrative meditation
b. opening up meditation
c. biofeedback
d. recollective analysis
   (page 546)

29. The essence of biofeedback is that:
a. it causes the production of neuromodulators
b. it causes increased relaxation
c. it makes otherwise unknown information available to consciousness
d. it results in an altered state of consciousness
   (page 547)

30. When the researchers at the Menninger Clinic observed the Indian Yogi:
a. he died because of failure in the biofeedback equipment
b. his concentration in the laboratory environment was impaired
c. he stopped his heart
d. he sent his heart into fibrillation that mimicked a heart stoppage
   (page 547)

ANSWER KEY

1.	a	6.	b	11.	c	16.	c	21.	c	26.	c
2.	b	7.	a	12.	d	17.	b	22.	b	27.	a
3.	c	8.	b	13.	a	18.	d	23.	d	28.	b
4.	a	9.	b	14.	d	19.	a	24.	a	29.	c
5.	d	10.	c	15.	a	20.	b	25.	b	30.	d